Our Common Humanity

Dedicated in the memory of
Professor William S. Hatcher, Dr Magdelene Carney,
Mírzá Abu'l-Faḍl, and Dr Jane Faily

Our Common Humanity

Reflections on the Reclamation
of the Human Spirit

Michael L. Penn

GEORGE RONALD
OXFORD

George Ronald Publisher, Ltd
Oxford
www.grbooks.com

A catalogue record for this book is available from the British Library

ISBN 978-0-85398-649-2

Cover design: Steiner Graphics

CONTENTS

Preface   vii
Acknowledgements   ix
Introduction   1

Part I: Unique Powers of the Human Spirit

1   The Capacity to Know   23
2   The Capacity to Love   43
3   The Nature of Will   61

Part II: Alternative Conceptualizations of Human Identity

4   The Psychoanalytic Perspective   83
5   The View of Evolutionary Psychology and Neuroscience   96
6   Discourses on the Problem of Evil   102

Part III: The Human Spirit and the Social Order

7   The Journey Out of the Racial Divide   119
8   Ideological Arguments that Seek to Justify and
     Sustain the Practice of War   132
9   Neo-Liberal Obstacles to Addressing Universal
     Human Needs   145

Part IV: Care of the Spirit

10 The Inner Life   157
11 The Logic of Prayer and Meditation   165

12   Consultation: An Instrument of Personal and Social
Transformation   179
13   A Final Word: Humanity's Spiritual Heritage   187

Bibliography   219
Notes and References   231
Index   247
About the Author   253

'The most exciting breakthroughs of the 21st Century will occur not because of technology but because of an expanding concept of what it means to be human.'

~John Naisbitt

PREFACE

Every historical epoch, noted the Brazilian educator, Paulo Freire, 'is characterized by a series of aspirations, concerns, and values in search of fulfillment . . . The epochs are fulfilled to the degree that their themes are grasped and their tasks solved.'[1] The themes that animate the present age flow out of the profound implications of the oneness and interdependence of humankind. The oneness of humanity is a biological fact affirmed by more than a century of study in the natural sciences; it is a moral truth upon which all claims to human rights rest; and it is a feature of social reality that the integrative forces of history will no longer permit us to avoid. As an ontological truth, the oneness of humanity is reflected in those universal moral and intellectual capacities that define the nature and needs of the human spirit. This book provides a rational, Bahá'í-inspired account of what might be meant by the human spirit, explores its relevance to our effort to meet the challenges that define this historical moment, and links the development and refinement of the human spirit to the realization of that which is most noble in each of us.

In previous works I have sought to define, in consultation with the works of others, the capacities that animate and define the human spirit. In a *Human Rights Quarterly* article, published in 2010, Aditi Malik and I suggested that a government's ability to create the conditions that foster the development of the human spirit ought to be the primary standard whereby its legitimate right to govern is evaluated, and I have drawn upon material from that article in framing the discourse that animates the present volume.[2] Earlier, in 2007, I co-authored a paper for the United Kingdom's Royal College of Physicians that demonstrated how the proliferation of psychopathic behaviour, and other extreme forms of moral disengagement, may arise, in part, from neglect of the conditions required for the healthy development of the human spirit;[3] and in 'Mind, Medicine and Metaphysics: Reflections on the Reclamation of the Human Spirit', published in the *American Journal of Psychotherapy* in 2003, and co-authored with one of my students, I outlined the history of the eclipse of the concept of the human spirit in psychiatry and psychology and suggested why the notion of the human spirit may be making its way back into these fields.[4]

The current project – undertaken on the heels of a conference I sponsored on the nature of human dignity in collaboration with Hoda Mahmoudi (holder of the Bahá'í Chair for World Peace at the University of Maryland) – draws upon some of the ideas that were shared at that conference and that have inspired many of my earlier works. In preparing for this collaboration, I drew upon the corpus of writings that constitute the Bahá'í teachings on the human spirit. This work, however, makes no effort to impose a Bahá'í point of view. I offer the novel perspectives contained on this theme in the Bahá'í writings alongside the perspectives of other traditions of thought that have contributed to our understanding of the nature, needs, and development of the human spirit across the ages.

The desire to prepare such a work began during my years of undergraduate studies, first at Brandeis University where I studied philosophy, and later at the University of Pennsylvania where I studied psychology, history, and religion. I went on to graduate school in clinical and experimental psychopathology in the hope that my study of these varied fields might provide insight into the nature of the human spirit, but found in these academic encounters no mention of it. Indeed, the sense that I got from my very able professors was that discourse on the human spirit is both antiquated and unnecessary, and that everything that had once been associated with the human spirit is best understood today in terms of neurobiology and cognitive science. Having been drawn to the insights into human identity that emerge from the world's religions, as well as traditions of Eastern and Western philosophy, I came to believe that these schools of thought continue to have much to say about human identity that deserve our serious consideration. When, as a student at the University of Pennsylvania, I encountered the vast reservoir of material on the human spirit contained in the Bahá'í writings, the hope emerged that I might be able to write about the phenomenon in a way that would honour the unique perspectives contained in these writings alongside the rich diversity of other philosophical, epistemic, and moral traditions that have contributed to our understanding of the nature and needs of the human spirit over the ages. This book is an attempt to satisfy that longing.

I write at a time when notions of identity, grounded in socially constructed conceptualizations of race, gender, class, and nationality continue to pose serious threats to our collective future. My sense is that a deeper appreciation of the nature and needs of the human spirit can contribute to our ability to work more closely together in pursuit of that which honours and upholds the dignity inherent in each of us. I should note at the outset that I have come of age in the United States as an African-American; and so, as a consequence, the American experience has provided many of the examples from which I draw as I describe the human condition. My hope, however, is that the insights that are embodied in my examples will prove to be relevant to peoples living in diverse settings around the world.

ACKNOWLEDGEMENTS

In addition to those gems in whose names this work is dedicated, I owe a great debt of gratitude to many others. Among these are Mr Hooper Dunbar, who provided encouragement for pursuing this project during a visit to his office on Mt. Carmel; Dr Hooshmand Sheshbaradaran, whose insights and suggestions led to the transformation of nearly every chapter of this book; Homa Tavangar, who read an early draft and critiqued it in so many valuable ways; and my editor at George Ronald, May Hofman, whose patience, generosity of spirit, and professionalism have been critical to its successful completion. I would also like to remember my brother, David, for his fortitude and good will; as well as my illumined and courageous wife, Kathy, whose qualities of character evoke in those of us who know her both admiration and respect.

INTRODUCTION

A significant discovery of the twentieth century is that many of our actions are governed, not by reality, but by our fundamental beliefs about reality. These inner models of reality have been variously labelled 'theories of reality', 'structures of meaning', 'social imaginaries' or 'worldviews'. A worldview provides the lens through which we perceive and understand the experience of life. It determines, to a significant degree, what we hope for, how we spend our time, how we relate to the natural and social environment. Worldview provides the overarching conceptual matrix within which we come of age. It determines, to no small degree, the trajectory of our individual and collective development and provides the visionary material out of which is formed the kind of human beings we aspire to become. Worldviews are not created anew with each individual but are transmitted from one generation to another via the mechanism of culture.

A worldview is designed to provide answers to some of the most fundamental problems or questions of life. But reality will not tolerate just any conception of it. Some inner models of reality, some worldviews, will prove more useful, more in harmony with well-established truths. Some will facilitate the achievement of human prosperity and development. Others will provide moral justification for bigotries, violence and destruction.

An ideology is the most destructive expression of a worldview. When social, political or religious systems function as ideologies they conceive of morality as the belief in and defence of particular doctrines. These doctrines are viewed as the supreme value and morality is conceived as their propagation and dissemination by all possible means. From this perspective, an ideology may be understood as any philosophy or worldview that holds that certain doctrines, ideas or propositions are more important than human beings. Since any moral system affirms that lesser values may be sacrificed to obtain greater values, an ideology sanctions – at least implicitly – the deliberate sacrifice of human beings if it is deemed necessary for the propagation of the doctrines of that ideology.[1]

The nearly 250 million people who were sacrificed in the wars and violence of the twentieth century were sacrificed principally in the name of one or more ideologies – communism, racialism, or nationalism. If the twenty-first century is to be any different from the century just ended, it will be so, in part, because ideologies will have lost the power to justify acts of brutality, terror and violence. In addition, if human security and development are to find a firm and stable foundation, the protection and development of the human spirit will have to emerge as an appropriate focus for adjudicating the moral legitimacy of any human act, any social policy, or any cultural or religious practice. This book seeks to explicate and justify these claims.

By 'human spirit' is meant two things: first, a capacity of consciousness that enables the human species, as distinct from all other known species, to consciously strive to attain that which is perceived to be true, beautiful and good; and second, a set of psychological and spiritual faculties that generate a psychological sense of 'self' and 'community' with hopes and aspirations that transcend the struggle for mere existence and continuity as a biological organism. As has been argued in various ways by H. B. Danesh,[2] Julio Savi,[3] William Hatcher[4] and others, we suggest here that the human spirit consists of three basic capacities: the capacity to know, to love, and to will. When awakened and nurtured, the capacity to know stirs humanity in its ceaseless search for knowledge and wisdom; the capacity to will motivates us to pursue that which is thought to be good; and the capacity to love animates our attraction to beauty and our longing for connection to nature, to one another, and for many, to that which is sacred.

The development of the human spirit results from the maturation, cultivation, and refinement of these universal capacities. As these capacities unfold and express themselves in the life of the community, we see the emergence and efflorescence of the sciences, arts, and systems of ethics and law upon which civilization depends. We also witness the appearance of those virtues that redound to human honour and dignity, and which give order and harmony to the social world. Inasmuch as the human spirit is that one aspect of identity that transcends race, class, culture, and religion, the capacities that animate the human spirit provide the ontological basis for the oneness of humankind.

I begin in this introduction with a brief overview of a Bahá'í-inspired perspective on human identity, and bring this perspective into greater discourse with other schools of thought as the book unfolds.

In the late eighteenth and early nineteenth centuries psychiatry emerged out of neurology as a new branch of medicine. This new field, which made possible the emergence of novel approaches to understanding and treating mental illnesses, required reconceptualizations of the human mind. If they were to prove useful, theories of mind had to be liberated from the superstitious ideas that had, for centuries, hampered the development of a science of psychopathology. And while the new conceptualizations of mind that grew out of psychiatry during this period would be effective in rendering the mind an appropriate object of empirical study and clinical concern, the assumptions that these theories embodied would also divest the discourse on mind from consideration of those unique features of consciousness that distinguish human minds from all other phenomena in nature.[5]

During this same period, however, a unique view that sought to recover the mind from the materialistic philosophies of the era while also harmonizing with the rational and evidential demands required of modern empirical science began to appear in the writings of the Bahá'í Faith. At the heart of the Bahá'í model is an ontological order that provides for causality and law in the sphere of nature, and for a relatively high degree of freedom and responsibility in the human realm. It affirms that human beings belong both to the realm of nature as well as to a transcendent dimension of existence made possible by the unique capacities associated with the human soul or spirit.

The Bahá'í writings suggest that the human soul is the most essential and enduring aspect of human identity. It is described as 'a sign of God, a heavenly gem whose reality the most learned of men hath failed to grasp'[6] and is among the most profound of all mysteries;[7] and yet, like all other phenomena, it can be known, in part, by the effects that it produces in the world. The soul provides each human being with the core identity that is the self, and it is through the instrumentality of the human brain and body that the character and capacities of the soul are gradually developed and revealed. Inasmuch as the soul is not a thing, it cannot, in the Bahá'í view, either enter or leave the body. Rather, it is said to enjoy a relationship with the body that is akin to the relationship that light has to a mirror. It is useful, in this regard, to consider the nature of light as described by the physicist Arthur Zajonc:

> As part of what I call 'Project Eureka', a friend and I have designed and constructed a science exhibit in which one views a region of space filled with light. It is a simple but startling demonstration that uses only a carefully fabricated box and a powerful projector whose light shines directly into it. We have taken a special care to ensure that light does not illuminate any interior objects or surfaces in the box. Within the box, there is only pure light, and lots of it. The question is: What does one see? How does light look when left *entirely* to itself?
>
> Approaching the exhibit, I turn on the projector, whose

bulb and lenses can be seen through a Plexiglas panel. The projector sends a brilliant light through optical elements into the box beside it. Moving over to a view port, I look into the box and at the light within. What do I see? Absolute darkness! I see nothing but the blackness of empty space.

On the outside of the box is a handle connected to a wand that can move into and out of the box's interior. Pulling the handle, the wand flashes through the dark space before me and I see the wand brilliantly lit on one side. The space clearly is not empty but filled with light. Yet without an object on which light can fall, one sees only darkness. Light itself is always invisible. We see only things, only objects, not light.[8]

From a Bahá'í perspective, the human soul or spirit (and here we shall use these terms interchangeably), like light, cannot be known directly. In order for it to manifest itself, a vehicle is required. Thus, the human brain and body make possible the manifestation of the powers of the human spirit in much the same way that a mirror provides a means for the manifestation of the qualities of light.

In the empirical sciences, we call phenomena that can only be known by the signs or effects that they produce 'hypothetical constructs'. Hypothetical constructs include forces like love, intelligence, memory, and so forth. Insofar as these phenomena are never accessible to direct sense inspection, we must intuit their existence by examining the effects that they produce in the world. For example, we know that something that we call 'gravity' must exist because we observe that all unsupported objects move toward the earth. This ordered behaviour, this systematic deviation from chance, justifies our invocation of a cause; and so we say that this behaviour is due to gravity – even though no one has ever seen or heard or touched or smelled gravity.[9] Similarly, from a Bahá'í perspective, because the soul is not a thing, its existence can only be known by its effects. The greatest sign of the soul's existence is human civilization and all the arts and sciences that are the harvest of human thought. Lacking the unique capacities associated with the human soul, no other creature known to nature has been able to produce such signs.

During the period of existence when the immortal soul is in relation to the human body it produces a phenomenon of mind that is unique to the human species. The mind, noted 'Abdu'l-Bahá, who was the son of the Founder of the Bahá'í Faith and led the Bahá'í world community from 1892 to 1921, 'is the power of the human spirit'.[10] He goes further to note that the human spirit may be likened to a lamp and that the mind is 'the light that shines from the lamp'.[11] Light provides a particularly apt metaphor here for several reasons. For example, though the properties of light may be seen through the instrumentality of a mirror, the mirror and the light that it reflects are independent of one another. If the mirror is harmed, no harm can come to the light. However, if the full spectrum of light is to be seen in a mirror, a clear and polished mirror is required. In a similar way, if the capacities and properties of the soul are to be fully revealed in the mirror of the mind (in the mirror of the self), then the brain and body must be healthy and sound. Thus, any imperfections in the structure or functioning of the body may be reflected in the functioning of the mind. To use another metaphor, one could also liken the body to a musical instrument. The only way that a great musician can reveal her musical prowess is by having a sound, finely tuned instrument. The instrument becomes the vehicle through which the spiritual and wholly abstract creative capacities of the artist can be made manifest.

There are other reasons why light, in particular, provides an especially excellent metaphorical device for reflecting on the capacities of the human soul. For example, just as the light of the sun serves to cultivate potentialities that are latent in nature, so also does the light of a healthy and well-developed mind serve as a creative force in the life of a family, society, or civilization. In addition, light has the peculiar quality of being both wave-like (much like pure energy) and particle-like (much like matter) in its nature. That is, it manifests, as does the human brain and mind, attributes commonly associated with both the concrete and abstract forces of existence.

. The body and mind develop together. Indeed, the existence and development of the body render the development and refinement of the mind possible. In this sense, the relationship between the mind and body reveals a fundamental truth about the relationship between the physical and spiritual aspects of human existence. That is, from a Bahá'í point of view, the physical world provides the concrete foundation upon which spiritual powers are revealed and spiritual understandings and insights are gradually built. It is, perhaps, for this reason that 'Abdu'l-Bahá affirms that the mind comes to comprehend the abstract 'by the aid of the concrete'.[12]

In his book *The Purpose of Physical Reality*, John S. Hatcher has explored the role of the physical world in the development of spiritual knowledge and wisdom. He notes that the natural world provides the metaphorical tools that enable us, as sign users, to begin the process of understanding the metaphysical truths, abstract laws, and spiritual principles that are reflected in the things and processes of nature.

In other words, the mind is not a passive recipient of the forces that operate upon it. Drawing on the unique, rational powers of the soul, the human mind is endowed with the capacity to understand those forces and to resist and overcome whatever would be a source of physical or existential harm. Yet, on the other hand, because the mind is at once a reflection of the human soul, the human body, and the society into which it is born and develops, the powers of the mind can never be fully revealed in an individual or a society that is not physically sound, intellectually mature, or morally healthy.

While the human soul is not a composite entity, the properties and capacities of the human mind are, in part, the epiphenomenal byproduct of the *composition* of the human brain and body. Properties can be said to exist by composition when their existence depends on the proper blending of diverse elements.

For example, water exists by the composition of hydrogen and oxygen in the proper proportion. So long as these conditions are satisfied, the properties of water will be manifest. As soon as the bond between hydrogen and oxygen is broken, all the properties associated with water disappear. Thus, we say that the properties of water are *compositional qualities.*

In a similar way, the properties that are associated with the functioning of the human mind depend on the blending of diverse elements in a precise fashion because the brain and nervous system are the instruments that make possible the manifestation of the powers of mind in the natural world. Indeed, deviation from the ideal complement of elements will result in illness and sometimes death. It is well known, for example, that if levels of naturally occurring neurotransmitters (such as serotonin, dopamine, GABA (gamma-aminobutyric acid), and so forth) are not in the proper amount and proportion, the human brain will often lose its capacity to manifest reason or sound judgement. One may lose the capacity to control one's emotions or may be overwhelmed by inordinate degrees of anxiety, depression, and worry. The Bahá'í writings point out that these disorders result from improper composition of the body's essential elements and have nothing to do with the life or health of the human soul.

In this regard, the Bahá'í writings note that 'the soul . . . is exalted above, and is independent of all infirmities of body or mind . . .' and that 'every malady afflicting the body . . . is an impediment that preventeth the soul from manifesting its inherent might and power. When it leaveth the body, however, it will evince such ascendency, and reveal such influence as no force on earth can equal.'[13] The human soul is immortal because it is not a composite entity and does not come into being through the affinity of molecular elements. Since it is not composed, it cannot be decomposed and is thus 'not subject to disintegration'.[14] In a letter addressed to one inquirer, 'Abdu'l-Bahá wrote: 'Verily the body is composed of physical elements, and every composite must needs be decomposed. The spirit, however, is a single essence, fine and delicate, incorporeal, everlasting, and of God.'[15]

Thus, from a Bahá'í point of view, the mind is not a thing that is coequal with the brain; nor is it simply the by-product of the evolution of organic matter. Rather, it is said to be a spiritual power that is drawn to the human form even as the rays of light are drawn to a mirror: 'It is the same reality which is given different names, according to the different conditions wherein it becomes manifest,' notes 'Abdu'l-Bahá. 'Because of its attachment to matter and the phenomenal world, when it governs the physical functions of the body, it is called the human soul. When it manifests itself as the thinker, the comprehender, it is called the mind. And when it soars into the atmosphere of God and travels in the spiritual world, it becomes designated as spirit.'[16] Shoghi Effendi, who led the Bahá'í community from 1921 to 1957, clarifies this idea further: 'What the Bahá'ís do believe . . . is that we have three aspects of our humanness, so to speak, a body, a mind and an immortal identity – soul or spirit. We believe the mind forms a link between the soul and the body, and the two interact on each other.'[17]

Without the unique and transcendent powers of the human soul, human beings are logically unable to transcend the iron law of causality that determines and governs the phenomena of nature. At the same time, without the unique features and limitations of 'mind' – which serves as an intermediary between the natural world of the body and the spiritual reality of the soul – there could be no way to resolve the paradoxical problem of causality and determinism on the one hand, and human agency and freedom on the other. Understood as neither solely an emergent property of biological processes, nor as a force separate from, and alien to, the forces inherent in all of reality, the concept of mind as articulated in the Bahá'í writings enables us to understand how biological and social forces can influence the health, development, and expression of the human psyche, while at the same time affirming that the psyche or mind cannot be reduced to a series of biochemical events.

In contrast, therefore, to the existing nature–nurture, bi-partite conceptualization current among most Western intellectuals, the competing ontology referenced in the Bahá'í teachings affirms that *three* processes interact to form and shape human identity: (1) compositional and evolutionary processes, which include biological and genetic influences (nature); (2) social processes, which include experiential, educational, and cultural forces (nurture); and (3) innate processes associated with the life, development, and activity of the human soul or spirit. In order to provide a more adequate account of the notion of the human spirit as described in the Bahá'í writings, it is helpful to explore a few philosophical concepts.

The role of 'spirit' in a concept of mind

Aristotle, whose work is praised in the Bahá'í writings for some of the contributions it makes to the foundations of philosophy,[18] held that if we want to know the true identity of a thing, we must know its four causes: the material, formal, efficient, and final cause. Material cause is existence itself. It is that passive, undifferentiated matter that makes possible all other causes – it is the 'stuff' of existence without form or function. Aristotle held that inasmuch as something cannot be brought forth from nothing, to 'create' simply means to add to material cause formal cause (or structure) and final cause (or purpose). That cause which transforms unformed matter into 'something' is thus the efficient cause for that thing's existence. All processes of creation, suggested Aristotle, operate according to this same principle.

For example, an artist creates a sculpture by adding his or her conscious vision of form to unformed clay. In this case, the sculptor's hands and consciousness become the organizing energies that are the proximal sufficient cause for the coming-into-being of the sculpture. And although the clay certainly had existence prior to the work of the sculptor, it did not have existence as art. 'Abdu'l-Bahá notes that existence is thus relative, rather than absolute, and depends on the attributes, qualities, and capacities of the entities under consideration.

'Abdu'l-Bahá notes, for example, that persons exist and so

also do stones, but there are significant differences between the existence of a person and that of a stone. Though a stone exists, in relation to the existence of a person one could say that it is nonexistent. Thus do we say of a person who has passed from the human kingdom to that of the mineral that he or she has died. Of course, inasmuch as everything in the natural world is made of fundamentally the same matter (or the same basic elements), the capacities of an entity are determined not solely by the substance (or material cause) but by the energy, information, or consciousness responsible for an entity's organization and functioning.

A modern version of Aristotle's perspective is captured in the Second Law of Thermodynamics, or Carnot's theorem. This principle requires that if matter is to have form and order, it must be organized by some force or energy.[19] Manifested in one of its simplest forms (e.g. electromagnetic energy, the strong nuclear force, and/or gravity), this organizing energy is the cohesive force that results in the capacities apparent in the mineral kingdom. 'Abdu'l-Bahá explains that in the plant kingdom this same force manifests itself in the capacity for both cohesion and growth; in the animal kingdom, this power is manifested in the power of cohesion, growth, plus sense perception. Last, in the human person, this force is manifested as the power of cohesion, growth, sense perception, and the unique qualities of consciousness required for rationality and meta-cognition – or the consciousness of consciousness.

Let us note that at each level of ontology, moving from the mineral to the human kingdom, there is a corresponding increase in both complexity and freedom. Relative to the plant, which has, for example, the capacity to reorient its leaves and roots in order to take advantage of the light and water resources available in the environment, the mineral is a captive of its immediate circumstances. Similarly, as we move from the plant kingdom to that of the animal, we observe another significant leap in the degree of freedom. The powers of mobility and sense perception that characterize the animal kingdom permit animals to exercise a wider range of freedom in interacting with their environment; they have the capacity, for example, to form relational bonds with other beings of the same or different species. The 'kingdoms', often referred to in many of the world's wisdom and philosophical traditions, may thus be understood as spheres of awareness, freedom, and capacity that determine the essential identity of living things.

In the human kingdom, the power of consciousness gives the human person the potential for development along unique lines. This special type of consciousness is referred to in contemporary psychology as the power of meta-cognition – or the consciousness of consciousness. Meta-cognitive powers enable us not only to know the nonmaterial aspects of ourselves (such as our values, beliefs, attitudes, and so forth) but to have objective knowledge of metaphysical principles, laws, and processes – such as the abstract laws that govern the universe; the principles and qualities associated with assessments of beauty; and the underlying logic of systems of governance, ethics, and value. Our knowledge (as opposed to mere experience) of the operation of non-sensible forces, such as the forces of gravity and intelligence, requires the use of meta-cognitive powers that appear to be unique to human beings. Indeed, abstract thought, a capacity of the human spirit, is the source of human creativity, of all arts and sciences. In a discourse on this theme, 'Abdu'l-Bahá made the following observation:

> . . . know ye that the world of existence is a single world, although its stations are various and distinct. For example, the mineral life occupieth its own plane, but a mineral entity is without any awareness at all of the vegetable kingdom . . . In the same way, a vegetable entity knoweth nothing of the animal world, remaining completely heedless and ignorant thereof, for the stage of the animal is higher than that of the vegetable, and the vegetable is veiled from the animal world and inwardly denieth the existence of that world – all this while animal, vegetable and mineral dwell together in the

one world. In the same way the animal remaineth totally unaware of that power of the human mind which graspeth universal ideas and layeth bare the secrets of creation – so that a man who liveth in the east can make plans and arrangements for the west; can unravel mysteries; although located on the continent of Europe can discover America; although sited on the earth can lay hold of the inner realities of the stars of heaven. Of this power of discovery which belongeth to the human mind, this power which can grasp abstract and universal ideas, the animal remaineth totally ignorant . . .[20]

The healthy development of the human spirit

Development is gradual. During early stages of human development, the essential and universal capacities of the human spirit – which, as we have suggested, include the power to know, to love, and to will – are manifested in ways that are indistinguishable from the qualities of mind that characterize other species. The power of knowledge during infancy, for example, tends to be limited to 'instinctual awareness', and classical conditioning tends to be the primary mode of learning. Similarly, the power of will at early stages is marked by automatism, and love is manifested primarily in the instinctual form of 'bonding'. As childhood emerges out of infancy, an individual's innate intelligence becomes manifest and expresses itself in explorations of the world and the expansion of sensory-motor capabilities. Reactions, which, under healthy physical and environmental conditions, are increasingly mediated by a maturing will, tend to be emotion-based, and bodily desires, which are centred on the pursuit of pleasure and the avoidance of pain, tend to provide the primary incentives for action. In these early stages, love, too, appears to be under stimulus control and fluctuates as a function of that which provides sensual gratification.

In early adolescence, as the powers of consciousness expand and the capacity for meta-cognition strengthens, healthy individuals begin to reflect on the abstract dimensions of life. During this stage of development, the capacities that distinguish humans from other forms of life begin to become more pronounced. The human capacity to know, for example, transcends knowledge of that which is concrete and begins to encompass abstract systems of thought and of value. The power of will blossoms into the power to decide, based on consideration of an array of aesthetic, intellectual, and moral features; and love, which was previously a largely sensual and emotion-based phenomenon, becomes more consciously associated with a set of values and a worldview.

If the powers of mind broaden further, consciousness is illumined by universal ethical principles, and an individual may begin to manifest wisdom. Love also becomes enlightened by a genuine concern for the well-being and happiness of others, and the capacity for self-sacrifice becomes increasingly manifest. Under conditions that are optimal for human development, large groups of individuals begin to show evidence of what the sacred traditions refer to as 'spirituality'.

The concept of spirituality

Concern for the spiritual dimensions of existence is uniquely human; that is, only humans concern themselves, in any conscious way, with the non-material aspects of life. On the most basic level, spiritual concerns are embodied in our attraction to that which is perceived to be good, beautiful, and true. We seek the good, not only because that which is good brings pleasant feelings, but also because it appears to attract many of us in the way that the gravitational pull of the earth attracts those things that belong to it.[21] Indeed, we may pursue that which is thought to be good, even at considerable cost of comfort and personal well-being. The Bahá'í writings have suggested that we are attracted to the good because we belong to the good and cannot really be at peace unless we come to rest in it. As humans, we want our lives to be in harmony with the good; we generally want it said of us that we are reflections of the good, and when we are healthy and mature, we wish our days to be spent in promoting that which is good. Humanity's attraction to the good is embodied in the universal human concern for values.

Every society seeks to impart to its children its values, not only as a strategy for protecting the social order but also because we believe that by adhering to values, the inherent potentiality of our children – that which is fundamentally good in them – will best be realized. Values are thus taught in every society as part of the humanizing process. Our concern for spirituality is a concern for those transcultural, transhistorical values that would redound to the fullest development of human potential. When we speak of the cultivation of spirituality, we are speaking, in part, of the creation of the moral context in which human development can most effectively take place.

According to the world's spiritual traditions, there are certain moral conditions without which healthy human development is nearly impossible. Among the most important of these moral prerequisites are truthfulness, trustworthiness, compassion for other living beings, commitment to social justice and freedom from the tyranny of selfish desires. The cultivation of these social goods, or virtues, has been seen as important throughout the ages and across all civilizations. It is the eternality and cross-cultural nature of their importance to human life that leads us to regard virtues as spiritual qualities, without which human civilization is impossible.

Spirituality is manifested in our capacities of heart or feeling. These emotional capacities reflect themselves most potently in our longing for connection with other human beings, with our quest for union with God, and with our striving to surround ourselves with what is beautiful. Indeed, as Naguchi, Hanson, and Lample note, an attraction to beauty – the beauty of an object, an idea, an act – in many cases activates our will and motivates us to work and to strive so that we might be the creative authors of beauty or manifest beauty in the quality of our own lives. When we speak of spirituality, we are thus speaking, in part, of the heart's attraction to beauty.

When it is properly developed, the attraction to beauty may serve not only as an aesthetic lens through which to view the world, but as a guiding light or standard whereby individuals may judge their own work and behaviour. Attraction to beauty, the authors mentioned above write,

> manifests itself in love for the majesty and diversity of nature, the impulse to express beauty through visual arts, music and crafts, and the pleasure of beholding the fruits of these creative endeavors. It is also evident in one's response to the beauty of an idea, the elegance of a scientific theory, and the perfection of a good character in one's fellow human beings. On another level, attraction to beauty underlies the search for order and meaning in the universe, which extends itself to a desire for order in social relations.[22]

The phenomenology of spirit

The human soul provides humanity with another important power – the capacity to have a felt or phenomenological sense of the *presence* of spirit. Such a sense is what shall be referred to here as *a consciousness of the sacred*, which may be manifested in a variety of ways. It may be manifested in the uniquely human emotions of awe, wonder, and humility that accompany the perception of the presence of forces of truth, beauty, and/ or goodness that transcend the self; it may be awakened by an encounter with what Rudolph Otto refers to as the *mysterium tremendum* in his classic work *The Idea of the Holy*; or it may be a more regular part of a highly developed person's consciousness as described by William James in his discussion of 'saintliness' in *The Varieties of Religious Experience*. Whatever their nature, encounters with the sacred have been an undeniable feature of human development and transformation from the earliest days of recorded history. Indeed, an encounter with the sacred often has generated in human beings the courage, commitment, and vision necessary to begin their lives anew and to contribute in selfless ways to the evolution and development of society.

In the Bahá'í view, at least two expressions of spirit embody a sense of the sacred. These are referred to as the 'heavenly spirit' or the 'spirit of faith'; and the 'Holy Spirit'. The heavenly spirit or the spirit of faith is manifested when an individual's thoughts, actions, and intentions are in harmony with that which is good, beautiful, and true, as set forth in the holy texts. This convergence of the human will with the Will of God is said to attract to the centre of human action a transcendent spiritual force that serves to contribute to human advancement while also edifying the souls of others. Bahá'ís often refer to this unique form of spiritual assistance as 'the confirmations of God', and they believe that such confirmations are enjoyed by anyone of any faith or philosophy who labours for the good of the world. In a talk delivered in New York and recorded in *The Promulgation of Universal Peace*, 'Abdu'l-Bahá made the following statement:

> Consecrate and devote yourselves to the betterment and service of all the human race . . . for when your motives are universal and your intentions heavenly in character, when your aspirations are centred in the Kingdom, there is no doubt whatever that you will become the recipients of the bounty and good pleasure of God . . . Therefore, be ye assured and confident that the confirmations of God are descending upon you, the assistance of God will be given unto you . . . Be ye confident and steadfast; your services are confirmed by the powers of heaven, for your intentions are lofty, your purposes pure and worthy. God is the helper of those souls whose aim is to serve humanity and whose efforts and endeavors are devoted to the good and betterment of all mankind.[23]

Without the capacity to serve that which is sacred, or that which is, in some abstract sense, authentically and enduringly true, beautiful, and good, civilization would be impossible. Indeed, unless a significant proportion of a people are inspired on the level of the heart to be seekers after truth, lovers of beauty, and doers of good, the social order deteriorates into a discordant cacophony of competing interests, useless ideas, and vulgar acts. In such a context, the larger project of human development is neglected, and the civilizing process retards or reverses. For this reason, the Bahá'í writings affirm that spiritual inclinations, unencumbered by superstitious ideas and useless ideologies, are as vital to the protection and development of civilization as are sciences, arts, and technologies. In his explication of this principle, 'Abdu'l-Bahá said:

> Among other principles of Bahá'u'lláh's teachings was the harmony of science and religion. Religion must stand the analysis of reason. It must agree with scientific fact and proof so that science will sanction religion and religion fortify science. Both are indissolubly welded and joined in reality. If statements and teachings of religion are found to be unreasonable and contrary to science, they are outcomes of superstition and imagination . . . That which is found to be real and conformable to reason must be accepted, and whatever science and reason cannot support must be rejected as imitation and not reality. Then differences of belief will disappear. All will become as one family, one people, and the same susceptibility to the divine bounty and education will be witnessed among mankind.[24]

One should note that in the Bahá'í view, the body, brain, and mind are not ends in themselves; rather, they are means for the manifestation and cultivation of spiritual capacities. The Bahá'í writings claim that spiritual capacities constitute the real (or ideal) forces or powers of existence and that they represent the enduring harvest of a human life. 'In the world of existence', according to 'Abdu'l-Bahá, 'there is nothing so important as spirit, nothing so essential as the spirit of man. The spirit of man is the meeting between man and God. The spirit of man is the animus of human life and the collective centre of all human virtues. The spirit of man is the cause of the illumination of this world.'[25] Thus the cultivation of the human spirit (or of human consciousness) may serve as a discernible telos of evolution and development. Viewed in the light of this perspective, it may be argued that progress is 'the expression of spirit in the world of matter'[26] and that the central role of society is to provide the moral, political, economic, and institutional resources that best facilitate the protection, development, and refinement of the human spirit as it struggles in its self-conscious effort to evolve.

In the Bahá'í teachings, the 'Holy Spirit' is another level of spirit that is said to be the intermediary between the world of humanity and the realm of God. 'Abdu'l-Bahá briefly explains this idea:

> the Holy Spirit . . . brings the created earth into relation with the 'Unthinkable One', the Divine Reality.
> The Divine Reality may be likened to the sun and the Holy Spirit to the rays of the sun. As the rays of the sun bring the light and warmth of the sun to the earth, giving life to all created beings, so do the 'Manifestations' [of God] bring the power of the Holy Spirit from the Divine Sun of reality to give light and life to the souls of men.[27]

In the chapters that follow, we explore the unique capacities of the human spirit with greater care by examining the three powers most closely associated with it. These powers include the power to know, love, and will.

PART I

UNIQUE POWERS OF THE HUMAN SPIRIT

I

THE CAPACITY TO KNOW

In its capacity to know, the human spirit seeks knowledge of reality. As Noguchi, Hanson, and Lample note, an innate desire for knowledge motivates each human being to acquire an understanding of the mysteries of the self and of the universe. An individual motivated by a thirst for knowledge, they observed, approaches life as 'an investigator of reality and a seeker after truth'.[1]

While the Bahá'í teachings are in harmony with the postmodern observation that truth is always relative rather than absolute, the Bahá'í perspective departs from postmodernist thinking in affirming that the relativity of truth results, not from *its* state, but from ours. Truth is always relative to us because we necessarily approach it with the limitations of human consciousness, human maturation, and human needs and concerns. As human consciousness matures, and as our instruments for investigating reality advance, we naturally come to recognize that what we once regarded as true requires modification, and sometimes even outright rejection. In addition, as the number and diversity of truth seekers who are given voice expands, what we understand as truth is also likely to expand. Nevertheless, it is our striving to attain an apprehension of truth that has inspired our scientific, philosophical, and religious quests throughout the ages. The hunger for truth is reflected in our disdain for those who wittingly distort the truth for personal gain; it is reflected in our dissatisfaction with our own selves when we fail to be truthful; and it is manifested in the vast personal and collective resources that we expend in the search for truth as we explore the natural, social, and spiritual dimensions of life. The Bahá'í writings suggest that the longing for truth is also a reflection of the human longing for God. And while God is described as essentially unknowable, the human spirit can grow in its capacity to appreciate the *signs of God* which are reflected, to varying degrees, in all the phenomena of life.

The search for truth

Humans are unique in the capacity not only to think – but also to think about our thinking. When the power of human thought takes as its object thought itself, this capacity, as noted above, is known as the capacity for *meta-cognition*. Meta-cognitive abilities distinguish human beings from all other known species because they enable us not only to acquire knowledge and beliefs about the world and ourselves, but also to reflect critically upon our knowledge and beliefs. Thus, we may ask ourselves whether our thinking is internally consistent or logical; whether it is in conformity with what we observe through our senses; whether our inner convictions conform to our outward behaviour, and so forth.

Humanity's unique intellectual capacity for use of language and complex symbol systems thus enables the acquisition of two distinct but interrelated types of knowledge: knowledge of those things which can be perceived by the senses, and knowledge of intellectual or abstract realities (such as thought, gravity, justice, beauty, etc.). All other animals are limited in their mental manipulations to observable phenomena. Consider, for example, humanity's capacity to engage in scientific investigation. By careful observation, accompanied by critical reflection on that which we observe, humans are able to discover the operation of forces that are not themselves directly observable. Thus the human intellect brings forth from nature her hidden secrets (e.g. nature's laws) and enables us to harness natural forces for benefit or harm.

Consider an example. Astronomers tell us that the distance between the moon and the earth varies between 222, 042 miles on 21 January (perigee) and 251, 211 miles on 4 December (apogee). We know that this is correct because we have been able to land a spaceship on the moon using these distances for making the necessary calculations. You will note that there is nothing that we can observe through the use of the senses alone that can provide us with this information. In order to discover these truths, we have to deploy powers of reflection and analysis that have no parallel in the rest of the natural world. The signs that provide evidence of the existence of these unique powers justify the invocation of a unique cause which we are referring to here as the power of the human spirit.

To continue, we note that meta-cognitive capacities develop as a result of at least three interrelated mechanisms: first, biological processes associated with human evolution and maturation; second, the deliberate, systematic, and conscious effort of human beings to develop our capacity for critical thinking and the transmission of these capacities over time via the instruments of culture; and third, the intervention in history of those mystical Beings that are the founders of the world's religions (Abraham, Krishna, Zoroaster, Buddha, Jesus, Muhammad, the Báb, Bahá'u'lláh, and so forth). These unique souls, Bahá'ís believe, embody the capacity to extend the reach of human consciousness into new spheres of awareness and understanding. In addition, they fertilize the human spirit with new creative capacities that result in the emergence of new arts and sciences in much the same way that the sun in springtime brings forth the hidden potentialities of nature. The Bahá'í writings suggest that these Holy Ones also endow the human mind with new moral, social, and spiritual concepts that give rise to new forms of civilization. We explore this claim with some degree of care in a future chapter.

The conceptual development of critical thinking

The formalized process of critical thinking was perhaps first associated with the practice of *hermeneutics*. And although the term 'hermeneutics' entered common scholarly discourse in the beginning of the seventeenth century, the practice of hermeneutics may be traced to the earliest days of *exegesis*. In his discourse on the nature of religious intuitions, for example, Plato distinguished what we now call hermeneutic knowledge from what he called *Sophia*. Intuitive knowledge, which may be derived from the practice of hermeneutics, was said to be a form of knowledge that one receives from a critical examination and explication of the *meaning* of an utterance or text. This type of knowledge does not depend upon the truth-value of the interpretation – as the meaning of an ambiguous or metaphorical text may be subject to a variety of legitimate interpretations. *Sophia*, by contrast, was said to be knowledge of the actual nature of reality and thus must be grounded in objective truth. From this perspective, when what is in a thinker's mind corresponds to the reality of things, this correspondence could be referred to as *knowledge*. Philosophy, as conceptualized by the ancient Greeks, is thus the systematic process of interrogating one's beliefs about reality in such a way as to lead to knowledge of truth. Thus, we see from the outset two traditions of critical thinking – one centred in subjective interpretation (or exegesis) of metaphors and symbols; and the other centred in the search for objective truth concerning the nature of things. In all of nature, both these powers appear to be confined to human beings – and thus they are associated in the Bahá'í writings with the human spirit:

> The human spirit, which distinguishes man from the animal, is the rational soul, and these two names – the human spirit and the rational soul – designate one and the same thing. This spirit, which in the terminology of the philosophers is called the rational soul, encompasses all things and, as far as human capacity permits, discovers their realities and becomes aware of the properties and effects, the characteristics and conditions of earthly things.[2]

The formal intellectual roots of critical thinking are commonly traced to Plato's mentor, Socrates, whom Bahá'u'lláh describes as among the greatest of all philosophers:

> What a penetrating vision into philosophy this eminent man had! He is the most distinguished of all philosophers and was highly versed in wisdom. We testify that he is one of the heroes in this field and an outstanding champion dedicated unto it. He had a profound knowledge of such sciences as were current amongst men as well as of those which were veiled from their minds. Methinks he drank one draught when the Most Great Ocean overflowed with gleaming and life-giving waters. He it is who perceived a unique, a tempered, and a pervasive nature in things, bearing the closest likeness to the human spirit, and he discovered this nature to be distinct from the substance of things in their refined form. He hath a special pronouncement on this weighty theme. Wert thou to ask from the worldly wise of this generation about this exposition, thou wouldst witness their incapacity to grasp it.[3]

In his skilful use of systematic questioning, Socrates discovered that people were not particularly good at justifying their confident claims to knowledge. To the contrary, he found that 'confused meanings, inadequate evidence, or self-contradictory beliefs often lurked beneath smooth but largely empty rhetoric'.[4] Employing a method of questioning that was to be named in his honour ('Socratic dialogue') Socrates established that it is not always wise to depend upon those in authority to have sound knowledge and insight. In a series of discussions captured by the pen of his student, Plato, Socrates demonstrated time and time again that although persons may be in positions of power, they may be nevertheless confused and irrational. Socrates thus established the importance of asking challenging questions that require the knower to probe deeply into the ground of one's thinking before accepting an idea as worthy of belief.

As have many of the world's wisest, Socrates suffered martyr-dom for his rigorous assault on the presumptions to knowledge that animated the minds of many in the Greek aristocracy. In his place Plato was to stand and, soon after the death of Socrates, establish the revered centre of learning known as *Akademia*. For approximately 900 years it was the scholars of the Academy who were to preserve the Socratic and Platonic traditions of critical thought.

At the Academy Plato instructed Aristotle and the Greek sceptics – each of whom argued, as have the Bahá'í writings – that the realities of things are often very different from the way they appear. Plato promulgated the view that it is only the disci-plined mind that is prepared to see beyond surface appearances to the deeper realities of life. From this ancient Greek tradition there thus emerged the need for those who aspire to understand the deeper realities 'to think systematically, to trace implications broadly and deeply, for only thinking that is comprehensive, well-reasoned, and responsive to objections can take us beyond the surface'.[5] In emphasizing the 'search for truth' as a spiri-tual principle, and as an antidote to the crippling influences of useless dogma, ancient prejudices, and moribund superstitions, the Bahá'í writings proved to be in harmony with many Platonic epistemic prescriptions. 'Abdu'l-Bahá once said:

> Man must cut himself free from all prejudice and from the result of his own imagination, so that he may be able to search for truth unhindered. Truth is one in all religions, and by means of it the unity of the world can be realized.
>
> All the peoples have a fundamental belief in common. Being one, truth cannot be divided, and the differences that appear to exist among the nations only result from their attachment to prejudice. If only men would search out truth, they would find themselves united.[6]

Another of the contributions to critical thinking that was to emerge from the Socratic tradition was the recognition of the close relationship between epistemology and ethics. In other words, the early Greek philosophers brought to human consciousness the realization that the quality and reliability of human thought and knowledge depend, to a significant degree, on the moral qualities that animate the inner life of those who would be seekers after truth. When the process of critical thinking is sullied by selfish motives it may well deteriorate into a skilful and self-serving manipulation of ideas. Such was the condition of the Sophists, who, according to one encyclopedia of philosophy,

> undertook to provide a stock of arguments on any subject, or to prove any position. They boasted of their ability to make the worse appear the better reason, to prove that black is white. Some, like Gorgias, asserted that it was not necessary to have any knowledge of a subject to give satisfactory replies as regards it. Thus, Gorgias ostentatiously answered any question on any subject instantly and without consideration. To attain these ends mere quibbling, and the scoring of verbal points were employed. In this way, the sophists tried to entangle, entrap, and confuse their opponents, and even, if this were not possible, to beat them down by mere violence and noise. They sought also to dazzle by means of strange or flowery metaphors, by unusual figures of speech, by epigrams and paradoxes, and in general by being clever and smart, rather than earnest and truthful. Hence our word 'sophistry': the use of fallacious arguments knowing them to be such.[7]

Commensurate with the view that ethics and epistemology are intertwined, some of the wisest philosophers have taught that what we can know depends, to a significant degree, on our moral status; they have taught that knowledge of the true, beautiful and good is, in part, dependent upon such factors as the purity of our motivation and the sincerity of our purpose. Indeed, like Plato and Socrates, the founders of the world's religions have affirmed that ethics, epistemology and aesthetics are not separate spheres but are intimately intertwined. These three domains of inquiry are said to find a common ground in what the Bahá'í teachings refer to as 'the city of the human heart'.[8]

From this point of view, the heart may be conceptualized as the seat of the kind of knowledge that enables us to live a life that is honoured by spiritual excellence, nobility of character, contentment and inner peace, as well as wisdom and good relations with other living beings. Without this form of knowledge, which is sometimes called 'enlightenment', the little bits of knowledge that we gather can swell the ego and render us incapable of living well – either with ourselves or others.

It is, perhaps, this special type of knowledge that Christ sought to awaken when He taught: 'Blessed are the pure in heart, for they shall see God.'[9] To 'see God' in this sense is to have the capacity to recognize that which is true, and beautiful, and good. In this regard, it is instructive to note that when the Nuremberg trials were underway, twenty-one of the most senior Nazi leaders were administered IQ tests by prominent specialists in mental health. These examinations, conducted by different teams, led to similar conclusions – the Nazi leaders were sane, unusually intelligent, but also suffered from deep character flaws which were reflected in the unresponsiveness of their nervous systems to the suffering of others. In such men the light of the intellect was strong but the faculties of the heart were gravely impaired. In this way their knowledge proved not to be a resource but was a society-destroying power that nearly brought the 'civilized' world to ruin.

The Middle Ages in Europe was to witness the birth and life of one of the most significant figures in the history of critical thought. We refer here to an early apologist of Christian theology – St Thomas Aquinas (1225–1274). 'Aquinas lived at a critical juncture of western culture,' notes the *Stanford Encyclopedia of Philosophy*, 'when the arrival of the Aristotelian *corpus* in Latin reopened the question of the relation between faith and reason . . .'[10] Among Aquinas's many contributions was his insistence that his own thoughts, and even those upon which his faith was grounded, must be exposed to critical examination. Only those convictions that were capable of withstanding deliberate, systematic and public scrutiny, asserted Aquinas, deserve the believer's continued endorsement. Relying heavily upon the insights and proofs that had emerged centuries earlier from the mind of Aristotle, Aquinas introduces to theological discourse the requirement of 'justifiable belief'. His work is among the earliest attempts, therefore, to reconcile faith and reason.

Commensurate with this view, the Bahá'í teachings note that faith and reason are powers through which the human soul may gain knowledge and insight into the physical and spiritual dimensions of life. Reason, the Bahá'í writings affirm, is 'the first faculty of man'[11] and the power to reason 'singles man out from among created beings, and makes of him a creature apart'.[12] 'Abdu'l-Bahá noted that 'God has given us rational minds . . . to penetrate all things, to find truth. If one renounce reason,' he continued, 'what remains?'[13]

From a Bahá'í point of view, faith and reason are both necessary in order to advance the sciences, arts, and technologies that are at the foundation of civilization building. Rather than blind belief, the Bahá'í writings describe faith as conscious knowledge acted upon.[14] As one acts upon one's knowledge, knowledge is refined, new questions and challenges emerge, and the instruments that are required for human advancement may be brought into being. From this point of view, the practice of science is, itself, an act of faith.

Returning to Aquinas, one might note that among the most important of his contributions to critical thinking was his theory of analogy. Much critical thinking in the sciences, arts and humanities is dependent upon analogy. Analogies empower us to apply knowledge gained in one field of study to questions in another; and since the meanings of well-formed analogies are sufficiently ambiguous to invite multiple interpretations, analogies serve as vehicles for the cultivation of insight and discernment. It was, perhaps, this power of analogy that attracted the mind of Aquinas.

The Bahá'í teachings affirm that it is not possible to speak deeply of human experience without the use of analogies. Analogies enable us to draw upon the sensible dimensions of life in order to understand those phenomena of life that are wholly abstract or what might be called 'spiritual'. 'Abdu'l-Bahá once said:

> ... when you wish to express the reality of the spirit and its conditions and degrees, you are obliged to describe them in terms of sensible things ... For example, grief and happiness are intelligible things, but when you wish to express these spiritual conditions you say, 'My heart became heavy', or 'My heart was uplifted', although one's heart is not literally made heavy or lifted up. Rather, it is a spiritual or intelligible condition, the expression of which requires the use of sensible terms. Another example is when you say, 'So-and-so has greatly advanced', although he has remained in the same place, or 'So-and-So has a high position', whereas, like everyone else, he continues to walk upon the earth. This elevation and advancement are spiritual conditions and intelligible realities, but to express them you must use sensible terms ...[15]

It is thus our capacity to engage in metaphorical and analogous thinking that gives us access to understandings that transcend the material realm. In this way, we may use our knowledge of the things of nature to convey insights into what is, itself, otherwise ineffable.

In addition to Aristotle, another scholar who was to have a significant influence on both Aquinas and the literature on critical thought was the great Jewish scholar, rabbi, and physician Moses Maimonides (1138–1204). Having lived for a time among the Moors in Cordoba, Spain, Maimonides came under the influence, not only of the Greeks whose works were preserved and translated by Muslim scholars, but also under the influence of some of the greatest Muslim thinkers ever to live, such as Avicenna. Maimonides was convinced that there could be no contradiction between the truths revealed by God and the discoveries that flow from the human mind as a consequence of the practice of science and philosophy. Many are his contributions to critical thinking. For example, Maimonides demonstrated a keen sensitivity to the value of paradox and showed a remarkable capacity to reconcile what appeared to be contradictory ideas. In this way did Maimonides introduce to critical thinking a degree of nuance and tolerance for ambiguity that served as a 'guide for the perplexed'.

In the period following Maimonides and Aquinas, significant movement in the direction of a commitment to *empiricism* (as opposed to philosophy) as *the foundation* for knowledge claims can be discerned. Sir Francis Bacon (1561–1626) was to be an important thinker in consolidating this epistemological shift. Inasmuch as Bacon had been a contemporary of Galileo and had observed in Galileo's life the church's resistance to the unfettered search for truth, Bacon knew well that both human minds and human institutions tend to use a variety of strategies to justify convenient, self-serving beliefs. In addition, as Fulton Anderson would note in his edited volume, *Bacon: The New Organon*, when Bacon entered Cambridge University at twelve years of age he would be subject to university exercises designed to train the student in disputation. These methods, shackled as they were to the rules of syllogistic logic, Bacon would come to deplore:

> A respondent was required to defend theses, with terms defined, against two or more opponents. The candidate's first disputations were rhetorical exercises, considered preparatory to later disputational 'demonstrations of truth'. 'Truth' in this conjunction consisted largely of a collection of prepositions traditionally taken from the physical, ethical, political and metaphysical works of Aristotle. The contexts of these propositions in the original writings were more often than not unfamiliar to candidates and not always

remembered, if ever known, by presiding officers. Against this method of testing and examination Bacon rebelled.[16]

What Bacon wished to see was the deployment of a method of inquiry that would enable the validation of beliefs, not so much against the demands of logic and rhetoric, but against the hard reality of observable facts. In his book *The Advancement of Learning*, Bacon was thus to insist that truth claims be justified by means of empirical validation. The corpus of his writings earned Bacon recognition as one of the founders of scientific method.

Following closely on the heels of Bacon, René Descartes (1596–1650) would contribute new insights that support the epistemological foundations of empirical methods. In *Rules for the Direction of Mind*, Descartes developed an approach to critical thought that was based upon the principle of systematic doubt. Having loosed himself from the fetters of any aspects of knowledge for which there was reason to doubt, Descartes then built his empirical approach upon that about which there could be no doubt (*Dubito, ergo cogito, ergo sum* – I doubt, therefore I think, therefore I am). Concerning Descartes' contribution to the emergence of scientific epistemologies, William Hatcher writes:

> There can be no serious doubt that the modern period, both in philosophy and science begins with René Descartes . . . Descartes' philosophy was really a form of Platonism, in which innate ideas, implanted in the mind of God, played a similar role to the universal forms of Plato's philosophy. The important shift, however, was that Descartes' approach was bottom-up instead of top-down. It began with the undisputable facts of the human condition (we are conscious, self-aware beings with no intrinsic measure of absolute truth), and moved upwards towards the absolute (whose existence we can deduce from the nature of our innate ideas). For Plato, empirical observation and logical analysis

were only exercises – vulgar approximations of the true knowledge that came only with the clear intuition of the forms. For Descartes, however, logical analysis and empirical observation were an integral part of true knowledge itself. For him, knowing meant knowledge of causal relationships between phenomena, the latter giving rise to laws which could be expressed in the exact language of mathematics.[17]

In addition to a growing commitment to empirical methods, by the seventeenth, eighteenth and nineteenth centuries the application of critical thought would be extended well beyond philosophical questions, or even matters related to the workings of nature, and would begin to include radical critiques of the social order. Enlightenment thinkers such as Voltaire, Diderot, Montesquieu, Paine, Rousseau and Hume, among others, would open the way to greater freedom to engage in intellectual explorations. These philosophers thus sought to liberate the human mind from the muffling power of ecclesiastical and political authority. In the view of Peter Gay, the Enlightenment broke through 'the sacred circle' whose dogma had imprisoned thinking.[18] In this way did the Enlightenment philosophers open an age of free and open inquiry that many have referred to as the 'modern age'. As has been noted by a number of scholars, this effort to liberate the human mind and spirit so that it could freely explore reality would prove critical to the effort to advance human rights.

Liberation of the intellect from constraints imposed by various ecclesiastical systems is a value often expressed in the Bahá'í teachings. Indeed, in remarks delivered in Paris on 12 November 1911, 'Abdu'l-Bahá noted:

Many religious leaders have grown to think that the importance of religion lies mainly in the adherence to a collection of certain dogmas and the practice of rites and ceremonies! Those whose souls they profess to cure are taught to believe likewise, and these cling tenaciously to the outward forms, confusing them with the inward truth.

35

Now, these forms and rituals differ in the various churches and amongst the different sects, and even contradict one another; giving rise to discord, hatred, and disunion. The outcome of all this dissension is the belief of many cultured men that religion and science are contradictory terms, that religion needs no powers of reflection, and should in no way be regulated by science, but must of necessity be opposed, the one to the other. The unfortunate effect of this is that science has drifted apart from religion, and religion has become a mere blind and more or less apathetic following of precepts of certain religious teachers, who insist on their favorite dogmas being accepted even when they are contrary to science. This is foolishness, for it is quite evident that science is the light, and, being so, religion *truly* so-called does not oppose knowledge.

We are familiar with the phrases 'Light and Darkness', 'Religion and Science'. But the religion which does not walk hand in hand with science is itself in the darkness of superstition and ignorance.

Much of the discord and disunion of the world is created by these man-made oppositions and contradictions. If religion were in harmony with science and they walked together, much of the hatred and bitterness now bringing misery to the human race would be at an end.[19]

The twentieth century witnessed the emergence of a generation of thinkers who would amplify the relationship between knowledge and power (such as William Sumner, Michel Foucault, or Paulo Freire). Others, following in the intellectual wake of the eighteenth-century philosopher Immanuel Kant, would demonstrate how human categories of thought or human methods of empirical investigation (Werner Heisenberg), or human needs, values and commitments (Koltko-Rivera) tend to impact the search for truth. Still others would begin to question whether truth could exist at all independently of what we say about the world.[20] Thus, it was during the twentieth century that the optimistic forecasts of the Enlightenment, which were grounded in the assumption that science and reason, unencumbered by superstition, would lead humanity out of ignorance and misery, began to come under doubt.

Into this growing confusion, the Bahá'í writings sought to offer models of reality and ways of thinking that sought to integrate and harmonize a diversity of epistemological approaches. Persuaded of the postmodern observation that the pursuit of truth is, of necessity, conditioned by a range of limitations – including those imposed by nature on the human mind, those associated with particular methods of observation and analysis, biases that are largely theoretical and that limit and structure what might be regarded as data, and a range of human interests, needs and concerns that incarnate themselves in the questions we ask – the Bahá'í writings encourage earnest *pursuit of truth*, unsullied by selfish motives, as human life depends upon it. Indeed, our protection of the right to pursue truth, our capacity to embody truth in our speech and actions, the development of centres of learning that advance the acquisition of knowledge of truths, and the development and refinement of methods for the investigation of the truths that undergird reality are necessary preconditions for sustaining what we have come to regard as 'civilization':

> Consider carefully: all these highly-varied phenomena, these concepts, this knowledge, these technical procedures and philosophical systems, these sciences, arts, industries and inventions – all are emanations of the human mind. Whatever people has ventured deeper into this shoreless sea, has come to excel the rest. The happiness and pride of a nation consist in this, that it should shine out like the sun in the high heaven of knowledge . . . And the honour and distinction of the individual consist in this, that he among all the world's multitudes should become a source of social good. Is any larger bounty conceivable than this, that an individual, looking within himself, should find that . . . he

has become the cause of peace and well-being, of happiness and advantage to his fellow men? No . . . there is no greater bliss, no more complete delight.[21]

To aid in the development of the capacity to pursue truth, societies for the cultivation of critical thinking have begun to emerge. In emphasizing the intellectual traits or virtues that should animate the search for truth, many of these societies promote values that are in harmony with Bahá'í epistemic ethics. Among these virtues are intellectual integrity, intellectual humility, confidence in reason, intellectual perseverance, fairmindedness, intellectual courage, intellectual empathy, and intellectual autonomy. In their explication of these intellectual traits, Richard Paul and Linda Elder have provided a variety of useful guides and distinctions:

- *Intellectual humility versus intellectual arrogance*: Having a consciousness of the limits of one's knowledge, including a sensitivity to circumstances in which one's native egocentrism is likely to function self-deceptively; sensitivity to bias, prejudice and limitations of one's viewpoint. Intellectual humility depends on recognizing that one should not claim more than one actually knows. It does not imply spinelessness or submissiveness. It implies the lack of intellectual pretentiousness, boastfulness, or conceit, combined with insight into the logical foundation, or lack of such foundation, of one's beliefs.
- *Intellectual courage versus intellectual cowardice*: Having a consciousness of the need to face and fairly address ideas, beliefs or viewpoints toward which we have strong negative emotions and to which we have not given a serious hearing. This courage is connected with the recognition that ideas considered dangerous or absurd are sometimes rationally justified (in whole or in part) and that conclusions and beliefs inculcated in us are sometimes false and misleading. To determine for ourselves which is which, we must not

passively and uncritically 'accept' what we have 'learned'. Intellectual courage comes into play here because inevitably we will come to see some truth in some ideas considered dangerous and absurd, and distortion or falsity in some ideas strongly held in our social group. We need courage to be true to our own thinking in such circumstances. The penalties for nonconformity can be severe.

- *Intellectual empathy versus intellectual narrow-mindedness*: Having a consciousness of the need to imaginatively put oneself in the place of others in order to genuinely understand them, which requires the consciousness of our egocentric tendency to identify truth with our immediate perceptions of long-standing thought or belief. This trait correlates with the willingness to remember occasions when we were wrong in the past despite an intense conviction that we were right, and with the ability to imagine our being similarly deceived in a case at hand.

- *Intellectual autonomy versus intellectual conformity*: Having rational control of one's beliefs, values and inferences. The ideal of critical thinking is to learn to think for oneself, to gain command over one's thought processes. It entails a commitment to analysing and evaluating beliefs on the basis of reason and evidence, to question when it is rational to question, to believe when it is rational to believe, and to conform when it is rational to conform.

- *Intellectual integrity versus intellectual hypocrisy*: Recognition of the need to be true to one's own thinking; to be consistent in the intellectual standards one applies; to hold oneself to the same rigorous standards of evidence and proof to which one holds one's antagonists; to practice what one advocates for others; and to honestly admit discrepancies and inconsistencies in one's own thought and action.

- *Intellectual perseverance versus intellectual laziness*: Having a consciousness of the need to use intellectual insights and truths in spite of difficulties, obstacles, and frustrations; firm adherence to rational principles despite the irrational opposition of others; a sense of the need to struggle with confusion and unsettled questions over an extended period of time to achieve deeper understanding or insight.

- *Confidence in reason versus distrust of reason and evidence*: Confidence that, in the long run, one's own higher interests and those of humankind at large will be best served by giving the freest play to reason, by encouraging people to come to their own conclusions by developing their own rational faculties; faith that, with proper encouragement and cultivation, people can learn to think for themselves, to form rational viewpoints, draw reasonable conclusions, think coherently and logically, persuade each other by reason and become reasonable persons, despite deep-seated obstacles in the native character of the human mind and in society as we know it.

- *Fairmindedness versus intellectual unfairness*: Having a consciousness of the need to treat all viewpoints alike, with reference to one's own feelings or vested interests, or the feelings or vested interests of one's friends, community or nation; implies adherence to intellectual standards without reference to one's own advantage or the advantage of one's group.[22]

The search for truth and two traditions of learning

In addition to exploration and cultivation of nature's resources, the development of the human spirit is reflected in the acquisition of noble qualities and the refinement of human character. However magnificent it may be in arts and sciences, no civilization can long endure if it neglects this aspect of human learning. Thus, a comprehensive approach to human development must embody processes of learning that encompass knowledge and refinement of the self as much as it stresses knowledge and refinement of the world. The Baháʼí writings suggest that if it is to be effective, education of the human spirit must reflect an appreciation of both of these dimensions of learning. The complementary nature of these two traditions has been captured succinctly in the Analects, one of the books that embody the teachings of the Chinese sage Confucius:

> The ancients who wished to illustrate illustrious virtue throughout the empire, first ordered well their own States. Wishing to order well their States, they first regulated their families. Wishing to regulate their families, they first cultivated their persons. Wishing to cultivate their persons, they first rectified their hearts. Wishing to rectify their hearts, they first sought to be sincere in their thoughts. Wishing to be sincere in their thoughts, they first extended to the utmost their knowledge. Such extension of knowledge lay in the investigation of things.[23]

The 'investigation of things' takes many forms and requires the use of reason, the empirical tools of science, the insights into reality contained in the works of pre-modern and contemporary philosophers, and the new perspectives that emerge in an atmosphere of humble consultation that is animated by a sincere desire to discover and then act upon new truths.

In his twelve-volume classic, *A Study of History* (1934–1961) the English historian Arnold Toynbee noted that like all complex systems, human civilizations are subject to the forces of entropy and thus require periodic renewal and reinvigoration. The historical record would suggest that such renewal is fuelled not only by paradigm shifts in the sciences which make possible technological revolutions, but by the intervention in history of the luminaries, prophets, and enlightened ones who have founded the world's great religions. Whatever deterioration and corruption their teachings may have suffered following their initial impact, no fair-minded observer can deny that Buddha, Jesus, Zoroaster, Muhammad, and a host of other sages have, throughout the ages, promoted greater commitment to the common good, cultivated deeper insight into moral and spiritual truths, and nurtured greater capacity to express, both individually and collectively, human compassion, wisdom, and love.

The Bahá'í teachings affirm that human prosperity can never be achieved without the harmonious interplay of the scientific and spiritual impulse, because each of these faculties constitutes integral, interrelated and essential aspects of human longing and identity. The proper expression of these faculties requires that the one hold in check and inform the other. Indeed, both religion and science may well need philosophy to ensure these systems of thought are put to good uses. The development of science and technology without the concomitant evolution of moral insight and spiritual wisdom leads to misuse of the creative powers of mind; while religion, without the tempering, evidenced-based, systematic and critical powers of science leads to the proliferation of suffocating dogmas, useless speculation, unbridled fanaticism, superstition, and intolerance of uncertainty. Each of these epistemic systems concerns itself with a dimension of human existence that cannot be neglected if the social, spiritual and intellectual capital that sustains community life, and indeed nature itself, are to be protected.

The capacity to know is animated and fuelled by another human capacity, which is the capacity to love. In the chapter that follows we outline the essential nature of that capacity and explore the relationship of love to knowledge.

2

THE CAPACITY TO LOVE

Love is *a power of attraction* and, according to the Bahá'í writings, all things that exist owe their existence to this power. The properties of water, for example, which provide the basis of organic life, come into existence through the union of hydrogen and oxygen. Gravity, which holds the planets and stars in orbit, is thought to be another manifestation of this power and it operates wherever matter can be found in the universe. Indeed, all phenomena derive their existence from union of some kind – and so when the phenomenon of *love* is invoked in the Bahá'í writings it is often referring to that force of attraction that makes connection and union in the world possible. 'Abdu'l-Bahá wrote:

> Love is . . . the unique power that bindeth together the divers elements of this material world, the supreme magnetic force that directeth the movements of the spheres in the celestial realms. Love revealeth with unfailing and limitless power the mysteries latent in the universe. Love is the spirit of life unto the adorned body of mankind, the establisher of true civilization in this mortal world, and the shedder of imperishable glory upon every high-aiming race and nation.[1]

The attraction that is love confers life because all creatures are dependent upon other creatures for their existence. That is, the existence of any particular thing is dependent upon the existence of something else – and thus no being, with the exception of God is in itself self-sufficient. Another way to put this is to say that all power and ability in this world is derived from association. In this sense the power of attraction, the bonding power in the world, can be said to be an expression of the power of love; and this power, as has been noted, makes all forms of existence possible.

In the biological realm love is manifested in the organization of organic matter into complex structures capable of signal detection and goal-directed movement in the service of survival, development, and reproduction. Over millennia simple organic systems have enhanced their mutual survivability by organizing into ever more complex systems that form organs, and diverse organ systems, working together in harmonious patterns, make possible forms of life that embody capacities that are greater than the sum of parts.[2] For example, in higher levels of organization organic systems manifest the capacity for conscious awareness of the environment through sense perception.

In *A General Theory of Love*, Thomas Lewis, Fari Amini, and Richard Lannon have argued that love begins to appear in a conscious way with the evolution of the limbic system. 'Reptiles', they write, 'don't have an emotional life. The reptilian brain permits rudimentary interactions: displays of aggression and courtship, mating and territorial defense.'[3] In order to see behaviour that approaches anything that we would call conscious love, one must have the complex brain and hormonal structures that enable mammals to 'care' for organisms that are not themselves. These 'others' are, of course, their own young, and these young ones begin life within the mammalian womb where there is no distinction between mother and child. The same authors note that a fresh neural structure blossomed within the skull as mammals split off from the reptilian line. This new kind of brain transformed both the mechanics of reproduction and the organismic *orientation* toward offspring:

> Detachment and disinterest mark the parental attitude of the typical reptile, while mammals can enter into subtle and elaborate interactions with their young. Mammals bear their young live; they nurse, defend, and rear them while they are immature. Mammals, in other words, *take care of their own*. Rearing and caretaking are so familiar to humans that we are

apt to take them for granted, but these capacities were once novel – a revolution in social evolution. The most common reaction a reptile has to its young is indifference; it lays its eggs and walks (or slithers) away. Mammals form close-knit, mutually nurturant social groups – families – in which members spend time touching and caring for one another. Parents nourish and safeguard their young, and each other, from the hostile world outside their group. A mammal will risk and sometimes lose its life to protect a child or mate from attack. A garter snake or a salamander watches the death of its kin with an unblinking eye.[4]

When a mother is removed from her litter of kittens or puppies, they note, the young ones begin to yowl and this *separation cry* communicates distress to the mother, which she responds to as if the distress were her own. 'But take a baby Komodo dragon away from its scaly progenitor, and it stays quiet. Immature Komodos do not broadcast their presence because Komodo adults are avid cannibals.'[5]

The development of the limbic system facilitated the further evolution of the thalamus and cortex, which empower mammals to use limbic-related biofeedback in the service of complex emotions that facilitate 'social learning'. Social learning aids in survival and development because it minimizes in-group violence, enhances coordinated protection of the young, and contributes to the ability of large groups to endure harsh environments. Thus, in the evolution of primates, we see the rudiments of 'society' and the emergence of love as an *emotion*. By 'emotion' we mean that in this stage of evolution and development, love is a *motivating* power – it gets organisms to do things they would not do if this power were absent. As an emotion, love inspires organisms to sacrifice their personal comfort, safety, and even life, so that the object of love may benefit.

The uniqueness of human love is revealed in the capacity to respond to the symbolic dimensions of relationships. In this way, we may come to love others and to sacrifice for them because we share a belief system, a set of values, a way of life, or a worldview. Furthermore, when humans truly love, according to Singer, 'In relation to the lover, the beloved has become valuable for his or her own sake.'[6] One would thus consider it a contradiction were one to say of a lover: 'She loves him, but she has little interest in his well-being and values him only insofar as he can satisfy her needs.'[7] In the words of mathematician and philosopher William Hatcher, whenever there is true love between humans, the lover perceives the *intrinsic value* of the loved one and it is the recognition of this intrinsic value that serves to attract the lover to the loved one and inspires the lover to make sacrifices so that this intrinsic value may be protected.[8]

In other words, loving another – whether the other is a child, a man or woman, a profession, nature, or a way of life – enables acts of self-transcendence; and whenever energies are expended on behalf of another, the other will grow and develop. If we take water that we could drink ourselves and give it to our plant, that plant will grow. If we teach someone something with the intention of being of benefit to them, they are more likely to develop their potential and capacities. If we spend time practising a science or an art, we will help that science or art to develop. Living systems expand or realize their potential in response to love. Whenever a person is truly loved for who they are, they discover and become who they truly are. In this sense, one could say that we create one another by loving one another. Loving brings us into a kind of relationship with others that causes them to 'come forth'. The point that we are making here is that, according to the Bahá'í teachings, which is a teaching that is in harmony with findings from the natural sciences, love is *necessary* for all forms of existence, health, and development. By *necessary* we mean that love is a cause, without which human existence and development are impossible. In stressing the supreme importance of the renewal of love, 'Abdu'l-Bahá wrote:

> The world is wrapped in . . . thick darkness . . . and swept by
> a whirlwind of hate . . . Therefore must the friends of God

engender that tenderness which cometh from Heaven, and
bestow love in the spirit upon all humankind. With every
soul . . . must they show forth kindness and good faith; to
all must they wish well.[9]

Hatcher has argued that human love has two dimensions – a
passive dimension which he calls 'acceptance', and an active
dimension which he calls 'concern'. The passive component is
reflected in our acceptance of the other without prejudgment
or preconditions. The active component is manifested in our
willingness to make sacrifices and allowances on behalf of the
welfare of the other. Authentic love, notes Hatcher, is acceptance plus concern:

> Though it may seem difficult to conceive at first, the two
> components of love are quite independent of each other . . .
> Acceptance without concern is what is usually called *toler-
> ance*, while concern without acceptance is *conditional love*.
> Tolerance occurs when we renounce the desire to change,
> convert, or dominate the other but have not yet developed the
> capacity to work actively for the improvement of his or her
> well-being. Conditional love means that, while we have rec-
> ognized the spiritual potential of the other and are concerned
> for the development of that potential, we have not yet recon-
> ciled ourselves to what we perceive as the other's limitations.[10]

Of course, it is also possible for situations to exist where there is
neither acceptance nor concern. In this case we have a condition
of *hatred*.

	Concern	Acceptance
Authentic love	+	+
Conditional love	+	-
Tolerance	-	+
Hatred	-	-

As history reveals, when hatred animates the relationship between racial, cultural, religious, or national groups, we tend to see the grossest assaults on the common good. The cultivation of acceptance and concern for each member of the human race is thus indispensable if we wish to build prosperous societies. In a letter to an early Bahá'í, 'Abdu'l-Bahá wrote:

> Every imperfect soul is self-centred and thinketh only of his own good. But as his thoughts expand a little he will begin to think of the welfare and comfort of his family. If his ideas still more widen, his concern will be the felicity of his fellow citizens; and if still they widen, he will be thinking of his land and of his race. But when ideas and views reach the utmost degree of expansion and attain the stage of perfection, then will he be interested in the exaltation of humankind . . .
>
> Love ye all religions and all races with a love that is true and sincere and show that love through deeds.[11]

In his dialogues, Plato argues that when we begin to see the world through the eyes of the intellect, love may transcend the material realm and we may become attracted to those abstract essences that are said to animate the reality of things. With such development, the object of human love can rightly be said to be beauty – the beauty of an idea, the beauty of nature, the beauty of a scientific theory, the beauty of a way of life, and so forth.

In the previous chapter we explored the nature of knowledge; here we wish to suggest, with Plato, that knowledge of the good generally results in our attraction to it. For many, to know the good means that we cannot help but love it. Knowledge of the good thus transforms human aspirations and desires. But knowledge of the good is not awakened merely by way of the intellect. We come to know the good through the heart's association with it in family and community. We must see it reflected in the lives of our teachers, our parents, our political leaders, and our peers; we must witness the power of the good in the lessons and stories of history; and we must acquire the capacity to bear witness to it by observing the countless mysteries and metaphors that are embodied in the workings of nature.

In the Zen Buddhist tradition, this idea is captured in the subtle discourse on what has been called the *Tao*. The Tao is, in a sense, the spirit that animates everything in the universe that is good. And although it can never be fully described, awareness of the Tao, and attraction to its benevolent spirit, is thought to be within the reach of human consciousness. Indeed, according to Zen, the cultivation of a consciousness capable of perceiving the Tao is at the foundation of the development and refinement of humanity's moral sensibilities:

Tao is empty
     yet it fills every vessel with endless supply
Tao is hidden
     yet it shines in every corner of the universe
With it, the sharp edges become smooth
     the twisted knots loosen
     the sun is softened by a cloud
     the dust settles into place
So deep, so pure, so still
     It has been this way forever
You may ask, 'Whose child is it'? –
     but I cannot say
This child was here before the Great Ancestor[12]

≈

The great Tao flows everywhere
It fills everything to the left
     and to the right
All things owe their existence to it
     and it cannot deny any one of them
Tao is eternal
It does not favor one over the other

It brings all things to completion
    without their even knowing it
Tao nourishes and protects all creatures
    yet does not claim lordship over them
So we class it with the most humble
Tao is the home to which all things return
    yet it wants nothing in return
So we call it 'The Greatest'
The Sage is the same way –
He does not claim greatness over anything
He's not even aware of his own greatness
Tell me, what could be greater than this?[13]

            ∾

Grabbing and stuffing –
    there is no end to it
Sharpen a blade too much
    and its edge will soon be lost
Fill a house with gold and jade
    and no one can protect it
Puff yourself with honor and pride
    and no one can save you from a fall
Complete the task at hand
Be selfless in your actions
    This is the way of Heaven
    This is the way to Heaven[14]

When the power of attraction that is love takes as its object knowledge, we develop our capacity to discover new truths about ourselves and the world; when this power takes as its object beauty, the capacity for the arts unfolds; and when we are attracted to that which is good, humanity's inner capacities for moral reflection and noble action are revealed. Since the capacity to love is an inherent and inseparable feature of the human spirit, human beings are always in a state of loving something.

The challenge is to refine our sensibilities so that the power of love is focused on that which would redound to our mutual development, well-being and happiness. Inasmuch as love guides our value choices, love and human values are intertwined.

Love and the problem of value

When I make a value choice, I sacrifice something that is perceived to be of lesser value for something that is of greater value. For example, if I wish to go to medical school, I will have to sacrifice some sleep. And while sleep has its own value, unless I am willing to dispense with some of it, it is not likely that I will be able to achieve the kind of learning that is necessary to gain mastery in chemistry, biology, anatomy, and so forth. Thus, whenever value choices are made, the effect is to sacrifice one thing, or one set of possibilities, for another.

Over the course of the twentieth century the discourse on value has been centred on three questions: does value exist independently of the observer or is it merely a function of personal and/or collective preferences; what *should* be valued and why; and is there anything that should be valued above all else, and if so, what should this be? Here we are seeking to advance the thesis that it is useful to distinguish between what is commonly referred to as 'socially constructed' value and value whose existence is independent of human preferences but conditional upon human learning and refinement.

In his article 'The Typology of Moral Ecology' Svend Brinkmann has described the human world as 'a moral ecology; as a meaningful world with moral properties that present human beings with moral reasons for action'.[15] Thus, in contrast to the perspective which holds that all values are impositions of human will, Brinkmann has suggested that human life is saturated with moral reasons for action and that we cannot achieve our potential excellence unless we acquire the capacity to respond appropriately to the moral imperatives of human existence. For example, Brinkmann writes that some human acts are acts of 'brutality' and that we must recognize brutality when it is present. To perceive brutality requires the cultivation of compassion and concern. Without this inner development, acts of brutality do not awaken in us the proper response. Further, the claim that all values are cultural constructions threatens the rational and pragmatic basis of human and civil rights – as such a perspective renders it possible to legitimize acts of exploitation and brutality so long as culturally coherent rationales can be adduced in their defence.

For more than a century and a half, the Bahá'í community has been reflecting on the values that make it possible for us to achieve our potential as a species. Reflecting on these values on behalf of the Bahá'í world community, the Institute for Studies in Global Prosperity notes: 'As a vision of society, the relentless pursuit of wealth in an impersonal marketplace and the frenetic experimentation with various forms of self-indulgence are being rejected as irrelevant to the awakening hopes and energies of individuals in all parts of the planet.' For in the face of mounting evidence, they continue, 'it is no longer possible to maintain the belief that the approach to social and economic development to which the materialistic conception of life has given rise is capable of leading humanity to the tranquillity and prosperity which it seeks.' [16] In another place, the Bahá'í International Community observed: 'Attention must now be focused upon that which lies at the heart of human purpose and motivation: the human spirit; as nothing short of an awakening of the human spirit can create a desire for true social change and instill in people the confidence that such change is possible.'[17]

Reflecting further on the most significant philosophical and pragmatic barriers to the emergence of a viable, global community in *The Century of Light*, the Trustees elected to serve the Bahá'í world community addressed, candidly, the problem of materialism.[18] What we see everywhere, the statement notes, 'is unbridled exploitation of the masses of humanity by greed that excuses itself as the operation of "impersonal market forces" . . .' What we find ourselves struggling against 'is the pressure of a dogmatic materialism, claiming the voice of "science", that seeks systematically to exclude from intellectual life all impulses arising from the spiritual level of human consciousness'.[19] The statement analyses the rise of this attitude:

Fathered by nineteenth century European thought, acquiring enormous influence through the achievements of American capitalist culture, and endowed by Marxism with the counterfeit credibility peculiar to that system, materialism emerged full-blown in the second half of the twentieth century as a kind of universal religion claiming absolute authority in both the personal and social life of humankind. Its creed was simplicity itself. Reality – including human reality and the process by which it evolves – is essentially material in nature. The goal of human life is, or ought to be, the satisfaction of material needs and wants. Society exists to facilitate this quest, and the collective concern of humankind should be an ongoing refinement of the system, aimed at rendering it ever more efficient in carrying out its assigned task . . .

In the absence of conviction about the spiritual nature of reality . . . it is not surprising to find at the very heart of the current crisis of civilization a cult of individualism that increasingly admits of no restraint and that elevates acquisition and personal advancement to the status of major cultural values . . . If leaders of thought were to be candid in their assessment of the evidence readily available, it is here that one would find the root cause of such apparently unrelated problems as the pollution of the environment, economic dislocation, ethnic violence, spreading public apathy, the massive increase in crime, and epidemics that ravage whole populations. However important the application of legal, sociological or technological expertise to such issues undoubtedly is, it would be unrealistic to imagine that efforts of this kind will produce any significant recovery without a fundamental change of moral consciousness and behaviour.[20]

Among empirical and theoretical studies that have explored the nature of materialism, three types have been identified: crass materialism, philosophical materialism, and scientific materialism. Crass materialism has been extensively studied by psychologists and is characterized by an excessive reliance on material goods, the tendency to pursue happiness via consumption, and a proclivity to place inordinately high importance on material possessions. Scientific materialism, by contrast, is not related to the proclivity to seek ownership of things, but has been articulated in order to specify the proper objects of scientific exploration. It seeks to limit the work of scientists to phenomena whose behaviour can be objectively validated. In other words, scientific materialism suggests that science can be concerned only with those phenomena that may be understood in terms of the laws that govern observable forces and entities. Philosophical materialism, however, goes further than scientific materialism in asserting that any true and useful explanation of any process in the universe must be understood as the result of the interaction of material substances and that all other explanations for events are, *a priori*, superstitious. Here we concern ourselves solely with the implications of philosophical and crass materialism, as it is in the interaction between these two approaches to life that many of the challenges adumbrated above may be found.

'Today the world is assailed by an array of destructive forces,' writes the Universal House of Justice:

> Materialism, rooted in the West, has now spread to every corner of the planet, breeding, in the name of a strong global economy and human welfare, a culture of consumerism. It skillfully and ingeniously promotes a habit of consumption that seeks to satisfy the basest and most selfish desires, while encouraging the expenditure of wealth so as to prolong and exacerbate social conflict.[21]

In another place they write: 'true prosperity, the fruit of a dynamic coherence between the material and spiritual requirements of life, will recede further and further out of reach as long as consumerism continues to act as opium to the human soul . . .[22] At the same time, the Bahá'ís share the view that spiritual discourse that is grounded in various forms of superstition and dogma are at the root of innumerable problems plaguing the world.

Mindful of the current confusions, we have sought throughout this discussion to approach these questions rationally. And while we have suggested that humanity's limitless potential for transformation is linked to the powers that animate and define the human spirit, we have attempted to define these powers in ways that are in harmony with well-established facts and insights from a variety of fields.

One might hypothesize that the concept of 'spirit' is integral to many of the world's wisdom traditions because such a construct enables one to capture the multidimensional nature of the power that animates life across different levels of ontology, or different qualities of existence. We may therefore speak of the qualities of existence that characterize the mineral, plant, animal, and human kingdoms as being due to the presence of different qualities (or manifestations) of a single, unitary force responsible for the life, awareness, and development of living things.

Viewed from the foregoing perspective, as the most evolved, complex, and refined entity in nature, the human brain and body naturally provide for the manifestation of spirit in its highest form. This highest form is the appearance in nature of the phenomenon of 'self'. In the next chapter on the nature of will, we explore the notion of self and outline the ways in which the emergence of the unique capacities associated with a self confer upon human beings powers and responsibilities found nowhere else in nature. Here, suffice it to say that in the life of the individual, when the powers of the self and the animating forces of the human spirit are eclipsed by an unhealthy body, unhealthy ideas, unhealthy relationships, or other impediments, the mind shows signs of illness and dysfunction and the processes of personal development suffer.

Freud's work, for example, which was among the earliest to lead to the discovery of the social roots of trauma-related disorders,[23] enhanced our ability to understand and treat assaults to the human spirit brought on by pathological relationships. This development in medicine not only enabled psychiatry to emerge out of neurology, but can be viewed as a discovery of the impact of oppression and injustice on the life of the mind and the developing self. Freud's patients were not, as he himself clearly established, suffering principally from biological disorders; rather, they were grappling with assaults to the psyche brought on by sexual exploitation and violence.[24] Of course, inasmuch as matter and spirit (or body and mind) constitute an integrated whole, psychological injuries will quite naturally have somatic consequences, and vice versa.

Insofar as these issues are beyond the scope of this volume, suffice it to say here that integrating Bahá'í metaphysics into the broader scope of the natural and clinical sciences is a task that awaits Bahá'í-inspired researchers and clinicians of the future. For example, identifying mechanisms and/or principles that help illuminate how the soul, mind, and body might interact – especially insofar as these interactions may have clinical implications – is an important aspect of theory and research. Useful, perhaps, in our understanding of the soul/body relationship will be an integration of neuroanatomy, neurochemistry, and the ancient notion of the 'subtle body' found principally in Eastern philosophy.

The subtle body, as discussed in the yoga traditions and in various other disciplines – such as the martial and healing arts of the East (shiatsu, reiki, and acupuncture, among others) – refers to the energy currents that flow through and around and emanate from all beings. The subtle body may be conceptualized as existing between the physical and metaphysical realities in much the same way that light exists as a phenomenon that unites the attributes of the material and non-material worlds. Within human beings, the subtle body is said to be sensitive and responsive to the physical, psychological, and spiritual dimensions of life, and plays a mediating role between the conditions of the physical body and the conditions of the psyche.

Understood as energy currents, or energy fields ('chi' or 'prana' in Eastern healing arts), the subtle body is described by various traditions as constituting a continuum of different energy layers and densities. If there is an ailment in either the physical or psychological dimension of human existence, that ailment will be reflected at the level of the subtle body in the form of energy disturbances or obstructions. Following this line of reasoning, it is possible, through treatment at the level of the subtle body, to provide therapy for both the physical and psychological dimensions of the human person. If left untreated, by contrast, disturbances in the subtle body may influence other dimensions, resulting, for example, in a psychological ailment manifesting itself as a pathophysiological process. Indeed, these aforementioned ailments have been described in the Western medical tradition as somatoform disorders, psychosomatic illnesses, posttraumatic stress disorder, or functional somatic syndromes.

In Bahá'í metaphysics, every spiritual phenomenon is said to have a correspondence in the physical world. A reasonable assumption, worthy of further study, is that the sympathetic nervous system, and the neurotransmitters that are responsible for the life and energy of the nervous system, are the physical correlates of the subtle body in the material world.

Neurotransmitter systems may be likened to the subtle body in five important ways. First, neurotransmitters are present in the human body in such small amounts that until very recently they were not directly measurable. They could only be detected by measuring the metabolites that they produce. Indeed, neurotransmitters appear in the body in traces equal to approximately one eye-drop in a 10,000-gallon pool of water. Yet, their presence in the body is so essential that if levels of neurotransmitters rise or fall to even an infinitesimal degree, either apathy, lethargy, and profound depression occur, or hyper-excitability, confusion, irritability, and motor dysregulation can result.

Second, neurotransmitters, like light, behave at the synapse – both as particles and as waves. They behave as particles in that they act as 'keys', unlocking ion channels that are critical for the transmittal of neuronal signals, and they act as waves because they lead to the manifestation of neuroelectrical properties that stimulate receiving neurons into action. Without this neuroelectrical stimulation, all human activity, both of a physical and a psychological nature, would immediately cease. Third, and most important, neurotransmitters are responsible for the activity of the sympathetic nervous system, which is described by 'Abdu'l-Bahá as being both of a physical and spiritual nature: 'The powers of the sympathetic nerve are neither entirely physical nor spiritual,' He writes, 'but are between the two (systems). The nerve is connected with both. Its phenomena shall be perfect when its spiritual and physical relations are normal.'[25]

Fourth, abuse, injustice, and other trauma-related pathogens tend to lead to psychoneurobiological disorders with corresponding somatic and psychological symptoms; and finally, psychoneurobiological disorders are particularly responsive to non-material therapies.

In addition to the neurological health of the individual, the pioneering work of Stephen Porges has led to increased understanding of the important role of the Vagus nerve in mediating healthy interpersonal relationships. Porges's research has demonstrated that the process of *neuroception*, which functions beneath conscious awareness, has evolved in mammals over millennia and that it serves to facilitate the detection of threat and safety when we are in the presence of others. The vagal complex thus determines, to a significant degree, how humans will act and feel toward each other when they meet. In his groundbreaking book on this theme Porges writes:

> By processing information from the environment through the senses, the nervous system continually evaluates risk. I

have coined the term *neuroception* to describe how neural circuits distinguish whether situations or people are safe, dangerous or life threatening. Because of our heritage as a species, *neuroception* takes place in primitive parts of the brain, without our conscious awareness. The detection of a person as safe or dangerous triggers neurobiologically determined prosocial or defensive behaviors. Even though we may not be aware of danger on a cognitive level, on a neurophysiological level, our body has already started a sequence of neural processes that would facilitate adaptive defense behaviors such as fight, flight, or freeze.[26]

We invoke Porges's work here because of the strong emphasis placed in the Bahá'í writings on the qualities of humanity that are required if we are to overturn the fear-mediated responses that may arise, unbidden, in us when we encounter people that are of a different race, culture, caste, and/or class. In many cases, such as we see between black and white Americans, these fear-mediated responses have been carefully and deliberately cultivated over centuries. They thus often evoke deep and often unconscious responses of fear and suspicion that are incongruent with the actual threat posed by racial differences. The Bahá'í prescription seeks to overcome these fears and prejudices by providing the kinds of spiritual and humanitarian responses to others that increase the probability that fear will be replaced with gratitude and appreciation for the beauty of diversity. Commenting on this, 'Abdu'l-Bahá offered the following counsel:

> If you beheld a garden in which all the plants were the same as to form, colour, and perfume, it would not seem beautiful to you at all, but, rather, monotonous and dull. The garden which is pleasing to the eye and which makes the heart glad, is the garden in which are growing side by side flowers of every hue, form and perfume, and the joyous contrast of colour is what makes for charm and beauty . . .
> Thus should it be among the children of men! The

diversity in the human family should be the cause of love and harmony, as it is in music where many different notes blend together in the making of a perfect chord. If you meet those of different race and colour from yourself, do not mistrust them and withdraw yourself into your shell of conventionality, but rather be glad and show them kindness. Think of them as different coloured roses growing in the beautiful garden of humanity, and rejoice to be among them.

Likewise, when you meet those whose opinions differ from your own, do not turn away your face from them. All are seeking truth, and there are many roads leading thereto. Truth has many aspects, but it remains always and forever one.

Do not allow differences of opinion, or diversity of thought to separate you from your fellow-men, or to be the cause of dispute, hatred and strife in your hearts.[27]

We turn now to the third capacity associated with the human spirit – the power to will.

3

THE NATURE OF WILL

Every human power is limited. Our capacity to know, for example, is constrained by the reach of the human mind and senses; it is limited by stages of psychosocial and intellectual development that have been achieved, as well as by the conceptual tools and scientific instruments that we have at our disposal for exploring reality. And while we may go on acquiring knowledge forever, we recognize that at no time will our knowledge encompass all there is to know about ourselves or the universe. Another way to put this is to say that we are not now, nor will we ever be, omniscient. Omniscience is not a state to which we can aspire.

Just as our capacity to know is limited, so also is our capacity to will. We cannot bring into being whatever we might wish or desire. The natural world imposes insuperable limits upon our freedom. Whatever we might wish we are compelled, for example, to sleep and to die. Furthermore, our power to choose is limited by a variety of natural, social, political, and economic forces that are usually well beyond the immediate control of any individual or small group. Thus, when we speak of the power to will, we are speaking, necessarily, of a power that reveals itself according to the limitations that define a human life. To argue, however, that we have *no* access to will is as absurd as it is to argue that our capacity to exercise will is without limits. In this chapter we explore what might be meant by *will* and associate the exercise of this capacity to the pursuit of that which we perceive to be good.

≈

In the small part of the universe that we occupy the sun is the source of all life and development. Indeed, it is both a necessary and proximal cause of every living creature. Notwithstanding the infinite bounty conferred upon us by it, we do not tend to congratulate the sun for its gift of life because we know that it could not have done otherwise. We know that all of the work of the sun is a function of its predetermined nature; we know that it is compelled by immutable laws to function in the way that it does and that it cannot deviate a hair's breadth from the course that is set for it. We know, in other words, that the sun operates perforce and without will of any kind.

A dog, by contrast, appears to have a greater range of possibilities within its behavioural repertoire. It may be trained, for example, to serve as a vicious attack dog; or its nature may be groomed so as to make it safe and playful around children. Dogs may be nurtured such that they take delight in sniffing out illegal drugs; they may be cultivated in such a manner as to cause them to pull sleds for hundreds of miles through the frozen tundra of Alaska, or they may be prepared to perform tricks on the stage at county fairs. The range of behaviours that are accessible to the common dog is much greater than the range of possibilities that are accessible to the sun. This is so because we can deploy *human understanding* of the principles of reward and punishment that shape the behaviour of many conscious creatures in order to impose upon dogs behaviours that they would never otherwise perform. This is why we usually hold owners and not dogs responsible for many of the things that dogs do. We act in similar ways towards the behaviour of computers, robots, and self-driving cars. We know that the 'autonomy' of these machines is derived from the choices that have been made by engineers and programmers – all of whom are people.

In a previous chapter we noted that humans are able to exercise so much control over the phenomena of nature because of the powers associated with human consciousness. This special type of consciousness we referred to as the power of meta-cognition and we noted that meta-cognitive powers enable us to know not only the non-material aspects of ourselves (such as our values, beliefs, attitudes, and so forth), but to have objective knowledge of the principles, laws, and processes that govern many phenomena of the natural world. Speaking of this power at a talk delivered in New York City on 15 April 1912 'Abdu'l-Bahá observed:

> The phenomenal world is entirely subject to the rule and control of natural law. These myriad suns, satellites and heavenly bodies throughout endless space are all captives of nature. They cannot transgress in a single point or particular the fixed laws which govern the physical universe. The sun in its immensity, the ocean in its vastness are incapable of violating these universal laws. All phenomenal beings – the plants in their kingdom, even the animals with their intelligence – are nature's subjects and captives. All live within the bounds of natural law, and nature is the ruler of all except man. Man is not the captive of nature, for although according to natural law he is a being of the earth, yet he guides ships over the ocean, flies through the air in airplanes, descends in submarines; therefore, he has overcome natural law and made it subservient to his wishes. For instance, he imprisons in an incandescent lamp the illimitable natural energy called electricity – a material force which can cleave mountains – and bids it give him light. He takes the human voice and confines it in the phonograph for his benefit and amusement. According to his natural power man should be able to communicate a limited distance, but by overcoming the restrictions of nature he can annihilate space and send telephone messages thousands of miles. All the sciences, arts and discoveries were mysteries of nature, and according to natural law these mysteries should remain latent, hidden; but man has proceeded to break this law, free himself from this rule and bring them forth into the realm of the visible.[1]

Our capacity to put conscious knowledge to work in pursuit of outcomes that we value is part of what we mean when we speak of the will; and it is the human 'self' that is at the centre of this power. Hossain Danesh has written about the unique powers of the self:

> Experience of selfhood is uniquely human . . . As human beings, we all have certain instincts that we share with animals. These instincts are essential for survival and continuation of the species. We get hungry and search for food; we experience pain, realizing something is wrong, and seek remedy for the pain. We have the capacity to sense danger, so we either face the danger and fight it, or escape the danger and seek a secure situation . . .
>
> At the instinctual level most advanced animals do the same. There is, however, a very fundamental difference between humans and animals. Animals do not deviate from instinctual laws. Humans, clearly, have a choice. Our response to basic instincts of hunger, pain, fight or flight, and sex are quite different from animals. We may decide to fast or diet rather than eat. Some may decide to fast to death to make a point, often to seek justice. Some people eat even when they are not hungry. Others do not eat even though hunger and food is accessible (as in anorexia nervosa). Still others do not share food with the starving masses even when they themselves have more food than they need. These are all unique to human behaviors.
>
> The same is true of pain. It should be added here that not all pain is a sign of illness. For example, growth is painful. The same is true of the pain we experience following strenuous physical activity. Masochistic human beings intentionally inflict pain upon themselves. Sadistic people inflict pain upon other people. From these few examples it is very clear that the human approach to pain is very complex and does not follow the simple laws of instincts.
>
> The fight or flight reaction is also different in humans. There are many occasions in which we choose to face dangerous situations even though we know that we would not

be able to protect ourselves. This is the way the followers of Gandhi faced the threat of British forces . . . We may ask why human beings respond so differently to these basic instincts. The answer, of course, lies in the fact that humans have consciousness and will. We have the capacity to choose . . .[2]

Notwithstanding the thoughtful critiques of *essentialism* that have emerged over the past twenty-five years,[3] and despite wide variation in morphological or cultural form, the characteristics that unite all human beings and that distinguish humans from all other forms of life are clearly evident when we examine the powers that are associated with the human self. Meta-cognitive capabilities bestow a consciousness of self and provide for the ability to direct the development of the self in ways that liberate humankind – at least to some degree – from the tyranny of biology (nature) and history (nurture).

Consider, for example, humanity's capacity to engage in scientific investigation. By careful observation of that which may be perceived by the senses, we humans are able to discover the operation of forces that are not themselves directly observable and enable us to make predictions about future states before they come into being. The power to predict the future states or conditions of many natural systems would be entirely useless if we did not also have the power to influence such systems on the basis of our goals and current understandings. This fact alone is sufficient proof that human beings must, to a significant degree, also have the power to exercise will. In this regard, William Hatcher has noted:

> By deliberately establishing, in the short run, certain particular conditions of a system, we can bring about, in the long run, certain desired future states of the system, i.e., configurations that are favorable to our goals and our [perceived] interests. This is the power that scientific knowledge gives us, the power to control our future – to participate in the

processes of the natural world and not just endure them. In other words, scientific knowledge has the effect of *increasing our autonomy with regard to the natural world.*[4]

C. J. Herrick had written in a similar way several decades earlier:

Man's capacity for intelligently directed self-development confers upon him the ability to determine the pattern of his culture and so to shape the course of human evolution in directions of his own choice. This ability, which no other animals have, is man's most distinctive characteristic, and is perhaps the most significant fact known to science.[5]

Furthermore, despite the proliferation of twentieth-century theories that attempted to divest humans of will, the ethical basis of human rights law is that human beings have an inherent degree of freedom to shape the direction and quality of their own lives and that this freedom ought not to be abridged arbitrarily.

Indeed, in the wake of the Holocaust of the 1940s some of the French and German philosophers began to reflect deeply upon the 'terrible freedom' that was revealed in the behaviour of the Nazis who used their power to dominate, kill, and oppress in ways that had been previously unimagined. Reflecting deeply on these things, many of these philosophers, who began to call themselves 'existentialists' (e.g., Camus, Heidegger, Jaspers) joined, in spirit, with 'third wave' psychologists of the 'humanistic' school (e.g., Fromm, Rogers, May) in order to try to steer the use of human freedom in directions that would better insure the protection of human rights and dignity.

As had many of the early philosophers before them, these intellectuals understood that the freedoms conferred by human thought require engagement with profound moral questions that cannot be avoided if we are to live human lives. These questions, however, were not simply about the nature of right actions, but included questions that were necessary for reimagining the ethical foundations of human society: 'What kind of life is worth living?' asked the existentialists; 'What constitutes a rich and meaningful life that is revealed in the flourishing of human character?' wondered the humanists; 'What are the human values that ought to be non-negotiable; and what are the aspects of social life that are more trivial, more peripheral, less essentially-related to the proper exercise of human freedom?'; 'What is the role of government and community in securing and protecting these rights; what is the role of education in ensuring that the exercise of human freedom does not destroy us?' In this way did the Holocaust of the twentieth century bring moral questions back to the centre of discourse on human freedom and responsibility.

Furthering this discourse in the 1950s, a group of philosophers at Oxford set out to construct a 'virtue ethics' that might be deployed in order to refine understanding of human freedom by articulating what might be meant by 'moral wisdom' and by fixing a role for education in the cultivation and refinement of it.[6] Realizing the impotence of laws that are unaided by the force of human virtues, virtue ethicists concerned themselves primarily with what might be required in order to realize the development of morally responsible *selves.* They reasoned that, insofar as the capacity to will takes as its object that which is perceived to be good, if we wish to advance the humanizing process we must seek the cultivation of *moral discernment* as opposed to mere adherence to laws. Such a perspective drew upon the work of Aristotle who, in the *Nicomachean Ethics* had written, 'the end of political science is the supreme good, and political science is concerned with nothing so much as with producing a certain character in the citizens or in other words with making them good, and capable of performing noble actions'.[7]

In addition to broad socio-historical processes that reawakened concern over the potentially destructive power of will, growing bodies of research undertaken in laboratories around the world also began to contribute to our understanding of the nature of this power. That research taught us much about the forces that can strengthen, weaken, or destroy human will. One such body of research came out of the labs of experimental psychopathologists where I had been trained.

Injustice: Destroyer of the capacity to choose

Experimental psychopathologists endeavour to create in the laboratory, sometimes using animals, conditions that mimic the onset of psychological disease and disability in humans. The condition of most interest concerns the impact of exposure to uncontrollable events on human health and development. To expose an organism to an uncontrollable experience is to render it helpless; and to be helpless is to be in a condition wherein our actions do not influence what happens to us. In such circumstances the outcomes that we experience are under the control of arbitrary or random forces. Over the last five decades a great deal of research has been done on the impact of helplessness on individuals and groups.

In the early helplessness experiments created by Martin Seligman, David Maier, and their colleagues, the *triadic design* is employed. This design enables researchers to expose one group of subjects to unpleasant controllable events, a second group of subjects to unpleasant uncontrollable events, and a third group to neither uncontrollable nor controllable events. What is illuminating about the triadic design is that the subjects that are in the first two conditions (the controllable and uncontrollable conditions) are exposed to exactly the same amount of an aversive experience (for example, a loud buzzing noise) for exactly the same amount of time. When the subjects in the controllable condition figure out what they can do to turn off the noise, the noise goes off for the subjects in the uncontrollable condition as well. We say that the subjects in this latter condition are *helpless* because there is nothing that they can do to stop the noise. Their destiny, with respect to the noise, is determined wholly by the actions of another.

At early stages of a helplessness experiment, the subjects will do all that they can to avoid or stop the noxious stimulus.

Sometimes they must solve a puzzle, or run through a maze, or jump over a barrier in order to turn off or avoid it. In the uncontrollable condition, subjects are exposed to situations in which they cannot solve the puzzle, go through the maze or get over a barrier, but they do not know that the experiment is designed for them to fail. When subjects in this uncontrollable condition come to realize that their actions do not have an effect, they stop acting and begin to suffer the noxious stimulus passively. We have seen helplessness deficits develop in a wide range of species and thus we know that controllability is fundamental to life at various levels of existence.

Controllability is vital to so many species because it is connected with the more pervasive and fundamental law of cause and effect. One might argue that the operation of the law of causality is the manifestation of the principle of justice in nature. Because of the operation of this law, the natural world is rendered orderly and predictable. This order and predictability renders the natural world a place wherein organisms can develop their inherent capacities. For organisms that have the cognitive capacity to prefer that some effects be realized while others avoided, effects (or consequences) take on hedonic or emotional value and may be experienced as rewards and punishments.

For humans, in particular, the expectation of reward and the fear of punishment are critical in sustaining the coherent processes that are associated with our conscious development. If we cannot trust, for example, that our behaviour is linked to outcomes that we can reasonably predict, the rationality that guides our behaviour will quite naturally suffer. For this reason, when policies, practices and laws are arbitrary, corrupt, or profoundly discriminatory, the social order becomes chaotic and the processes of individual and collective development are arrested.

Indeed, what the laboratory research revealed is that when humans are exposed to ongoing forms of injustice, which is really the only form of suffering that appears to inflict enduring harm, they often develop a kind of *paralysis of will* and may begin to imagine insuperable barriers to the development of their innate capacities. When these conditions obtain, it is often no longer necessary to actively block a people's progress. They will stop making progress because they no longer believe that their destinies are shaped by what they do or do not do. Indeed, they will begin to see themselves as powerless and will tend to be seen by their oppressors as deserving of their low estate. It is, perhaps, for this reason that the Bahá'í teachings have placed such a strong emphasis on justice. One might say that justice is realized when people have access to that which *empowers* them to satisfy their legitimate *needs*; that is, when they have access to that which is necessary for their full and healthy development. Let us explore this idea further.

Social justice and human needs

A need may be conceptualized as a form of assistance that is required for the development of a capacity. If the need is not satisfied, the capacity may be poorly developed or may never appear. In an earlier work on this theme, we provided the following example:

> If we plant an acorn and wish to see it develop, we will have to satisfy the acorn's needs. These needs include a certain amount of soil above, beneath, and around it. If the acorn is buried too deeply, it will never grow; if it does not receive sufficient water or sunlight, it will not grow; and if the spring winds do not blow upon it during its life as a sapling, it will not acquire the strength needed to stand against the fall and winter winds in its maturity. The evidences of its healthy development are its capabilities as an oak tree. If it does not develop bark and leaves and branches, and if it does not produce sap or acorns for the development of other oak trees, then we know that there has been a failure of development. Further, we would never plant an acorn and expect it to produce oranges, grapes, or bananas. The capacities of an entity thus fix both what it can and cannot become.

When the legitimate needs of a living system are satisfied it comes forth according to its nature. So it is also with human beings.[8]

The capacities to know, love, and will implicate needs. The capacity to know, for example, implicates a need for education. Unless this need is satisfied, the capacity to know will not develop fully. The capacity to love creates the need to belong, as well as the need to connect with nature, with other human beings, and with that which is sacred. Without the satisfaction of these needs, the capacity to love is stillborn or distorted. The capacity to will implicates the need for a certain measure of freedom. Without the proper exercise of freedom, the inner capacity for autonomy cannot unfold.[9] In the satisfaction of legitimate needs, we protect the development and refinement of the human spirit.

From this perspective, the ability to achieve happiness and good mental health depends, to no small degree, on the satisfaction of human needs at every stage of life – during gestation, infancy, childhood, youth, and adulthood. One must inherit healthy genes, be exposed to proper nutrition and loving relationships, and exercise the powers of the human spirit in ways that are in harmony with the ethical principles that animate the universe. To the degree that these conditions are satisfied, one's capacity for sound mental health and well-being are greatly enriched. Since we can never know all of the biological and social forces that have shaped an individual's mental health status, the Bahá'í writings encourage an attitude of humility and compassion when confronting one's own suffering and the suffering of others.

We note that serious mental illness is often characterized by an inability to control some normal aspect of consciousness at will (e.g. one's thoughts, emotions, memories, beliefs, imagination, appetite, and so forth). In this way, mental illness may be distinguished from the everyday fluctuations in psychological functioning and well-being that are an inevitable part of human life. Indeed, the Bahá'í writings point out that life is often both difficult and painful and that suffering is an integral part of the development of many living systems. We are suggesting here, however, that some forms of suffering are neither 'normal' nor inevitable. They result from the functioning of a profoundly disordered society that deprives human beings of the healthy exercise of will and the cultivation of productive forms of autonomy and freedom.

Across the world, for example, one of the most widespread forms of mental disability is post-traumatic stress disorder (PTSD). And while this debilitating disorder may develop as a consequence of exposure to natural disasters, the overwhelming majority of cases arises from exposure to violence in the home, in the community, or in response to wars. These well-established sources of PTSD reveal much about the moral and spiritual consciousness of the generality of humankind and tell us much about how delicate the human spirit actually is. Further, if this pervasive illness is to be adequately addressed, what will be required is a transformation of the values, attitudes, and beliefs that make it possible for large numbers of human beings to harm others – often while justifying acts of brutality by invocation of some high moral principle.

Other forms of mental illness that may be related to humanity's collective moral and spiritual health include such disorders as narcissistic personality disorder, antisocial personality disorder, and various forms of addiction. And while all human beings should be treated with respect and dignity no matter what illness they may have and no matter how such an illness may have been acquired, the Bahá'í writings suggest that many of these disabilities may be impossible to eradicate or to significantly reduce without consideration of the moral and spiritual responsibilities that are an inevitable concomitant of human freedom.

A prescription for the body politic

Aware of the importance of a noble vision if humanity is to use its freedom responsibly, the Bahá'í writings overflow with beautiful descriptions of the powers and capacities that lie hidden within the human spirit. Bahá'u'lláh writes, 'O friends! Be not careless of the virtues with which ye have been endowed, neither be neglectful of your high destiny . . .' He continues, 'Ye are the stars of the heaven of understanding, the breeze that stirreth at the break of day, the soft-flowing waters upon which must depend the very life of all men.'[10] I dwell here on this theme because psychology, in its materialistic heyday, has sought to divorce itself from its spiritual and philosophical roots. In doing so, it has also severed itself from the primary sources of the vision for humanity as articulated in all major religious traditions. It thus contributes, unwittingly, to the very ills that it seeks to remedy.

The human psyche is not a closed system; neither is it self-sufficient. If it is to remain vital, the psyche must be fed the food of meaning and understanding. The teachings and insights provided by the great seers, poets, and prophets are as food for the human spirit. Thus have the words of Christ been likened to bread from heaven; thus did the ancient Greeks describe the universe as the embodiment of the Logos; thus did Islam and Judaism liken the 'Book' to an ark of human salvation; and thus does Bahá'u'lláh affirm, 'should the lamp of religion be obscured, chaos and confusion will ensue'.[11] At a time in history in which violence, prejudice, materialism, and social despair are so acutely felt, no psychology that fails to tap the mysterious well-springs of the human spirit can possibly hope to serve as a catalyst for the regeneration of either the world or the individual. In stressing the oneness and interdependence of all humankind and the power of collective, unified action across lines of race, class, culture, and religion, the Bahá'í writings endeavour to awaken and nurture a social vision that is necessary for lifting humanity to a new stage of collective development.

In addressing the sorely distressed body of humankind, Bahá'u'lláh offers counsel: 'The best beloved of all things . . . is justice. Turn not away therefrom . . . and neglect it not'.[12] Why is justice 'the best beloved of all things', and what, for our purposes here, is the relationship between justice and the health of the human spirit?

One might say that in nature, justice is compelled and, as noted earlier, is manifested in the operation of the laws of causality. Precisely because of the causal laws, the universe is ordered and can be rendered meaningful. The wisdom traditions assert that the laws of nature are but a manifestation of the commandments of God in the contingent world. Because of the higher degree of freedom manifested in the human kingdom, justice is not compelled but must be consciously chosen. The sacred laws – which are articulated by the prophets and founders of the world's religions and which have traditionally provided a pattern for the articulation of civil law – are offered to mankind so that there may be justice and order in the world of humanity as there is in the world of nature.

'The purpose of justice', Bahá'u'lláh affirms, 'is the appearance of unity . . .'[13] He consummates this weighty counsel by pointing out that inner, interpersonal, and international unity is the cause of human development, the source of human prosperity, and the sign and cause of all forms of life. Inner, interpersonal, and intercommunity conflict, by contrast, is a major source of destruction, disability and disease. The strong emphasis placed on the role of justice in the attainment of human happiness and the importance of unity for development and prosperity suggests that human beings are so fundamentally interdependent that no one can fully realize his or her potential as long as the body politic is diseased. Bahá'u'lláh's prescription, therefore, is one directed not only at securing the well-being of the individual but at securing the felicity of all humankind.

≈

In addition to the bounties conferred by good physical and mental health, the wisdom traditions affirm that human happiness is conditioned by moral and spiritual behaviour. In a series of lectures offered in Paris in 1911, for example, 'Abdu'l-Bahá observed that 'Man is really a spiritual being, and only when he lives in the spirit is he truly happy.'[14] Referencing the moral laws that animate the Bahá'í teachings, the Universal House of Justice notes that, 'The laws do not represent a sterile and inhumane legal code, but rather the divine prescription, a definition of how an individual must act in order to achieve true freedom and spiritual happiness in this world and the next.'[15]

In this respect, the Bahá'í teachings are in harmony with a perspective on happiness that has animated many religions since the period of history known as the Axial Age.[16] Such a perspective suggests that enduring happiness is not an inevitable by-product of material conditions – such as a healthy brain and body, good weather, access to the resources necessary to sustain life, and so forth – but is conditional upon the development and exercise of moral and spiritual faculties. In the *Nicomachean Ethics*, for example, Aristotle avers, 'The good of man is the active exercise of his soul's faculties in conformity with excellence and virtue.'[17] Similar sentiments are expressed in *The Analects* of Confucius, the moral teachings of Judaism, Christianity, Islam, the Zoroastrian faith, and Buddhism. In our own work we have begun to explore the role of what are called 'moral emotions' in human happiness and mental health.[18]

Moral emotions are 'those complex emotions that reflect or arise in response to thoughts and actions that are ordinarily thought of as touching on concerns of right and wrong, or that can influence or motivate actions that touch on moral concerns'.[19] At the core of moral emotions are self-assessments and self-reflective judgements that centre on what one has done or failed to do, or the kind of person one has become.[20] From a clinical perspective the moral emotions that are of greatest interest include guilt, shame, regret, and remorse, because these emotions may play important roles in the pathogenesis or exacerbation of a range of psychopathological states – including anxiety, depression, substance abuse, and vulnerability to suicide. Acts of *akrasia*, which are acts that are voluntarily performed but that violate one's own moral standards, have long been hypothesized to awaken negative moral emotions.

The concept of akrasia was first articulated by the Greeks and refers to the problem of moral weakness or *weakness of will*. An agent's will is said to be weak if he or she acts, and acts intentionally, in ways that are contrary to his or her own best judgement. Under such circumstances it is sometimes said that the actor lacks 'self-mastery', or the willpower to do what he or she knows or believes would be best. The Roman poet Ovid captures the problem of akrasia in *Metamorphoses*: 'I am dragged along by a strange new force. Desire and reason are pulling in different directions. I see the right way and approve it, but follow the wrong.'[21]

When people act in ways that are inconsistent with their values they tend to experience intrapsychic discomfort that arises out of awareness that one's behaviour and one's ideal self are incongruent. Akratic behavior may thus awaken negative emotions that are strong enough to disturb happiness for significant periods of time and may also act as diatheses (or risk factors) in the development of psychological disorders – such as anxiety and depression.

Human emotions are useful because they orient us to our values and make it possible for us to protect those aspects of life that we perceive to be important. In this respect, negative moral emotions – such as guilt, shame, regret, and remorse – may play especially important roles in protecting our personal dignity while empowering us to pursue our highly valued 'hoped for selves'.[22] Given, however, the potentially corrosive, health-compromising influence of negative moral emotions, the Bahá'í writings tend to emphasize moral growth as a *process* that is beset by difficulties, setbacks, and disappointments.[23] The Bahá'í teachings thus encourage a spirit of compassion, patience, and persistent effort in the pursuit of moral and spiritual development.

～

One final area of research that has taught us much about human will focuses on the problem of addiction. Addiction researchers have learned that the human response to pleasure is subject to the influence of a region of the brain that is commonly referred to as the reward centre. The reward centre consists of the Ventral Tegmental Area (VTA) and the Nucleus Accumbens (NAcc). While many behaviours that are rewarding lead to alterations in these regions of the brain, the most significant alterations result from drug abuse.

All forms of drug abuse result in the release of neurotransmitters that generate pleasant feelings. The most common of these is dopamine. Other naturally occurring neurotransmitters that produce an artificial sense of euphoria when one takes a psychotropic drug include beta-endorphins, anandamide, and phenylethylalanine. These substances function in the brain as endogenous opioids, cannabinoids, and amphetamines respectively. Other rewarding behaviours, such as gambling, shopping, and consumption of pornography also facilitate release of these neurochemicals.

Over time, as one acquires an addiction, the rewarding effects of these sources of hedonic pleasure begin to replace other values, and addicts prove willing to sacrifice more and more of what they had once valued – their jobs, families, food, rest, and so forth – in order to gain access to the drug or behaviour that nourishes their addiction. Addiction is thus characterized by compulsive engagement in the search for pleasure-rewarding stimuli despite negative consequences. In the end, what is lost in addiction is the sense that one embodies a 'self' that is capable of protecting and directing its own development. When a person has lost volitional control in this way, we say that he or she has become ill with an addiction. Recovery from addiction often requires that the addict submit to the intervention of forces outside of the self. In this way, addiction may be understood as a disorder of both biology and will.

What has been discovered about recovery from addiction has also taught us a great deal about the ways that human minds differ from those of animals. In the 1970s, for example, Harry Frankfurt at Princeton noted that all conscious animals embody what he referred to as 'first-order desires'. These are desires to do or not do something. However, a peculiar characteristic of humans, he observed, is their ability to form what he called 'second-order desires' – the desire to desire or not desire to do something. Frankfurt also made a distinction between 'desires' and 'volitions', in which the former describes a 'want' while the latter describes a 'will'. A second-order volition is present when someone not only desires to desire to do something, but also wants it to be their will to do something, regardless of whether or not they actually have the ability to do it. The capacity for second-order volition is the basis of Frankfurt's conceptualization of a person.

Consider the potential difference between two addicts. One addict, which Frankfurt calls the 'unwilling addict', has the first-order desire to take a drug, but he also *wants it to be his volition to not take the drug*. In Frankfurt's view, for this addict, 'It is the latter desire, and not the former, that he wants to constitute his will; it is the latter desire, rather than the former, that he wants to be effective and to provide the purpose that he will seek to realize in what he actually does.'[24] The second addict, by contrast, is one who also has the first-order desire to use a drug, but does not have the will to stay sober. In this way does Frankfurt identify the meta-cognitive capacities that are associated with willing that is unique to human beings. Animals, such as the rats that are commonly used in laboratory studies of addiction, do not have the capacity to overcome their addiction 'at will' because they cannot take themselves as objects of concern or value. They cannot perceive for themselves a future that is different from what they are already living; they cannot entertain values that inform them of the benefits of being drug free.

In other words, lacking the ability to conceptualize a *self*, they can only respond to whatever desires that are present in them by pursuing these desires. In this sense, they lack the capacity that we are referring to here when we use the term 'will'. Humans, it seems, are the only creatures known to nature that can abandon what they desire by shifting their awareness to a value that becomes a source of biology-transcendent motivation. This capacity to be motivated both by what we desire and what we envision for ourselves in the future is a major source of human freedom.

PART II

ALTERNATIVE CONCEPTUALIZATIONS OF HUMAN IDENTITY

The educator and developmental psychologist Daniel Jordan use to tell the story of a man who lives in the country and is thus isolated from the benefits of modern technology. Such a man learns shortly after he gets electricity and a radio that he has won a refrigerator from one of the nearby radio stations. When the refrigerator is delivered to his door the new owner instructs that it be placed on the porch whereupon he brings out his hats, overalls and shoes and fills it. And while a refrigerator can certainly be used to store these things, use of it in this way betrays a lack of understanding of the full identity and nature of a refrigerator.

The question of identity is so critical here because confusion about the nature of human identity has been at the root of some of the world's most destructive ideologies – racism, sexism, and nationalism. Indeed, such confusion has fuelled nearly all the human rights abuses of the twentieth century. In the next chapters we outline some influential alternative perspectives on human identity that gained ascendency over the course of that century. Our hope is to say something about how these perspectives have come to shape widely held views on human nature and to thereby further clarify the alternative view that we are seeking to advance. We begin with the highly influential but largely discredited psychoanalytic account in this chapter and follow in Chapter 5 with brief overviews of the perspectives embodied in contemporary neuroscience and evolutionary psychology.

4

THE PSYCHOANALYTIC PERSPECTIVE

Among the most significant works published in the last century was Dudley Fitts' and Robert Fitzgerald's translation (first published in 1939) of *The Oedipus Cycle,* a trilogy by the Greek dramatist Sophocles, which included *Oedipus Rex, Oedipus at Colonus,* and *Antigone.*[1] The widely read translations of these works reintroduced the story of Oedipus to Western audiences. These new translations were important because, in their totality, they captured a dimension of the human spirit that had been obscured at the end of the nineteenth century when Sigmund Freud chose the story of *Oedipus Rex* to serve as the root metaphor for the theory of mind that would animate the early days of psychoanalytic psychiatry. Inasmuch as no theory of the mind has had a greater impact on shaping modern views of the human condition, an analysis of *Oedipus Rex,* and of the uses to which the story was put in the making of psychoanalytic theory, is illuminating.

In formulating his influential theory of psychoanalysis, Freud was captivated by two aspects of the story of Oedipus. The aspect best known to most readers emerged after the death of Freud's father in October 1896. Although Freud's father was by then an old man, and although his death was not unexpected, during the year following his father's death Freud found himself in a state of inner conflict and unanticipated turmoil. During that year he also had what he came to regard as a significant dream. He dreamed that he was late for his father's funeral. In his attempt at self-analysis, Freud arrived at the disturbing conclusion that at some level of his personality, he was not unhappy about his father's death. Indeed, he was to confess to himself that his father's death represented the fulfilment of a long-standing wish that had begun in childhood – a wish that his father would be out of the way so that he would be the sole possessor of his mother. It became apparent to Freud that this pattern of wishes paralleled the plot of Sophocles' play *Oedipus Rex,* in which Oedipus discovers that he has unwittingly slain his father, Laois, and married his mother, Iocaste, Queen of Thebes. At the same time, as the enthroned King of Thebes, Oedipus brings down the wrath of the gods on his kingdom. 'The play', writes Raymond Fancher, 'portrays the agonizing process by which Oedipus realizes the nature of his deeds,' a terrifying self-appraisal not unlike Freud's own self-analysis. When Oedipus learns the true nature of his deeds, he is so horrified that he puts out his own eyes. In Freud's view, Oedipus's horror was symbolic of 'the dread that always accompanies the revelation of repressed ideas and wishes'.[2]

The second aspect of the Oedipus story that captured Freud's imagination concerns the way in which it depicts the power of a person's past to determine his or her future. It is this dimension of the story of Oedipus, the dimension that would come to embody Freud's notion of 'psychic determinism', that is of concern here. For it was, in many respects, the notion of psychic determinism that rendered Freud's theory of the mind pseudo-scientific and that enabled the mind to become a legitimate object of empirical study and clinical concern.

Oedipus as root metaphor in the birth of psychoanalytic psychiatry

In the early nineteenth century, medicine – as a professional discipline – was just beginning to be consolidated. There were only three firmly established branches of medicine: internal medicine, surgery, and neurology. One of the notions that was to appear early in nineteenth century medicine and that was to pave the way for the emergence of the young field of psychiatry was the concept of *Functional Delta*.

Functional Delta can be explained by noting the difference between a *symptom* in medicine, which is some kind of verbal or behavioural report of physical dysfunction or distress, and a *medical* or *pathophysiological sign*, which is some physical evidence that stands in causal relation to the reported symptom and accounts for it. If, for example, Mrs Stephens enters the hospital and reports that she has blurry vision and a bad headache, she has reported two symptoms. If upon physical examination it is found that she has a tumour growing in the occipital lobe, the tumour is the pathophysiological sign that accounts for these reported symptoms. Under normal circumstances, there is a causal and logical relationship between the severity of symptoms that are reported or evidenced by patients and the pathophysiological signs that are discovered upon physical examination. If patients manifest a variety of symptoms but evidence no pathophysiological signs, the discrepancy between their reported symptoms (or illness-related behaviour) and the observable signs is referred to as a *Functional Delta*.

During the late eighteenth and early nineteenth centuries physicians believed that patients could manifest a high Functional Delta in two ways and for two reasons: when pathophysiological signs were minimal or absent but the intensity and range of symptoms and illness behaviour were high, patients were often accused of being malingerers who were playing the part of a sick person for some primary or secondary gain; conversely, when pathophysiological signs of disease were high but symptoms and illness-related behaviour were absent or relatively low, patients were said to be, for whatever reason, unaware of the severity of their actual disease.

In the late 1800s, however, medical science began to identify a particular configuration of symptoms – without corresponding pathophysiological signs – that could not be understood by invoking either malingering or a patient's unawareness as sufficient logical explanations. This constellation of symptoms was known as *hysteria;* and while these symptoms had been observed in women for many centuries, they had not been understood as constituting a legitimate medical disorder. It was the meticulous observational and diagnostic work of one of the great physician-teachers of the time, Jean-Martin Charcot, that led to the acceptance of hysteria as an authentic medical illness and that precipitated an intense clinical search for its natural cause.

Charcot carried out his work at a massive hospital complex in Paris known as Le Salpêtrière, which, by the end of the nineteenth century, had become a well-established asylum for the poorest of the Parisian proletariat. Among those seeking refuge in Salpêtrière, no patients were of greater interest to the leading physician–intellectuals of the time than the many women who suffered from hysteria.

For more than two thousand years hysteria had been considered an incomprehensible disease the cause of which was explained at various times by invoking a variety of mystical entities or illogical processes such as evil spirits or wandering uteri. During the eighteenth and nineteenth centuries, however, neurologists began to search for the causes of hysteria, and all other diseases, in natural, observable processes. Understanding of hysteria advanced greatly at Salpêtrière, due, in large part, to the meticulous clinical work of Charcot. Judith Herman, one of the foremost authorities on the history of trauma-related disorders, has affirmed that Charcot's approach to hysteria 'was that of a taxonomist. He emphasized careful observation, description, and classification. He documented the characteristic symptoms of hysteria exhaustively, not only in writing, but also with drawings and photographs.'[3] Because Charcot was one of the most entertaining lecturers of his time, every Tuesday afternoon when he held his public lecture–demonstrations on hysteria many distinguished physicians would make the pilgrimage to Salpêtrière to behold the great master at work. Among those visitors were two young neurologists, Pierre Janet and Sigmund Freud. As Janet, Freud, and a variety of fascinated male physicians looked on, Charcot and his interns performed the public, grand-rounds examination that was intended to reveal the symptoms of a convulsive hysterical attack. After witnessing many of these examinations, Freud returned to Vienna and resumed his practice with a new mission. He set for himself the goal of going beyond a mere description of hysteria to demonstrating, unequivocally, its cause.

For nearly a decade Pierre Janet in France and Sigmund Freud in Vienna were to search for the causes of hysteria. Their search, however, would be conducted in a manner wholly different from the usual way of proceeding in nineteenth-century medicine. Rather than examining their patients' bodies for physical or pathophysiological signs, the neurologists, operating on little more than a hunch, undertook their search by examining the stories that their patients told about their lives.

In listening to such stories, Freud, Janet, and Joseph Breuer came to affirm that the pathogenesis of hysteria can be traced to early sexual experiences that are traumatizing, not so much to the body, but to the 'mind'. In order to make such a claim, these neurologists would have to invoke aspects of the mind–body dualism that Descartes had proposed more than two centuries before – but they would embrace dualism in a completely new way.

Freud's description of the human reality was similar to the perspective advanced by Descartes in that it suggested that human ontology consists of two dimensions: a somatic dimension and a psychological one. Each dimension, though related to the other, was said to have its own anatomy, its own dynamics, and its own set of illnesses. Freud was the first in medicine to describe an 'anatomy' of the psyche – which he conceptualized as being the by-product of biological processes and thus wholly contingent upon the body for its functioning and existence. By rendering the psyche dependent entirely upon the body's biological processes, Freud's model suggested that the body produces psychological phenomena in much the same way that it produces saliva and heat. Further, by rendering the mind an epiphenomenon of the functioning of the body, Freud provided a partial solution to the problem of Cartesian dualism. Thus, Freud's conceptualization would prove acceptable to the leading European intellectuals of the time as it embodied a materialistic notion of the psyche that held that no special entity, process, or force was necessary to explain the psyche's existence, nature, or function.

In 1896 Freud announced to the world the results of his study on hysteria. In his report, entitled 'The Aetiology of Hysteria', he wrote:

> I therefore put forward the thesis that at the bottom of every case of hysteria there are one or more occurrences of premature sexual experience, occurrences which belong to the earliest years of childhood, but which can be reproduced through the work of psycho-analysis in spite of the intervening decades. I believe that this is an important finding, the discovery of a *caput Nili* in neuropathology.[4]

Notwithstanding Freud's later retreat from this thesis,[5] the discovery of the etiology of hysteria was revolutionary in that it contained the idea that human pathology may originate not only from diseased tissue, organs, and pathophysiological processes, but also from stressful experiences and social relationships.[6] In this way did Freud's reconceptualization of the psyche, as well as his adumbration of its role in human disease, launch a century of study on the role of psychological processes in disease and the practice of medicine, and open exploration into the impact of biological and social processes on the mind's health and development.

The loss of human volition and responsibility

Notwithstanding Freud's revolutionary contributions, two significant problems with his somato-psychic conceptualization can be identified. Inasmuch as he, and most of those who followed him, conceptualized the psyche as nothing more than the byproduct of biological and social processes, Freud's theory deprived the human person of volition and responsibility. Thus, while proving successful in rescuing the study and treatment of mental illness from the superstitious ideas that had plagued the field for centuries, in conceptualizing the psyche as an epiphenomenon of somatic processes, human consciousness was reduced to an *effect of preconscious biological processes* and was given little or no causal role in the calculus of human action. In brief, it could be said that psychoanalytic psychiatry emerged in Europe through sacrifice of the powers commonly associated with the human spirit or soul.

In contemporary times, the perspective on human nature that is embodied in Freud's theory is captured in the longstanding nature versus nurture debate. *All human attributes,* affirmed the sociobiologists*, must be explainable by invoking individual biological heritage;* no, retort the environmentalists, *it is experience which best accounts for the acquisition of distinctly human characteristics.* The most sophisticated in this debate have come to affirm that human characteristics and behaviour are best explained by invoking the *interplay* between nature (biology) and nurture (history).

Here we suggest that in the absence of a theory of mind that allows the possibility of transcending the influences of natural and social processes, an individual's present and future must be seen as an inevitable result of the present or past. Such thinking was captured in Freud's notion of 'psychic determinism' and was also embodied in the story of *Oedipus Rex*, the first play in Sophocles' Oedipus cycle, which served as the root metaphor in the development of psychoanalysis.

Adherents to the principles of psychic determinism – whether they be *soft* (nurture-centred) or *hard* (nature-centred) – suppose that human action can be explained using roughly the same causal principles that underlie the actions of other mammals. In the view of determinists, just as the biology and history of baboons and chimpanzees are sufficient to explain and predict their actions, in like manner can we understand

and predict the psychological and social lives of human beings.[7] Karl Popper discussed this as the problem of *historicism* – the doctrine according to which socio-historical events are as fully determined by their antecedents as are physical events by theirs.[8]

The transcendent possibilities associated with human life can have no place within a deterministic framework. Indeed, in reflecting on a kind of hope that is unique to the human spirit, the philosopher Calvin Schrag wrote that human hope

> shows itself as a horizon of social consciousness, bearing implications for the wider cultural life of man. Understood within this modality, hope is the site from which the thought and action of interacting social selves transform the present in response to an envisioned condition of life in the future ... The future is envisioned as the coming of the era of emancipation from bondage to an alienated present. Hope is thus postured as a simultaneous awareness of the insufficiency of the present and an anticipation of future fulfillment.[9]

Schrag goes further to distinguish between human hope and calculative social planning. In both cases, he observes, there is dissatisfaction with the present and an orientation toward the future. 'However, in the case of social planning, the orientation toward the future is in the mode of a calculation of empirical probabilities that can be manipulated within a simulated plan. In the phenomenon of hoping,' by contrast, 'the possibilities of the future remain incalculable from an empirico-experimental standpoint. Hope struggles against odds that appear overwhelming from the perspective of calculative thinking and technological control.' In this sense, 'hope discloses an openness and transcendence of the future which imposes limits on calculation and prediction'.[10] It is this transcendent dimension of hope that is a unique feature of human consciousness and that is lost in Freud's reading of the story of Oedipus.

Oedipus Rex served Freud as a root metaphor because it demonstrates the power of biology and history to fix the destiny of even the most sincere and high-minded among human beings. One sees through the play that Oedipus, like most children, is a goodhearted lad, who, upon hearing the terrible prophecy of the Oracle at Delphi, flees his home to avoid it. The prophecy was given in two parts: the first was that Oedipus would murder his father, marry his mother, and sire a child who would be his sister; the second was that he would be buried in the city of Colonus. Despite Oedipus's efforts to escape his destiny, he unconsciously and unwittingly fulfils the prophecy precisely as the Oracle had given it. Thus, Oedipus's efforts and good intentions have no influence whatsoever over his destiny.

Oedipus Rex opens with a crowd of suppliants who have brought the king branches and chaplets of olive leaves and who 'lie in various attitudes of despair':

> Great Oedipus, O powerful King of Thebes!
> . . . Your own eyes
> Must tell you: Thebes is tossed on a murdering sea
> and cannot lift her head from the death surge.
> A rust consumes the buds and fruits of the earth;
> the herds are sick; children die unborn,
> and labor is vain. The god of plague and pyre
> raids like detestable lightning through the city,
> and all the house of Kadmos is laid waste.
> All emptied and all darkened; Death alone
> battens upon the misery of Thebes.
> Therefore, O mighty King, we turn to you . . .[11]

Thebes suffers, one later learns, from 'an old defilement' that is sheltered there – a defilement that must be expelled if the land is to be healed. This defilement, it turns out, is the result of the deeds of Oedipus, who, in a fit of rage many years earlier, had murdered King Laios and was enthroned in his stead. At its heart, *The Oedipus Cycle* symbolizes the movement from childhood to maturity. As such, Sophocles' trilogy begins by affirming the power of biology (nature and the passions) and of family history (nurture) in shaping an individual's early life.[12]

The story of Oedipus is the story of every human being, for every person begins this life as an unconscious slave to nature. That Oedipus is a slave to nature's passions is symbolized by the reckless abandonment with which he slays, unwittingly, his father, King Laois. Oedipus describes this moment to his wife (and, as it transpires, mother), Queen Iocaste:

> I will tell you all that happened there, my lady.
> There were three highways
> coming together at a place I passed;
> and there a herald came towards me, and a chariot
> drawn by horses, with a man such as you describe
> seated in it. The groom leading the horses
> forced me off the road at his lord's command;
> but as this charioteer lurched over towards me
> I struck him in my rage. The old man saw me
> and brought his double goad down upon my head
> as I came abreast.
> He was paid back, and more!
> Swinging my club in this right hand I knocked
> him out of his car and he rolled on the ground.
> I killed him.[13]

Inasmuch as Freud's theory of the psyche is fundamentally a theory of the psyche in childhood and adolescence, it was fitting for him to invoke the story of *Oedipus Rex* as root metaphor in the development of psychoanalysis; but the other two plays in the trilogy (*Oedipus at Colonus* and *Antigone*) go beyond this simple narrative. They illustrate how the mind and heart of Oedipus, and of his daughter, Antigone, mature as a consequence of the terrible hardships that they must face.

Sophocles wrote *Oedipus at Colonus* as sacred theatre in the late evening of his life. At eighty-nine years of age, he was certain that this mystic drama would represent his final work. It is no wonder, then, that, for his wise and surrogate voice, Sophocles has old Oedipus, his body blind and bent with age, address the people of Colonus about the life that is so quickly fleeting and the life that is to come. Sophocles shows through *Oedipus at Colonus* that the former king, having been in exile for many years, and having, in willing fulfilment of the Oracle's second prophecy, arrived finally at the city of Colonus, has matured and has, indeed, become a very great man. In this ironic moment of contentment, Oedipus begins his final address with a prayer that is directed both to Apollo – who had guided him mysteriously to that hallowed ground – and to the people of Colonus, that he might fulfil his destiny, which called for him to be buried in their venerated city. Oedipus has thus arrived at Colonus after a long and painful journey, not merely as an exile, a refugee, and a fallen king, but as a noble, chastened, and illumined spirit in service to that which is greater than himself:

> Ladies whose eyes
> are terrible: Spirits: Upon your sacred ground
> I have first bent my knees in this new land;
> therefore be mindful of me and of Apollo,
> for when he gave me oracles of evil,
> he also spoke of this:
> A resting place,
> after long years, in the last country, where
> I should find home among the sacred Furies:
> That I might round out there my bitter life.
> Conferring benefit on those who received me,
> a curse on those who have driven me away.
> Portents, he said, would make me sure of this:
> Earthquake, thunder, or God's smiling lightning;
> but I am sure of it now, sure that you guided me
> with feathery certainty upon this road,
> and led me here into your hallowed wood.
> How otherwise could I, in my wandering,

have sat down first with you in all this land,
I who drink not, with you who love not wine?
How otherwise had I found this chair of stone?
Grant me then, goddesses, passage from life at last,
and consummation, as the unearthly voice
Foretold;
unless indeed I seem unworthy of your grace:
Slave as I am to such unending pain
as no man had before.[14]

Hearing the words of this strange traveller, the people of Colonus recognize that he is none other than Oedipus of Thebes, fallen king, disgraced in all the world. To the plea of Oedipus and Antigone, his faithful daughter and sister, they reply that because Colonus is sacred ground, one such as Oedipus cannot be buried there.

In that hour of searing and final disappointment, Oedipus reaches deep into the reservoir of the human spirit and delivers to the people of Colonus words that appear to those who hear him to be inspired by the gods. As he persuades the people of Colonus to grant him, in their compassion, a final resting place, he breathes into them the spirit of life; and as he takes his last breath, they take within themselves that vitalizing force necessary for resurrection and renewal. The people of Colonus are revitalized because in caring for Oedipus and in helping him to realize his destiny, they rediscover the noble qualities in themselves that had made the people of Colonus so great. In addition, the words of Oedipus inspire the people of Colonus in the ways that all great prophets and holy ones inspire. Their words are as manna for the soul; as light to the understanding; as water to the parched, longing heart.

Through this second drama in the Oedipus trilogy one learns that the apparent injustice that Oedipus suffered in childhood and youth was actually a more refined form of justice that made possible the maturation of his faculties. What rendered the maturation of these faculties possible was not the arbitrary manipulation or intervention of the gods, but Oedipus's own striving in the face of untold and apparently senseless difficulty. In this sense, the story of Oedipus is also the story of Job, and of Socrates, and Nelson Mandela, and the Apostle Paul, and all others who have suffered injustice and taken from it a harvest.

Sophocles followed *Oedipus at Colonus* with *Antigone,* the final play in the trilogy. *Antigone* covers the period after Oedipus's burial at Colonus and represents, in part, the biological, social, and spiritual heritage passed from Oedipus to his faithful sister/daughter, Antigone. But it also represents the qualities that Antigone wins for herself as she struggles, in her own way, to fulfil her responsibilities to that which she believes is right and good. In the ultimate act of freedom, Antigone chooses to sacrifice her own life so that Polyneices, a brother whom she loves, might be properly buried. The play opens in front of the palace of Creon, the new King of Thebes. Creon, whose kingdom had been rendered secure after the successful defeat of the Argive army – an army led by Polyneices – orders that no one should bury the fallen leader and that no one should mourn him. Rather, must his body 'lie in the fields, a sweet treasure for carrion birds . . . '[15]

Though well aware that she will have to die for it, Antigone decides, nevertheless, to bury her brother's body. In witnessing this noble act, the reader notes that, although in his youth her father slew a man in blind rage, in her youth Antigone sacrifices herself, in full consciousness, that something of transcendent value – namely, human honour and dignity – might live. In this manner does Sophocles, in his final play, describe the development and refinement of the human spirit and its capacity for self-transcendence and self-sacrifice. It is this will-centred, transcendent dimension that is lost in Freud's deterministic theory that is being reclaimed here in our discourse on the human spirit.

5

THE VIEW OF EVOLUTIONARY PSYCHOLOGY AND NEUROSCIENCE

In his widely read and influential book *The Selfish Gene*, Richard Dawkins noted that the central argument of his book is that 'we, and all other animals, are machines created by our genes' and that 'it is not the survival of the species that is the focus of evolution, but rather the survival of the individual (or, more specifically her genes)'.[1] Dawkins goes further to argue that:

> . . . a predominant quality to be expected in a successful gene is ruthless selfishness. This gene selfishness will usually give rise to selfishness in individual behaviour. However . . . there are special circumstances in which a gene can achieve its own selfish goals best by fostering a limited form of altruism at the level of individual animals. 'Special' and 'limited' are important words in the last sentence. Much as we might wish to believe otherwise, universal love and the welfare of the species as a whole are concepts that simply do not make evolutionary sense.[2]

While evolutionary theory provides indispensable and inarguable insight into how the complexity of form and function that facilitate survival and reproduction have emerged over millennia, the discovery of the mechanisms of evolution do not, in themselves, qualify evolutionary psychologists to affirm, with the kind of confidence that many embody, that we are merely 'machines' that have been 'created by our genes' for *their* survival.

Such statements as these are not merely reports or interpretations of empirical findings; rather, they reflect a philosophical perspective. That is, they reflect a *worldview*.[3] Here we wish to suggest that the kinds of longings that are special to human beings – the longing, for example, to live a certain kind of life – even if life itself must be sacrificed in pursuit of this longing, cannot be understood from the perspective of a worldview that affirms that we are merely biological machines that have been created by our genes to ensure their survival. We challenge this perspective for two reasons: first, this minimalist view is incompatible with what we seek to protect when we advance claims to the conditions that would preserve human dignity; and second, such a perspective is incapable of explaining so many of the things that we do in order to be and become the kinds of beings that we suspect we can become as human persons. As we have suggested in our account of the human spirit, to be a person is to be animated by hopes and aspirations that transcend the struggle for mere existence and continuity as a biological organism. Elucidation of this perspective is aided by calling upon our old friend – Socrates.

What do humans want?

In *Beyond Evolution: Human Nature and the Limits of Evolutionary Explanation*, the philosopher Anthony O'Hear reminds us of the dialogue recorded in Plato's *Phaedo* that takes place on Socrates' final day on earth. In speaking his last words, Socrates is reported to have said: 'We ought to offer a cock to Asclepius.'[4] Asclepius, we are told, is the Egyptian god of healing; and so Socrates implies here that under certain circumstances, life itself can become a kind of disease, and in such cases, death becomes a cure. Since Socrates' life is not threatened by any physical threat that he could not easily avoid by saying the kinds of things that his accusers wished to hear, what this passage presupposes, writes,

O'Hear, is 'the thought that a certain kind of life might be so shameful that death is preferable'.[5] The evolutionary perspective, as given by many Darwinians, O'Hear notes, is incapable of giving an account of why the wise Socrates felt it better for him to die than to have to live a certain kind of life. Indeed, it seemed that Socrates desired more from life than mere survival could offer. O'Hear continues:

> . . . if it is said that from an evolutionary point of view Socrates was a failure, and that a nation of Socrateses would not survive (leaving aside that he had already produced children), this . . . does little to explain why Socrates is so widely admired a figure, and why many people even today, and in quite different social and religious circumstances, feel that Socrates was right to have done what he had done. Here we have the germs of a conflict, between a doctrine which says that there are considerations which ought to override survival and reproduction, and one which says that ultimately rational morality must have its edicts legitimated in terms of the contributions to the survival and reproduction of individual agents, actual and potential.[6]

The account advanced by evolutionary psychology seeks to explain human motivation in terms reducible to survival and reproduction. If we find some humans, as we often do, who are animated in their choices by values that transcend a pragmatic concern for personal survival, we will need to be able to explain this by thinking that, perhaps, under strong cultural influences human motivations can begin to grow roots in value systems that seek the survival, not just of human bodies and of human genes, but of human values and ideals.

In his book *Sapiens: A Brief History of Humankind* (2015), Yuval Harari has argued that what renders the human species unique is our ability 'to transmit information about things that do not exist at all'[7] and thus to create approaches to life that have their strongest motivational roots in the stories we tell about ourselves. These stories, myths, or worldviews come to influence human values, desires, and behaviours in ways that often override the biological imperatives that impose motivational limits on the behaviour of all other creatures. From this perspective, the human motivation to defend, sometimes with our lives, what is thought to be 'right', 'just', 'good', 'noble' and 'true' cannot be explained if our analyses are confined to the doings of our genes. The neuroscience perspective suffers from a similar problem when it appears in that overly reductionistic form that seeks to explain all human action by referring to what happens within the brain and nervous system.

In his recent international bestseller *We Are Our Brains*, for example, neuroscientist Dick Swaab provides a detailed, yet accessible, account of how many complex human functions may be understood in terms of the biochemical and neuro-electric events that take place in various regions of the brain. His purpose is to defend the claim that when neurophysiological processes are fully understood we may give a causal account rooted in neuroscience for any behaviour, whether rational or dysfunctional, that humans perform. We have suggested, by contrast, that while the basic cognitive and emotion-related capacities of the human brain have evolved to facilitate survival and are thus traceable to physiological functions that all primates share, many of the complex processes associated with self-consciousness, moral engagement, cultural formation, and the cultivation, preservation, and transmission of abstract knowledge are difficult to understand if we limit the causal discourse to biological evolution and neuroscience.

A reductionistic neuroscience perspective on human identity is called into question because we cannot ask the neuroscientists to explain more than can be expected from a discipline whose borders are limited to what can be perceived through the lens of a microscope, or the images of an fMRI, a CT-Scan, or an EEG. Any description of what humans *are* and any account of human behaviour will require an integration of knowledge from all the sciences – as well as appreciation for the insights that have emerged from humanity's diverse philosophies, literatures and arts. We are more than the most complex biological system known to nature. We are also a complex array of meaning, value, and teleological systems whose purposes and motivations can both facilitate and threaten the survival of our own and other species. A simple example from the author's own life will suffice.

After high school, I joined the US Navy and became a navigations petty officer aboard a ballistic missile submarine. And although our ship's homeport was in the north of Scotland, as we neared the end of my time in the military we took the submarine to a port in South Carolina for renovations and repairs. One night my crewmates and I went dancing. This occurred in the late 1970s and I was one of only a handful of African-American submariners at the time.

Unmindful of the problems that might be associated with race, my crewmates had elected to go to a dance hall that played country and western music and taught line dancing. And although I felt quite out of place, after they had been dancing for a while, I sheepishly joined them. Just when I had relaxed a bit and had begun to enjoy myself, a small group of white men surrounded me and asked what a n..... was doing in that place. They said that I should 'get the f... out', and their words, coming as they did after I had begun to imagine that I had been accepted, dismantled my naïve optimism and rendered me dazed and disoriented. With my heart pounding and my mind in disarray, I made it to the street and returned to the ship.

I recount that scene because a reductionistic perspective neglects the symbolic and worldview-related processes that render the experience both a biological event associated with perceptions of threat as well as a quintessentially human encounter that would have no parallel in the rest of the animal kingdom. In other words, I do not think it sensible to argue that what we experienced in that dance hall as black and white Americans can be adequately understood by reference to a range of neurochemical processes – however detailed and elaborate such a reference might be. If we wish to understand this phenomenon, we will need to know something of biology, yes; but we will also need to know something of history, ethics, psychology, economics, and aesthetics, as well as the functioning of the institutions of American society during the latter half of the twentieth century. In other words, we will have to know something of the various evolutionary, social, historical, and philosophical forces that have defined, nourished, and informed the development and character of the human spirit.

6

DISCOURSES ON THE PROBLEM OF EVIL

In reflecting on the ubiquity of conflict and violence over the ages some have wondered whether there is something about the nature of the human person, and of reality more generally, that renders violence and conflict essentially unavoidable. Those that espouse a traditional theological view, for example, tend to see conflict and violence as inevitable, as it is thought to reflect the struggle between two immutable and independent forces – the forces of good and evil. The forces of evil and the forces of good are said to be in a battle, and the arena of this battle is thought to be human history. History, from this perspective, is a narrative account of the doings – the failures and the successes – of these two fundamental forces. All conflict, from this view, is essentially the result of the friction produced inside the individual, the family, the community, or between nation-states when these two forces collide.

To say that there are two morally opposed forces operating in the world is to say that conflict is at the very heart of the structure of reality. It is to say that reality is simultaneously good and evil and that anyone who participates in reality will have to come to grips with this fundamental truth. From this view, God and his servants are generally said to be the progenitors of good, while Satan and his agents are said to be the progenitors of evil. This basic motif is manifested in many of the world's theological systems and is embodied, in part, in the problem that the philosophers have called the *problem of theodicy*, which states that if there is a God, He cannot be, at once, omniscient, omnipotent and good. For inasmuch as there is much evil in the world, if God is, indeed, all-powerful and all-knowing, God is responsible for this evil since He could prevent it if He chose to.

One way to resolve this problem is to say that if God is indeed all-good and all-powerful and that there is yet evil in the world, then this evil must actually be good in disguise. That is to say, what appears to be evil is actually another manifestation of good. Another way to resolve this problem is to say that while evil does exist, its existence is due to a force other than God. And, as has been noted, the origin of this additional force is said to be Satan or the devil.

There are many, many problems with these kinds of arguments and neither time nor training will permit a careful elucidation of them. Suffice it to say that from the perspective that we find most satisfying, there is no evil force at the foundation of the world. Evil becomes manifest in the world when the otherwise good powers and capacities that have been placed at the disposal of human beings are used recklessly, in immature ways, or in ways that are deliberately exploitative and self-serving. Because we have the capacity to choose the kinds of lives we will make for ourselves on earth, the same power to know that enables us to discover the secrets of the universe may be used to deceive; the capacity to will that empowers us to achieve great feats of endurance and courage can be marshalled in the service of domination and cruelty; and the power to love that inspires us to care for those who are helpless can be perverted in the direction of nationalism and racism. And so, from the point of view that we are seeking to advance, the conflicts that exist everywhere in the world are not due to a fundamental force that exists in opposition to the force of good. It is due to something else. What is this something else?

To put it simply, we could say that much of the conflict that is experienced in the world arises out of the conceptual, technical, and moral challenges that are associated with the special nature of human life. When we confront these challenges with a thirst for knowledge, compassion for the plight of others, and a determined and morally authentic will, the conflicts that we experience fuel development and are sources of good. By contrast, when we come to problems without the desire to see, and when we fail to respond to the manifest suffering of others in active and deliberate ways, we not only fail to solve problems, we tend to create social spaces – whether these be families, neighbourhoods, or nation states – where life grows increasingly dangerous and dark. In these settings, we see the ugly face of evil.

Conflict and development

There is a wonderful story that is told by Reverend C. L. Franklin (the late father of Aretha Franklin) about the way that eagles teach their eaglet offspring how to fly.[1]

According to Franklin, when eagles have eaglets they build their nests very high overlooking deep valleys. They also build into their nests briars and other sharp materials that are, at first, at the bottom of the nest. Once the eaglets hatch and begin to grow, their mothers begin to stir the nest so that the briars that were once at the bottom begin to move toward the surface. In this way is the nest into which the eaglets were born gradually transformed into a very uncomfortable place to be. Since the nests are built up high, and since eaglets do not appear to know at birth that they are capable of flight, as they look over the side of the nest into the valley below they become afraid, as the only way to go appears to be down. After much hesitation the eaglets throw themselves out of the nest into the deep valley below, and in an effort to save themselves they naturally begin to flap their wings. In this way eagles learn that they are capable of flight.

Reverend Franklin's point is that without an unavoidable confrontation with discomfort the eaglets would never be in a position to discover their capacity for flight. This simple story, whatever its literal veracity, embodies a truth – that difficulties, hardships and troubles are among the forces that fuel the development of living beings.

Consider another example from the plant kingdom. A few years ago scientists developed a self-contained ecosystem that they named Biosphere II. All was well in Biosphere II except for one problem that puzzled the scientists for quite a while. The problem was that the trees in Biosphere II, though growing tall, could not stand upright. After numerous studies, one of the researchers was struck by the realization that in this totally enclosed ecosystem, there was no wind. Since saplings acquire the strength to stand by resisting the wind, the lack of exposure to wind during their early development rendered these saplings incapable of fully functioning as adult trees.

In a similar way, human beings acquire emotional and psychological strength by encountering challenges in childhood and youth. When these challenges occur in situations of love and justice, and when we confront these challenges with the help of competent models, we acquire psychological robustness and emotional competence. These strengths are needed to face the more difficult challenges that attend the responsibilities of adulthood. When we confront adult challenges without these skills, our responses are often childish, maladaptive, and ineffective. Rather than benefiting from the conflicts that are generated by challenge, we respond in ways that only intensify these conflicts. Since we are social organisms, the internal conflict that we feel naturally finds expression in the ways that we relate to others. In this sense, conflict may become for us a mode of functioning that has little positive value and appears to make little sense either to ourselves or others. Since we cannot help but carry these immature and maladaptive ways of functioning into our work as adults, we see these tendencies manifest in the behaviour of village leaders, corporate executives, and heads of states. Under such circumstances it is easy to begin to feel that there is something fundamentally wrong with the world.

Because we are a moral species, there is another source of conflict that has its roots in the struggle to acquire virtues. No other species, so far as we know, is burdened with this struggle. The effort to master the lower self and to bring it under the stewardship of what the ancients have referred to as the higher self is a recognizable motif in every culture across time. Islam commands this struggle when it prescribes jihad or holy war; and while jihad is frequently invoked to justify acts of terrorism and violence, the jihad spoken of in the Qur'án may also be understood as a call to the holy war to conquer one's self. One who engages in jihad seeks to achieve self-mastery. Buddhists, Christians, Hindus, Jews, Zoroastrians, and the moralists of the humanistic school all address this struggle, as it is a universal one without which civilization is impossible. In the world's mystic, philosophical, and religious literatures, stories and parables abound about the difficulties that are related to self-purification and self-mastery.

In *The Republic*, for example, Plato is engaged in discourse with those who do not understand the necessity of this struggle and who therefore say that the best in life is to do injustice without penalty, while the worst is to suffer injustice without being able to take revenge. Inasmuch as the state would be poorly run if people committed injustice without fear of punishment, Plato's detractors affirm that the whole purpose of law is to prevent injustice by providing threats and punishments to those who would otherwise be unconstrained in pursuing their passions. To illustrate the force of their popular, albeit misguided argument, Plato draws upon a myth about the power that the ancestor of Gyges of Lydia possessed:

> The story goes that he was a shepherd in the service of the ruler of Lydia. There was a violent thunderstorm, and an earthquake broke open the ground and created a chasm at the place where he was tending his sheep. Seeing this, he was filled with amazement and went down into it. And there, in addition to many other wonders he saw a hollow bronze horse. There were windowlike openings in it, and, peeping in, he saw a corpse, which seemed to be of more than human size, wearing nothing but a gold ring on its finger. He took the ring and came out of the chasm. He wore the ring at

the usual monthly meeting that reported to the king on the state of the flocks. And as he was sitting among the others, he happened to turn the setting of the ring towards himself to the inside of his hand. When he did this, he became invisible to those sitting near him, and they went on talking as if he had gone. He wondered at this, and, fingering the ring, he turned the setting outwards again and became visible. So he experimented with the ring to test whether it indeed had this power and it did. If he turned the setting inward, he became invisible; if he turned it outward, he became visible again. When he realized this, he at once arranged to become one of the messengers sent to report to the king. And when he arrived there, he seduced the king's wife, attacked the king with her help, killed him, and took over the kingdom.

Let's suppose, then, that there were two such rings, one worn by a just and the other by an unjust person. Now, no one, it seems, would be so incorruptible that he would stay on the path of justice or stay away from other people's property, when he could take whatever he wanted from the marketplace with impunity, go into people's houses and have sex with anyone he wished, kill or release from prison anyone he wished, and do all the other things that would make him a god among humans. Rather his actions would be in no way different from those of an unjust person, and both would follow the same path. This, some would say, is a great proof that one is never just willingly but only when compelled to be. No one believes justice to be good when kept private, since, wherever either person thinks he can do injustice with impunity, he does it.[2]

In defence of his 'virtue is its own reward' perspective, Plato devotes *The Republic* to demonstrating that the virtuous life is one in which the elements of the soul are properly coordinated; that such a life is healthy and is characterized by wisdom, courage, and moderation; and that a life adorned by such virtues is one in which true happiness can be achieved. Only when this fundamental principle of life is understood, affirms Plato, will the inner psychological order of the individual and the outer social order of the state attain felicity.

Plato advances this thesis by invoking two metaphorical devices. The one that we will examine here is of a single being, a multicoloured beast that is an amalgam of different animals, some of which are gentle and some savage. These animals represent the various aspects of the human personality but are joined together such that anyone who sees only the outer covering and not what is inside will think that it is a single creature, a human being. Plato is in discourse with his student Glaucon:

> Then, if someone maintains that injustice profits this being and that doing just things brings no advantage, let's tell him that he is simply saying that it is beneficial for him, first to feed the multiform beast well and make it strong; and second, to starve and weaken the human being within, so that he is dragged along wherever either leads; and third, to leave the parts to bite and kill one another rather than accustoming them to each other and making them friendly. Yes, that is absolutely what someone who praises injustice is saying.
>
> But, on the other hand, wouldn't someone who maintains that just things are profitable be saying, first, that all our words and deeds should insure that the human being within this human being has the most control; second, that he should take care of the many-headed beast as a farmer does his animals, feeding and domesticating the gentle heads and preventing the savage ones from growing; and third, that he should make the lion's nature his ally, care for the community, and bring them up in such a way that they will be friends with each other and with himself? In light of this argument, can it profit anyone to acquire gold unjustly if, by doing so, he enslaves the best part of himself to the most vicious? If he got the gold by enslaving his son or daughter to savage and evil men, it wouldn't profit him,

no matter how much gold he got. How, then, could he fail to be wretched if he pitilessly enslaves the most divine part of himself to the most godless and polluted one and accepts golden gifts in return for a more terrible destruction than Eriphyle's when she took the necklace in return for her husband's soul?[3]

Plato's purpose is to show that human nature is an amalgam of qualities and that when an individual cannot regulate his own passions and must be regulated wholly by a force outside of the self – such as the force of law and threat of punishment – the noble and rational part of the self becomes enslaved, atrophied, and incapable. Furthermore, inasmuch as health, in any system, requires the proper balance and regulation of constituent forces, and health is a precondition of human happiness, such enslavement, while perhaps allowing for the uninhibited pursuit of pleasures, precludes the possibility of achieving a sense of inner peace and well-being. To the contrary, a life pulled in different directions by the force of desire is one that leads to various forms of torment, regret, shame, degradation and a dulling of human sensibilities.

Echoing Plato's observation more than two thousand years later, 'Abdu'l-Bahá wrote that one of the most essential attributes of a truly learned individual is that he 'opposes his passions'. In *The Secret of Divine Civilization*, which was written with an eye toward rehabilitating the civil forces of Persian society, he says that to oppose one's passions is the 'very foundation of every laudable human quality . . . the impregnable basis of all the spiritual attributes of human beings. This is the balance wheel of all behaviour, the means of keeping all man's good qualities in equilibrium.' He continues:

> For desire is a flame that has reduced to ashes uncounted
> lifetime harvests of the learned, a devouring fire that even
> the vast sea of their accumulated knowledge could never
> quench. How often has it happened that an individual who

was graced with every attribute of humanity and wore the jewel of true understanding, nevertheless followed after his passions until his excellent qualities passed beyond moderation and he was forced into excess. His pure intentions changed to evil ones, his attributes were no longer put to uses worthy of them, and the power of his desires turned him into ways that were dangerous and dark.[4]

In the *Mathnavi* of Rumi the story is told of four evil birds that, once put to death, are transformed into four birds of goodness. The allegory refers to the human quest to subdue self-centred passions and qualities and replace them with qualities that reflect due concern for others. This effort is one beset with hardships, trials and sometimes setbacks that may generate in the heart a surging sea of conflict. Such conflicts do not indicate the presence of evil forces. They reflect the forces of nature that the civilizing forces of culture, when they are functioning well, bend in service to the common good.

A common predicament

There is another source of conflict that arises out of competition for limited resources.

In an illuminating series of studies conducted in June 1954, Muzafer Sherif and his colleagues found that conflict over material resources is a primary source of intergroup hostility, prejudice and violence.

Sherif and his research team took two groups of 11-year-old boys to a summer camp called Robbers Cave located in the San Bois Mountains near Oklahoma City, Oklahoma. The Robbers Cave State Park provided a 200-acre site with fishing, swimming, canoeing, hiking and other camp games and sports for the unsuspecting participants in Sherif's experiment.

All those who went to Robbers Cave that summer were white, middle-class males with no record of psychological, school or behavioural problems. They became involved in the experiment

when their parents secretly agreed to let them participate in a
field study of intergroup conflict. None of the boys knew that
the camp counsellors and directors were all social psychologists;
and because Sherif had sent each group to camp on a separate
bus, for one week, neither group was aware of the other's presence.

In the first week at Robbers Cave, each group gave itself a
name. One group called itself the 'Eagles' and the other the
'Rattlers'. For a week the Eagles and the Rattlers took part in
separate activities designed to promote group cohesion. Each
group developed its own norms and leaders and each developed
its own flag. After the Eagles and Rattlers had established close
bonds among themselves, conditions were arranged so that they
would 'discover' one another.

When the Eagles first saw the Rattlers using what they regarded
as 'their' ball field and 'their' hiking trail, it sparked demands for
a competition. As had been planned, the staff arranged a four-
day tournament including basketball, tug-of-war, a treasure
hunt, and other events. The experimenters promised the winners
a trophy, badges, and multi-bladed pocketknives. Both groups
worked hard in practice, cheered on their teammates, and booed
and insulted the competition. Hostilities escalated as the tournament progressed, culminating in a flag-burning when the Eagles
lost the tug-of-war.

The Eagles ultimately won the tournament and collected the
trophy and pocketknives. But while they were celebrating their
victory, the Rattlers raided their cabins and stole their prizes. The
rivalry quickly escalated into a full-blown war. Name calling, fist
fights, cabin raids and food wars occurred around the clock. The
experiment had successfully transformed twenty-two normal
boys into two gangs of violent troublemakers, full of hostilities,
prejudices and resentments.

Sherif and his colleagues had set up this experiment to
understand how intergroup conflict and hostilities develop and
how they can be resolved. Conflict, Sherif found, arises out of a
perceived incompatibility of goals: 'what one party desires, the

other party sees as harmful to its interests'. The primary source of conflict is competition. In the conflict between the Eagles and the Rattlers, each group sought to defend its swimming and playing territory; each stole the other's most valued possessions, and each engaged in athletic competition with the knowledge that only the winners would receive new pocketknives. The resulting escalation in hostilities thus arose out of competition for limited material resources.

The Robbers Cave experiment, along with a variety of other studies that have been conducted on intergroup relations over the last half century, shows how easy it is for group competition to escalate into hostility, prejudices and violence. In situations of conflict, groups demand loyalty, solidarity and adherence to group norms. Group members 'close ranks' and present a united front. Interaction or empathy with the out-group is condemned, thereby widening the gap between the groups and making further conflict nearly inevitable. Group leaders take advantage of the unifying effect of conflict to consolidate and strengthen their personal power. This is what Sherif and his colleagues found in the Robbers Cave experiment. Historical evidence suggests that the same conditions tend to develop among competing groups in the wider society.

Having accomplished their first goal, Sherif set out to discover how these two antagonistic groups might be brought together. Their first approach to establishing intergroup harmony was based on the assumption that pleasant contacts between members of conflicting groups would reduce friction between them. Thus the Eagles and the Rattlers were brought together for social events: going to movies, eating in the same dining room, intergroup parties, and so forth. Far from reducing conflict, however, each time they were brought together the conflicts between them only multiplied. The Eagles and Rattlers simply used these situations as opportunities to further berate and attack one another. In the dining hall line they shoved each other aside; they threw food and paper at each others' tables; an Eagle touched by a Rattler was warned by his fellow Eagles to

brush 'the dirt' from his clothes. Thus, under pleasant conditions, the rift between the two groups grew wider and deeper.

Then Sherif and his research team hit upon an interesting
idea. They returned to the assumption that just as competition
creates conflict and friction, working in a common endeavour
should promote harmony. So they decided to create problems
that would adversely affect both groups and which could not be
solved until the Eagles and Rattlers worked together. To test this
hypothesis, Sherif created a series of urgent, natural challenges,
which required cooperative action on the part of both groups
of boys.

The first problem they created was a breakdown in the water
supply. Water had been delivered to Robbers Cave through
pipes connected to a tank about a mile away. The experimenters
arranged to interrupt it and called the rival groups together to
inform them of the crisis. Both groups immediately volunteered
to search for the water line trouble and worked together harmo-
niously until the camp's water supply had been fully restored.

Another problem emerged when the boys requested a movie.
When they were told that the camp could not afford to rent one,
the two groups got together, figured out how much each group
would need to contribute, chose the film by a vote, and then
enjoyed watching it together.

On another day, the two groups went on a hike to a lake
some distance from the camp. A large truck, they were told, had
been sent for the food. But at just the time when everyone was
getting quite hungry, they were informed that the truck (which
the experimenters had disabled) would not start. After a brief
consultation, the boys decided to get a rope and pull together in
an effort to start the truck. Interestingly, the same rope they had
used in their acrimonious tug-of-war was used in this cooperative effort to get the truck started.

These cooperative efforts between the Eagles and the Rattlers
did not immediately dispel all hostility. Following the resolution of the first few crises, the two groups would immediately
return to their bickering and name calling. But gradually, as

they faced and overcame an increasing number of wide-ranging problems, these cooperative acts began to reduce friction and conflict between them. Over time, the antagonism between the Eagles and the Rattlers gave way to a sense of collective pride and solidarity. From two contending groups, they were becoming one. Sherif noted that gradually the members of the two groups began to feel friendlier toward each other:

> The boys stopped shoving in the meal line. They no longer called each other names, and began to sit together at the table. New friendships developed, cutting across group lines. In the end, the groups were actively seeking opportunities to intermingle, to entertain and 'treat' each other. Procedures that 'worked' in one activity were transferred to others. For example, the notion of 'taking turns' developed in the dining hall and was transferred to a joint campfire, which the boys themselves decided to hold. The group took turns presenting skits and songs . . . [M]embers of both groups requested that they go home together on the same bus . . . On the way home a stop was made for refreshments. One group still had five dollars won as a prize. They decided to spend this sum on refreshments for both groups, rather than using it solely for themselves . . . On their own initiative they invited their formal rivals to be their guests for malted milks.[5]

There is much to be learned from this simple study. Crises create what Sherif and his colleagues call 'superordinate tasks'. Superordinate tasks are problems that are so difficult or complex that no group working alone can possibly solve them. Thus superordinate tasks force groups into cooperation who would otherwise be unwilling to work with, or even associate with, one another. Examples of superordinate tasks that have forced the whole planet into consultation include COVID-19, which has brought the world economy to near collapse and taken the lives of millions around the world; unprecedented threats to the ecosystem that reveal themselves in a myriad of ways across every environment across the planet; growing shortages of vital resources – such as water and oil, the proliferation of nuclear and non-nuclear weapons and wastes; threats to the life and health of millions of the earth's peoples due to terrorism, and intrastate violence; global economic crises occasioned by greed and corporate corruption; and mass migration of refugees from war-torn, economically devastated, or politically oppressive regions of the globe. It is becoming increasingly clear that these problems can never be addressed within our current worldview perspective. Across the United States the social, economic, and mental health costs associated with disunity are mounting.

Demographers tell us that during this century racial and ethnic groups in the United States will grow to outnumber whites. The Hispanic population will increase by about 21 per cent, the Asian minority will grow by 22 per cent, African-Americans by 12 per cent and Caucasian-Americans by less than 3 per cent. Within twenty-five years, the number of Americans who are Hispanic or non-white will have doubled to nearly 115 million, while the white population will have barely increased at all. In about 60 years, the typical American will no longer trace his or her ancestry back to Europe, but will have come from Asia, Africa, South or Central America, the Middle or Far East or the Pacific Islands. As *Time* writer William Henry III observed, 'The former majority will learn, as a normal part of everyday life, the meaning of the Latin slogan E PLURIBUS UNUM, one formed from many.'[6]

For many of the nation's students the 'browning of America' is already a visible reality. Forty per cent of New York's elementary and secondary schoolchildren are ethnic minorities. White students in California are presently outnumbered by Hispanics, Asians and Blacks. Large numbers of Vietnamese call San Jose their home and thousands upon thousands of Hmong refugees now live in St Paul, Minnesota. Every state, city and town in America has begun to feel the realization of the vision expressed by Emma Lazarus in her welcoming poem: 'The New Colossus' (1883):

Not like the brazen giant of Greek fame,
With conquering limbs astride from land to land;
Here at our sea-washed, sunset gates shall stand
A mighty woman with a torch, whose flame
Is the imprisoned lightning, and her name
Mother of Exiles. From her beacon-hand
Glows world-wide welcome; her mild eyes command
The air-bridged harbor that twin cities frame.
'Keep, ancient lands, your storied pomp!' cries she
With silent lips. 'Give me your tired, your poor,
Your huddled masses yearning to breathe free,
The wretched refuse of your teeming shore.
Send these, the homeless, tempest-tost to me.
I lift my lamp beside the golden door!

Every year about 100 million people will leave their native homes to escape deprivation or violence or in search of greater economic, political, or religious freedom. The destination of choice for many continues to be North America, but increasing millions are also migrating to the relatively homogeneous countries of Europe. Neither the United States nor the countries of Europe will be able to build walls that are tall enough or strong enough or long enough to keep the world out. If the nations are to respond intelligently to these trends, they will have to learn how to draw from the enormous human capital that new immigrants bring. In addition, if the nations wish to check the growing flood of immigrants, they will have no choice but to develop the global institutions that are necessary to promote the dignity, well-being and rights of all peoples, wherever in the world they happen to be born.

PART III

THE HUMAN SPIRIT AND
THE SOCIAL ORDER

7

THE JOURNEY OUT OF THE RACIAL DIVIDE

In 1924, Raymond Dart, an anatomist at the University of Witwaterstrand in South Africa, received some rocks containing fossils from a student who had been digging in a limestone quarry at a place named Taung, located 200 miles from Johannesburg. After careful examination, Dart concluded that the rocks contained three-million-year-old skull fragments that he named *Australopithecus Africanus*. Dart's discovery was important because it was among the first in a chain of discoveries that would establish the monogenesis, or common biological roots, of all people. From East Africa our human ancestors began to spread to all places across the planet.

The migration of early humans to different parts of the world led to the phenotypic, genetic, and cultural differences that are commonly referred to now as racial groups. Biologists tell us that without diversification of the gene pool human beings would have gradually become extinct. Biological diversity renders human groups more robust by increasing our resistance to the development of various types of genetic defects and environmentally induced diseases. The biological diversification of humankind thus played an important role in ensuring humanity's survival.

In the fifteenth century, after many millennia of evolution and development in relative isolation, the peoples of the world began to come back together again in large numbers. Advancements in ship building, map making, and navigation enabled increasing numbers of the world's peoples to have ongoing contact with one another. The early centuries of humanity's encounter with its own diversity have been marred by patterns of exploitation, cultural hegemony, and presumptions of inferiority and superiority of various sorts. In the fifteenth century we also saw the emergence of a new kind of prejudice, the especially virulent form that has come to be known as 'racism'. For more than five centuries racism would spread across the world largely unopposed. Acting as an ideological machete, racism would inflict a deep wound on the human spirit, would invade the functioning of social institutions across the planet; it would nearly cripple humanity's ability to cooperate in the advancement of civilization and the maintenance of life. Furthermore, during some of the darkest days of the twentieth century racism would contribute to the deaths of millions of people and would lead to the near annihilation of Europe.

As a form of prejudice, racism is distinguished from ethnocentrism in that it seeks to justify the superiority of a particular ethnic, cultural or religious group based on permanent biological, psychological or spiritual factors. By contrast, ethnocentrism, a form of prejudice practised by the ancient Hebrews, Christians and Greeks, allowed for ways of overcoming alleged inferiority by conversion to the superior group or by assimilation into the dominant culture's language, traditions and values. For example, the Greeks considered anyone who did not speak and write the Greek language a 'barbarian'. However, as one was integrated into Greek values and culture, one was thought to be 'civilized' and could be accepted as an equal.

In contrast to ethnocentrism, modern racism began to emerge in fifteenth-century Spain and was developed to deal with large numbers of Jews who had converted to Catholicism and who were rapidly becoming leaders of the Church. As the Jewish converts had achieved literacy in relatively large numbers because of their study, as families and communities, of the Talmud and Pentateuch in 'hermeneutic circles', and had enjoyed a long, distinguished history of religious scholarship, they were well prepared to advance rapidly not only within the Church but within the increasingly prosperous economic hierarchy. Since the absence of knowledge could not be used to discriminate between New Christians, or *conversos*, and Old Christians, it was decided that they would be distinguished on biological grounds. Anyone who had had a Jewish (or Muslim) ancestor in the previous five generations was considered a 'New Christian'. These conversos were deemed to be inferior and were gradually forbidden to attend college, join most religious orders, or hold government jobs. To prove that one did not belong to the inferior group, one had to produce 'certificates of purity of blood'. The Inquisition was established in both Spain and Portugal to ensure that those of Jewish ancestry were kept out of mainstream society, irrespective of their knowledge, beliefs, or church membership.[1]

As noted by Richard Popkin, this new form of discrimination differed from ethnocentrism in that it allowed no means for leaving the group discriminated against. And while some Jews did escape discrimination by changing their identities, going into hiding, or fleeing to different parts of the world, they had no opportunity to prosper while living in Spain or Portugal as converts or Jews. Since biological racism was contrary to Christian doctrine on the need to convert everyone to the 'brotherhood of Christ', theories were needed to support and justify this new form of permanent inferiority. Justifications were founded on the idea that biologically and spiritually Jews possessed characteristics that could never be completely changed; these characteristics, it was argued, would jeopardize the Christian community. On this premise, Jews were rendered permanent second-class citizens.

When the Italian explorer Christopher Columbus, supported by the Spaniards and the Portuguese, sailed to the New World in 1492, he and his crew brought these racial doctrines with them. 'Certificates of whiteness' were introduced and served as functional equivalents to the certificates of purity of blood. As Popkin noted in his essay 'The Philosophical Basis of Modern Racism',[2] and Francisco Bethencourt has argued in his seminal work, *Racism: From the Crusades to the Twentieth Century*,[3] the basis for racism against the Jews was easily established within a Christian paradigm since, as far back as the Middle Ages, the Jews had been widely viewed as the killers of Christ and eternal enemies of Christianity. When Columbus imported biological racism to the New World, however, no such justification for prejudice against the Native Americans existed. European explorers were thus faced with the need to establish the identity of the native inhabitants in a way that would justify genocide, cultural hegemony, and economic exploitation.

One theory advanced in justification of what was to occur was that the indigenous Americans did not derive their origins from the Biblical world of Adam and Eve; rather, they had a separate and independent origin. They were not Adamites, it was argued, but pre-Adamites. As such, they were not fully human in any Biblical sense. In this manner was the *polygenesis* theory born. It held that human groups cannot trace their origins to a single source; but rather, derive from separate evolutionary trees. At the cutting edge of evolution were European Christians. Everyone else fell somewhere below. In this way is the doctrine of white supremacy advanced.

In support of the view that Native Americans were subhuman, it was argued that they were incapable of abstract ideas, that they practised sodomy, that they offered human sacrifices, and thus could not practise proper morality. The Spaniards and Portuguese would thus have to bring 'Indian' society under their supervision and governance. Although some accepted the pre-Adamite, not-fully-human status of these peoples, others maintained that their inferiority derived, not from a separate origin, but from degeneration. When they arrived in the New World in 1619 as slaves, similar explanations for the assumed inferiority of Africans were also advanced. For example, the curse of Ham, a 'divine act', was frequently invoked in explanation of African inferiority. Commenting on this, Alexander Thomas and Samuel Sillen write:

As proof of the black's predetermined deficiency, it was once considered sufficient to invoke Scriptural authority. According to Genesis, Noah was so enraged at his son Ham for beholding him naked that he thundered a curse dooming all the descendants of Ham to be the servants of servants. This passage was interpreted with the customary latitude by plantation owners who identified their slaves with the doomed tribe of Ham, thus providing unassailable Biblical support for the thesis that blacks are inherently subordinate creatures.[4]

Thus, the philosophical basis for modern racism was articulated by those who rejected the Biblical account of a single origin for all humankind and replaced it with either a polygenic theory or a theory of degeneration. The associated claim was that non-Adamites, or those who had been cursed, were characterized by a different nature. Non-white non-Christians were thus to be regarded as inferior in ways that could not be remedied. This was a radically different way to think about human identity, in that prior to this period the masses of humanity did not tend to base their assessments of human nature on skin colour, facial features, or hair texture.

With the spread of scientific method during the Enlightenment, biological racism received increasing support from scholars, philosophers and statesmen from all over the Western world. By the eighteenth century, according to Popkin,

there was a vast amount of literature on why blacks are black, why people speak primitive and inferior languages, and such matters. The application of the experimental method of reasoning to these problems brought forth two kinds of results, one a highly elaborated degeneracy theory, and the other a polygenetic explanation that claimed that differences between whites and nonwhites were fixed and permanent. Part of the battle between these basic accounts involved the question of whether there is a basic unity of mankind or a basic diversity.[5]

For most of the last several centuries, the focus has been on the diversity of human nature, rather than its basic unity. With rare exceptions, for more than five centuries, philosophers, scientists and politicians affirmed the superiority of whites and the obvious inferiority of all others. In his essay 'Of National Characters' the influential British philosopher David Hume wrote:

> I am apt to suspect the negroes and in general all other species of men (for there are four or five different kinds) to be naturally inferior to the whites. There never was a civilized nation of any other complexion than white, nor even any individual eminent either in action or speculation. No ingenious manufacturers among them, no arts, no sciences. On the other hand, the most rude and barbarous of the whites, such as the ancient Germans, the present Tartars, have still something eminent about them, in their valour, form of government, or some other particular. Such a uniform and constant difference could not happen in so many countries and ages, if nature had not made an original distinction betwixt these breeds of men.[6]

In the 1800s an eminent physician and professor of anatomy at the Pennsylvania Medical College, Dr Samuel G. Morton, measured the cranial capacity of skulls by filling them with pepper seeds. Based on his craniometric research, he concluded that the brains of various races became smaller and smaller as one 'descended' from the Caucasian to the Ethiopian.[7] These differences in brain size were said to account for 'those primeval attributes of mind, which, for wise purposes, have given our race a decided and unquestionable superiority over all the nations of the earth'.[8] Continuing this research into the early twentieth century, R. B. Bean noted in the *American Journal of Anatomy* that the Negro brain was smaller, had fewer nerve cells and fibres, and was thus less efficient than that of the white man. 'We are forced to conclude', the author affirmed, 'that it is useless to elevate the Negro by education or otherwise, except in the direction of his natural endowments.'[9]

Yet despite the brutality of slavery, and in spite of the near annihilation of the people who first called America their home, the mass migration of the peoples of the world to the North American continent marked a new stage in the life and development of humankind. Prior to the fifteenth century, the peoples of the world, largely in response to the influence of great spiritual luminaries – such as Abraham, Moses, Buddha, Zoroaster, and Jesus (among others) – had successfully organized themselves into families or clans, then into tribes, city-states, and finally, under the influence of the Prophet Muhammad – into nations. In each of these levels of social organization, the scope of community, or what anthropologists call the 'fictive kinship' was successively expanded to include a wider range of the human community. Now that nation building is nearly complete it would appear that the next stage in the evolution of life on the planet is the establishment of a global community that is diverse, yet organically unified, in all the essential aspects of its life. The United States of America, a nation born out of the many nations of the world, both as a place and an idea, represents an important movement in this direction.

Although all the forces of history have been drawing us back together, we have resisted this pull for several reasons. First, because America's national psyche was developed on the foundation of racism, this ideology has infected all its institutions and clouds the nation's vision; second, many who confuse unity with uniformity fear the loss of cultural pluralism; third, it is difficult to forgive and remedy the historical and ongoing injustices perpetrated by cultural or racial groups against one another; fourth, many contemporary leaders derive their status from maintaining a spirit of race- and class-based contention and divisiveness; fifth, long-term institutionalized injustices continue to create economic disparities which keep races, cultures and nations in a constant state of conflict; and last, much of humanity lacks the spiritual vision, moral discipline or social maturity necessary to contribute to the creation of harmonizing relationships. This combination of factors has led to a weakening of faith in humanity and a consequent paralysis of the collective will.

Of course, people of African descent are not alone in the struggle against the dark forces of prejudice. Our Middle Eastern and Jewish brothers and sisters continue to suffer under its oppressive weight in Eastern and Western Europe, the United Kingdom and the United States, and many other parts of the world. Our Palestinian friends, the Muslims of China and Myanmar, the 'untouchables' of India, and many, many others across the earth carry the burdens imposed by the presumption of superiority conferred by race, class, caste, ethnicity, religion, or degree of educational attainment. Just this morning we woke to yet another report in the *New York Times* of a string of attacks against older people of Asian descent in San Francisco: 'Two grandmothers stabbed and a third punched in the face in broad daylight. An 84-year old man fatally shoved to the ground while on his morning walk.'[10] And while assaults to the safety, security, dignity and well-being of people of Asian background have been a perennial problem stretching across more than a century in the United States, the sad spectacle of this form of racism in the twenty-first century carries with it a kind of pain that is amplified by the realization of its absurdity.

The spirit that animates oneness

Of the many scientific truths discovered in the century recently ended, none is more profound in its implications than the knowledge of interdependence. From the smallest particles of matter, to the grandest stars and planets, the universe has proven to be a tightly woven fabric of interconnected energies, entities and processes. Recently, for example, astrophysicists have discovered that galaxies that are 10 and sometimes 20 million light-years away from each other interact. Indeed, a study published in the *Astrophysical Journal* reported that there are perhaps hundreds of galaxies that are rotating in sync with each other across vast distances.[11] One potential explanation is that these galaxies appear to be connected by what are called 'large-scale structures', which are the largest known objects in the universe. These structures, astrophysicists believe, serve to tie many galaxies together into a kind of cosmic web in ways that we do not yet understand. Reflecting on this, the journalist Zat Rana writes: 'It's a little bit like a symphony, where the Universe uses its invisible strings to harmonize the movement of its different objects in the chaos of spacetime.'[12]

In the biological realm, the unity of diverse parts is the cause and sign of life, while disunity is the cause and sign of death. If we want to know if an organism is dying, we examine whether its diverse component parts are able to function together in some coordinated fashion. In animals, we might monitor vital signs – respiration, heart rate, liver and kidney functioning, digestion, and so forth. These diverse systems cannot simply do their own thing. They must function in such a manner that the entire system benefits. In the absence of constant feedback concerning the health and needs of the whole, the functioning of each component part becomes increasingly impaired. As a result, the whole organism begins to die. In addition, a living system survives not because every component part has the same characteristics – but because every part is different.

On a societal level, the nations of the world, which are themselves made up of ethnic, racial, religious and cultural groups, constitute the diverse parts that must work together in some harmonious fashion if humanity is to fully prosper and evolve. A society whose member groups are in constant competition and conflict will be unable to cultivate or use its limited resources in the best manner. The conflicts that divide blacks from whites, women from men, Muslims from Jews, conservatives from liberals, the middle-class and wealthy from the poor, and so on, all pose serious threats to the future viability of the country and world.

While the natural sciences have illuminated the processes that facilitate unity in diversity in the mineral, plant and animal kingdoms, we are only recently beginning to understand the unifying forces that harmonize the diverse needs and interests of human beings. The most potent of these forces is love. Love is not a luxury reserved for starry-eyed youth. It is the power that binds the diverse elements of the universe and makes possible all forms of existence and development.

In the human realm, true love – as distinguished from mere infatuation – is reflected in a myriad of principles and values that make family and community life possible. Among these principles are justice, compassion, trustworthiness, the simple yet profound virtue of courtesy – as well as a willingness to pursue and defend what is right and true. Whenever these values are distorted or underdeveloped, the spirit of love begins to dissipate. The result is chaos, confusion, violence, and a gradual collapse of the social order. If ethnic and race relations in America, and indeed around the world, are in a critical condition, the situation can be improved only through a wider, more sincere application of these love-related principles.

In all spheres of existence, order, within the context of change, is rule-governed. The laws of thermodynamics, the laws of motion, the law of the conservation of mass and energy, and so forth, all regulate processes of change in nature. Likewise, the orderly transformation of individuals and societies must be governed by laws and principles. The principles of transformation that are applicable to this stage in humanity's evolution must facilitate the establishment of harmony between the blacks and whites of America:

> Let the white make a supreme effort in their resolve to contribute their share to the solution of this problem, to abandon once for all their usually inherent and at times subconscious sense of superiority, to correct their tendency towards revealing a patronizing attitude towards the members of the other race, to persuade them through their intimate, spontaneous and informal association with them of the genuineness of their friendship and the sincerity of their intentions, and to master their impatience of any lack of responsiveness on

the part of a people who have received, for so long a period, such grievous and slow healing wounds. Let the [blacks], through a corresponding effort on their part, show by every means in their power the warmth of their response, their readiness to forget the past, and their ability to wipe out every trace of suspicion that may still linger in their hearts and minds. Let neither think that the solution of so vast a problem is a matter that exclusively concerns the other. Let neither think that such a problem can either easily or immediately be resolved . . . Let neither think that anything short of genuine love, extreme patience, true humility, consummate tact, sound initiative, mature wisdom, and deliberate, persistent, and prayerful effort, can succeed in blotting out the stain which this patent evil has left on the fair name of their common country.[13]

The cost of our collective healing will be inner and outer transformation. Both black and white Americans have prejudices to overcome: 'one, the prejudice which is built up in the minds of a people who have conquered and imposed their will, and the other the reactionary prejudice of those who have been . . . sorely put upon.'[14]

For many years social scientists believed that the prejudices would spontaneously disappear through a process they called 'cohort replacement'. This theory is predicated on the notion that each successive generation, because of increasing interracial contact, would quite naturally be less prejudiced than the preceding one. While on the face of it such a theory sounds reasonable, the last several decades have taught us that mere contact between antagonistic groups is not sufficient to change deeply entrenched prejudices. What we are learning now is that the subtle and not so subtle prejudices that divide white and black Americans has penetrated deeply into the human psyche and has also been embodied in a myriad of social institutions; it will thus take a mighty effort and a great vision on the part of both races to completely overcome it. It will also require that we draw upon the vast potential for transformation that is embodied in what we have been referring to here as the human spirit. Insofar as America is one of the most diverse nations on earth, and inasmuch as it nurtures forms of racism that are especially deep and virulent, we might draw upon the American story as we contemplate the journey out of the racial divide.

For example, the ideals of freedom and liberty, of the equality and dignity of all peoples, expressed in the American Constitution; the humanitarian aspiration embodied in that inspired, welcoming poem, etched on the base of the Statue of Liberty; her beautiful and spacious landscapes, and her multi-coloured, multi-talented peoples, all bear witness to the greatness of that country and to the loftiness of the vision which has given it wings. On these wings, America has soared to great heights. Its future, one might imagine, will be more glorious still. If America is to realize her great destiny, she will do so not because a few wise and noble leaders – of whatever party, race or culture – have saved us. Nor 'can the effort of will required for such a task be summoned up merely by appeals for action against the countless ills afflicting society. It must be galvanized by a vision of human prosperity in the fullest sense of the term – an awakening to the possibilities of the spiritual and material well-being now brought within grasp.'[15] America's destiny, in particular, also hinges upon its ability to nourish, educate, and unify the untapped resources that lie fallow or stir restlessly in the nation's rural wastelands and neglected cities. The race and culture-related challenges that are now being faced by Americans are challenges that are also at the door of growing numbers of European, Asian, African, and Middle Eastern nations – and so we cannot neglect discourse on the problem of racism around the world.

One notes, for example, that notwithstanding the suffering that racism imposed upon the lives of millions of dark-skinned people for more than five centuries, its devastating effects would not be adequately appreciated among many whites until the painful lash of Nazism gave racism a bad name across Europe.

Without a doubt, Hitler's ruthless armies gave millions of Europeans the opportunity to feel the harsh implications of racism in their own lives. What was to be created out of the searing pain of the Second World War was the first global movement to extend what came to be known as 'human rights', not just for white-skinned people, or to people with wealth and power, or to those who are praised and admired for their unique gifts and talents, but to everyone.

Indeed, four thousand years prior to the suffering of the two World Wars the Babylonian King Hammurabi had articulated a set of laws that were designed to protect rights. The Hammurabi Codes provided for fair wages and protection for private property, and required that charges levelled against a person had to be proven at trial. However, as Schulz has pointed out, Hammurabi's Codes 'said nothing . . . about how Babylonians were to treat their archenemies, the Assyrians'.[16] Because the Assyrians did not enjoy the protection of these rights, they could be subject to any kind of treatment that the Babylonians wished to mete out. They could be slaughtered at will, deprived of their property, and convicted of all manner of crimes without recourse to justice.

These forms of discrimination based on nationality, racial characteristics, ethnicity, or class are, perhaps, not seen as starkly today but they still constitute an essential aspect of the way that humans treat one another across the earth. Without a radical transformation of these traditions a viable future for humanity can scarcely be imagined. What is required is the complete rejection of any philosophy, doctrine, policy, law, custom, or practice that contravenes the principle of the oneness of humanity.

Racism is, of course, not the only ideological threat that burdens the human spirit and blocks realization of humanity's limitless potential. In the chapters that follow we examine ideological commitments that keep us saddled to war and also explore how well-intentioned neo-liberal values also render it difficult to provide for the basic needs of all human beings.

8

IDEOLOGICAL ARGUMENTS THAT SEEK TO JUSTIFY AND SUSTAIN THE PRACTICE OF WAR

During the twentieth century, even as we endured the nightmares of World Wars I and II, political *'realists'* sought to persuade us that it is impossible to create the conditions necessary to avoid war because it is not possible to erect an international framework suitable for maintaining peace and collective security among nations. Realist foreign policy thus encouraged nations to maintain the status quo and to continue to invest vast resources in the military infrastructures required for war because the nature of world politics is said to be constrained by human nature, which, realists affirm, is fundamentally selfish and aggressive. *Idealists*, by contrast, have noted that political realism is increasingly incongruent with global realities and that global trends support the possibility of establishing an enduring peace based on principles of cooperation and justice. These trends include the gradual spread of democracy, a growing recognition of economic interdependence, the decreasing appeal of war, and the gradual rise of technologies and supranational institutions that make it possible to regulate and harmonize world affairs.

In his book on idealism, realism, and American foreign policy, David Callahan provides insight into the ideological struggle between idealism and realism during the twentieth century. Beginning with Alexander Hamilton, who dismissed 'Enlightenment ideals of how a community of nations should behave', and extending throughout much of the twentieth century, notes Callahan, realism has inspired the foreign policy of most of America's presidents and foreign policy makers. As early as 1910 Alfred Mahan warned that, unless America adopted a realist foreign policy, it might well find itself 'vulnerable to an "aggressive restlessness" that underlay the continuous struggle for survival among great powers'.[1] Theodore Roosevelt is said to have adopted Mahan's foreign policy perspective and became one of the first realist presidents of the United States.

Mahan's contemporary, Walter Lippmann, further advanced the aims of realism when he attacked the 'naïve' idealistic assumptions that were believed to characterize President Wilson's handling of the peace negotiations that followed World War I. Insisting that the world was considerably different from the one envisioned by Wilson, Lippmann wrote, with considerable sarcasm, that 'the Wilsonian vision is of a world in which there are no lasting rivalries, where there are no deep conflicts of interest, where no compromises of principle have to be made, where there are no separate spheres of influence, and no alliances. In this world there will be no wars except universal war against criminal governments who rebel against universal order.'[2]

Although idealism may have had strong, vocal supporters following World War I, the calculated, self-interested brutality of World War II led to the consolidation of a realist foreign policy among US leaders and policy makers. 'In a world of Hitlers and Tojos,' Callahan writes, 'it was hard to have faith in good intentions and high minded schemes for collective security'.[3] In his depiction of American vulnerability following World War II, Nicholas Spykman, a powerful US foreign policy analyst, complained that the international community was without a central authority to preserve law and order, to guarantee territorial integrity and political independence, or to secure basic rights under international law. 'States exist, therefore, primarily in terms of their own strength or that of their protector states,' Spykman wrote, 'and if they wish to maintain their independence, they must make the preservation or improvement of their power position the principal objective of foreign policy.'[4]

Although the United States was a significant contributor to the development of the United Nations following World War II, the Wilsonian vision of collective security was supplanted by an aggressive arms race that was to claim an increasing share of the world's economic, political, and intellectual resources. The United States, influenced by Hans Morgenthau, the most successful proponent of realism during the postwar period, and by US diplomat George Kennan, who was deeply suspicious of both the legal and moral ideals that had influenced US policy, pursued the Cold War strategy of containment for more than four decades.

The re-emergence of idealism

In the years preceding the attacks of 11 September 2001, realist doctrine had come under renewed scrutiny. Over the 1980s and 90s, and most especially as the new millennium approached, a respected cohort of scholars and analysts began to suggest that global trends toward greater economic interdependence cast serious doubts over the legitimacy of a realist foreign policy.[5] In support of their critiques of realist policies, they tended to cite the rising power of multinational corporations and the emergence of international nonstate actors – such as the various nongovernmental organizations, the Organization of Petroleum Exporting Countries, and the European Community. They also described a rapidly changing world in which advances in communication, transportation, and international trade have released irreversible forces of transnational integration.

The rapidly changing geopolitical and economic context led both idealists and realists to affirm that world politics is in a period of transition. In 1975 Henry Kissinger, perhaps the most powerful realist in recent years, affirmed that 'we are entering a new era' and that 'old international patterns are crumbling'. The world, Kissinger noted, 'has become interdependent in economics, in communications, in human aspirations'.[6] In his description of this shifting paradigm, Michael Allen, Professor of Political Science at Bryn Mawr College, asserts that while in the past, the foreign encounters which had the greatest consequences for welfare, security and consciousness of people . . . were those enacted by agents of states . . . Today . . . [m]erchants and bankers are both more numerous and have been joined by overseas managers, engineers and technical advisers. Together their trans-border encounters have greater consequences for the welfare, security, and consciousness of people around the world than most of the inter-governmental or domestic actions of states.[7]

Despite these noteworthy changes, 'essential realism', which is fundamentally Hobbesian in nature, continues to manifest itself as captains of industry, bankers, film makers, and other private actors have entered, *en masse*, the international arena.

Essential realism, according to Allen, sees states as the primary units of action, assumes an environment of mutual hostility or suspicion among states, seeks power as a means of security in a presumably anarchical environment, and assumes that state actors are rational – inasmuch as they are motivated by self-interest.[8] Since private citizens tend to be guided by many of these same assumptions, in spite of dramatic changes in the *form* realism may now take, the *spirit* of realism continues to inform the nature of relations among and between the peoples and nations of the world. Furthermore, neither the emergence of non-state actors nor the end of the Cold War has put to rest realists' concerns for international order and security. Indeed, as Callahan notes, from a realist's point of view, while the end of the Cold War may have changed the structure of world politics, it did not change its essential nature:

That nature is seen as governed by an inescapable reality: no central authority exists to manage the international system . . . [thus] each country must take responsibility for its own security, preparing for the use of military force or living at the mercy of stronger neighbors. The Cold War's end, far from increasing stability, is seen as creating new dangers by

replacing stable bipolar rivalry with a less predictable mul-
tipolar system in which many strong states compete for
position and all states feel less secure.[9]

Despite the century-long struggle between realism and idealism,
and notwithstanding the doubts cast by various forms of terrorism (cyber, chemical, biological, religious, nationalist, separatist)
on the possibility of developing a workable international order,
one might imagine that the realist's need for national and international security and the idealist's hope of achieving harmony
and cooperation among peoples and nations are not mutually
exclusive. On the contrary, and commensurate with a realist
perspective, it might be argued that a sustainable peace can only
be achieved when the practical means necessary for safeguarding
national borders and resolving international disputes peacefully
have been well established. At the same time, as the idealists are
well aware, peace is far more than the absence of war and thus
requires a conscious, moral commitment to the implications of
humanity's interdependence. Thus, any viable vision for a new
world order must lie, not only in the peace-keeping institutions
that are prescribed, but in the philosophical and moral foundations upon which these institutions are based. Such a system will
require both an expanding vision of the nature and implications
of the oneness of humanity, as well as an international governing
body with sufficient military backing to ensure collective security. It is in addressing both of these dimensions of international
order that both realists and idealists may find their highest hopes
realized.

During the nineteenth century, nearly one hundred years
before the height of the arms race, Bahá'u'lláh – who was himself
the victim of a range of human rights abuses for more than forty
years – wrote to the entire concourse of the rulers of the earth:

> We see you adding every year unto your expenditures and
> laying the burden thereof on the people whom ye rule; this
> is naught but grievous injustice . . . Be reconciled among

yourselves, that ye may need armaments no more save in a measure to safeguard your territories and dominions. Be united, O concourse of the sovereigns of the world, for thereby will the tempests of discord be stilled amongst you and your peoples find rest. Should any one among you take up arms against another, rise ye all against him, for this is naught but manifest justice.[10]

In an elaboration of this prescription for a 'new world order' embodying those institutions necessary to ensure collective security, Bahá'u'lláh's great-grandson, Shoghi Effendi, wrote:

What else could these weighty words signify if they did not point to the inevitable curtailment of unfettered national sovereignty as an indispensable preliminary to the formation of the future Commonwealth of all the nations of the world? Some form of a world super-state must needs be evolved, in whose favour all the nations of the world will have willingly ceded every claim to make war, certain rights to impose taxation and all rights to maintain armaments, except for purposes of maintaining internal order within their respective dominions. Such a state will have to include within its orbit an international executive adequate to enforce supreme and unchallengeable authority on every recalcitrant member of the commonwealth; a world parliament whose members shall be elected by the people in their respective countries and whose election shall be confirmed by their respective governments; and a supreme tribunal whose judgment will have a binding effect even in such cases where the parties concerned did not voluntarily agree to submit their case to its consideration.[11]

To those who suggest that such a framework is impractical, Shoghi Effendi called upon the rulers of the world to reflect on the federal system that binds the semi-sovereign states that make up the United States. Because there is interstate cooperation and greater loyalty to a national constitution and body of laws, it is possible for the northern, southern, eastern, western, and central states, as well as Alaska and the Hawaiian Islands, to conduct commerce, protect civil rights, educate the population, share resources, and protect the interests of both individual states and the union in a more efficient, cost-effective manner. On a global scale, what is impractical is having to carry out those processes necessary for the maintenance of nations without the legal, constitutional, and legislative framework that would facilitate and inform the nature of international relations. Indeed, 'Laying the groundwork for global civilization calls for the creation of laws and institutions that are universal in both character and authority.'[12] For example, among the most important fruits of such a global framework would be internationally accepted and enforceable laws on human rights; a common global currency; a common universal auxiliary language; a common system of weights and measures; a common commitment to cultivating, safeguarding and sharing the earth's natural resources; and a universally supported international peace force, accountable to the dictates of a world parliament. Would not the business of sustaining and supporting life on earth be facilitated by such collective arrangements?

Although mindful of the grievous slaughter and exploitation of America's original inhabitants, Shoghi Effendi also suggested looking at the early history of the United States to develop greater confidence in the feasibility of a global federal system. In 1931 he wrote:

> How confident were the assertions made in the days preceding the unification of the states of the North American continent regarding the insuperable barriers that stood in the way of their ultimate federation! Was it not widely and emphatically declared that the conflicting interests, the mutual distrust, the differences of government and habit that divided the states were such as no force, whether spiritual or temporal, could ever hope to harmonize or control? And

yet how different were the conditions prevailing a hundred and fifty years ago from those that characterize present-day society! It would indeed be no exaggeration to say that the absence of those facilities which modern scientific progress has placed at the service of humanity in our time made of the problem of welding the American states into a single federation, similar though they were in certain traditions, a task infinitely more complex than that which confronts a divided humanity in its efforts to achieve the unification of all mankind.[13]

On human nature

Despite the urgent need and growing feasibility of establishing a global system of governance, the central concern expressed by realists that may cast doubts on the vision of peaceful co-existence is human nature. Realists tend to regard human nature as incorrigibly selfish and aggressive – thus, they argue that peace initiatives that depend on human beings for their success are bound to fail.

In spite of its wide acceptance, the realist perspective on human nature is one that fails to comport either with history or with the most recent developments in psychology. A large and growing body of research has demonstrated that human behaviour (including either aggression or altruism) is a function of the relationship between malleable attitudes and social norms and prevailing social and/or political conditions. Thus, in most cases, if one wants to explain why a person, a group, or a society has acted aggressively, one must know something about the interaction between the actors' beliefs and values and the social conditions prevailing at the time. Since all human qualities can be strengthened or weakened by training and are subject to immediate and historical social, political, and moral influences, aggression, selfishness, and violence are not unalterable features of human life. Rather, in most cases they are characteristics that are as remediable as is the inability to read and write.[14]

In *The Better Angels of Our Nature: Why Violence Has Declined*, Steven Pinker has shown that interpersonal, international, and intercultural violence has decreased dramatically over the past 150 years. Pinker links these trends to three socio-historical factors – 'the civilizing process', 'the humanitarian revolution', and 'the rights revolution'.

In describing the *civilizing process*, Pinker invokes the work of the Jewish sociologist Norbert Elias (1897–1990) who was born in Breslau, Germany but fled the country in 1933 to escape the Holocaust. Pinker notes that Elias's magnum opus, *The Civilizing Process*, was published in Germany in 1939, 'at a time when the very idea seemed like a bad joke'. The work, which examined the experience of everyday life in medieval Europe by examining manuscripts of etiquette, revealed how animalistic and violent the Europeans had been in the Middle Ages with respect to their tendencies toward extreme forms of violence for relatively minor assaults to their reputation or status. The work revealed that as social etiquette became part of common discourse, there was a corresponding decline in the homicide rate among Europeans. In exploring this work, Pinker notes that while today we think of etiquette books as 'sources of handy tips for avoiding embarrassing peccadilloes', they were once 'serious guides to moral conduct, written by the leading thinkers of the day'.[15]

The etiquette books of the Middle Ages provided rules for behaviour that began to shape human sensibilities in significant ways. They served to civilize relationships among Europeans of all classes. Commenting on Elias's work, Pinker notes:

> Elias's theory . . . attributes the decline in European violence to a larger psychological change . . . He proposes that over a span of several centuries, beginning in the 11th or 12th and maturing in the 17th and 18th, Europeans increasingly inhibited their impulses, anticipated the long-term consequences of their actions, and took other people's thoughts and feelings into consideration. A culture of honor – the

readiness to take revenge – gave way to a culture of dignity – the readiness to control one's emotions.[16]

In other words, violence in Europe began to decline, in part, as a function of a conscious effort to advance what has long been described as the 'humanizing' process.

Pinker goes further to explain that statistics from every contemporary Western nation show that interpersonal violence varies significantly with class and that the overwhelming majority of homicides and other violent crimes are committed by people in the lowest socio-economic classes. He notes:

> The main reason that violence correlates with low socio-economic status today is that elites and the middle class pursue justice with the legal system while the lower classes resort to what scholars of violence call 'self-help'. This . . . is another name for vigilantism, frontier justice, taking the law into your own hands, and other forms of violent retaliation by which people secured justice in the absence of intervention by the state.[17]

A second trend that Pinker associates with dramatic decreases in violence over recent centuries is what he has called the 'humanitarian revolution' associated with the European Enlightenment whose ideas and ideals reduced humanity's appetite for state-sponsored violence and torture and opened human hearts so that 'people began to *sympathize* with more of their fellow humans, and were no longer indifferent to their suffering'.[18] Commensurate with this view, in her important book *Inventing Human Rights: A History*, the historian Lynn Hunt noted that as people began, for example, to read novels that captured the lives and experiences of everyday people the sphere of human compassion began to widen and people began to 'imagine' human equality. The penning of the Declaration of Independence in America in 1776 and the promulgation of the Universal Declaration of Human Rights in 1948 were, in Hunt's view, seminal moments during which broader aspirations for human freedom and dignity were couched in terms so noble and beautiful that these documents won for the human rights movement many new adherents.

Last, Pinker associates the decreases in violence around the world to the 'rights revolution' – a revolution in the mid and late twentieth century that touched many parts of the world and that involved the successive rise of movements to advance civil, gender and children's rights, as well as the rights of animals. These movements were responsible for dramatic decreases in state-sponsored violence, lynchings, hate crimes, battering and gender-based assaults of various kinds. And while these social problems are no doubt still very much with us and continue to be serious threats to people's health and development, there can be little doubt that the effects of the civilizing process, the humanitarian revolution, and the rights revolution on prevalence rates of violence show that human aggression cannot be understood as an inevitable byproduct of 'human nature'.

Furthermore, if humanity is one, indivisible, organic whole, its growth, like that of all organic systems, is likely to be characterized by different stages of development. Just as the individual must pass through infancy, childhood, and adolescence, so it might be argued that humanity has also had to pass through analogous stages.[19] During the developmental process, if a human being is subject to the proper education he or she grows from a state of relative helplessness into a being capable of the most subtle and exquisite thoughts and actions. If one had not witnessed a newborn infant grow into a mature adult, one would not easily believe that a creature who can neither hold up its head nor control its own sputum could someday be able to play the harpsichord, fly an aircraft past the speed of sound, or transplant a kidney from one living person to another. This is the miracle of human life and development.

The true nature of a thing, noted Aristotle, is connected to its final cause – its end or purpose. To know the nature of an acorn, for example, one must know that it has the potential to become an oak tree. Final cause thus embodies a sense of *potential*. When one understands a developing organism's final cause, one is able to nurture its development with faith and confidence. One does not, for example, discard one's children because they are helpless, or bothersome, or sometimes even rude, arrogant, and violent; nor does one say that such characteristics are part of the child's immutable nature. The children are educated because there is a vision for their potential. The development of the body politic must be understood in much the same way.

Among the most important prerequisites for peace is the full and equal participation of women in all aspects of society – including the international political arena. Indeed, examination of the historical record reveals that much of the bellicose behaviour attributed to 'human nature' by realists is largely the reflection of only one half of the world's population. Rarely have women been the progenitors of war and systematic violence. On the contrary, while men have been waging war, women have been resolving disputes peacefully, nurturing the development and well-being of others, and teaching children the qualities of character necessary to get along with their siblings, classmates, and friends. As a result, the women of the world have developed many of the skills now needed to erect a global society based on principles of cooperation and justice.

Toward a blending of the practical and the visionary

Peace is a practical possibility because modern technology has made available material means for organizing and safeguarding the planet. Moreover, as is evidenced by the frequency and variety of global summits that have taken place over the past 30 years, in particular, a consciousness of interdependence has begun to shape the thinking of those concerned with all aspects of life on earth. Despite the possibilities for advancing the cause of peace that result from these developments, the turmoil convulsing human affairs cannot be overlooked. Indeed, 'Dangers unimagined in all history gather around a distracted humanity.'[20]

The greatest error that could be made at this juncture would be to allow recurring crises to cast doubt on the ultimate outcome of the process that is occurring. While an old world is passing away, a new world is struggling to be born. This new approach to life, this emerging global civilization, must be animated by a consciousness of the oneness of humanity.

9

NEO-LIBERAL OBSTACLES TO ADDRESSING UNIVERSAL HUMAN NEEDS

In *Human Rights: Beyond the Liberal Vision*, Judith Blau and Alberto Moncada, senior leaders of *Sociólogos sin Fronteras* (Sociologists without Borders), offer a critical analysis of the ways that American liberalism – as embodied in the country's ethos, its social institutions, and its approach to politics and economics – tends to foster a worldview that is incompatible with the promotion of humanity's collective interests. Insofar as various forms of neo-liberalism have come under scrutiny in recent years for some of the rarely recognized threats that they may embody to the collective, we invoke the work of Blau and Moncada and others in order to address those elements of neo-liberalism that may stand as obstacles to realizing satisfaction of universal human needs.

The critique by Blau and Moncada takes as its focus, not the usual connotations of *liberal* which commonly refers to those who tend to favour government spending for domestic pro-grammes, are apt to support progressive taxes, oppose war, and are generally pro-labour and against big business; rather, their critique is focused on *liberalism* 'in its historical and comparative sense, namely a political and philosophical commitment to indi-vidualism in the spheres of politics, economics and in society'.[1] Such a commitment or 'ideology', they suggest, 'powerfully binds together two spheres of freedoms – economic freedoms and political freedoms – in ways that threaten, and sometimes undermine, social cohesion'.[2] Since the effort to promote the best interests of humanity requires a sense of responsibility for the commonwealth, liberalism, as a worldview that prioritizes individualism over communal values, places a powerful check on the pursuit of humanitarian goals that would ensure that all have access to those basic needs without which the human spirit cannot flourish. This chapter provides an overview of Blau and Moncada's challenging perspective.

They begin their critique by distinguishing between *humanitarian justice*, which takes as its focus extreme violations of human rights – such as crimes against humanity and genocide – and the more ordinary human rights concerns that prevent large numbers of people from realizing their potential. Such concerns may include food insecurity, chronic unemployment, inability to make a living wage, inadequate access to a decent education, the right to live free of equality-defying oppressive ideologies, freedom from exposure to health-compromising environmental wastes, among others. The authors note that while the political, social, and economic culture allows most Americans to appreciate that the torture and killing of civilians are incompatible with American values and should be punished, 'yet', they write, 'that same culture is a serious impediment to Americans when it comes to understanding and fully appreciating that fundamental rights, such as the right to food security and to a job, are necessary to achieve a full life of freedom and dignity'. They go on to argue that America's relative lack of participation in what has come to be known as the human rights revolution can be understood in terms of the values that are at the heart of liberalism. Their critique thus centres on liberalism as a *social point of view* that is embodied in American socio-economic and political practices and is reflected in the functioning of many of its major institutions.

As a worldview, a *weltanschauung*, liberalism, they suggest, is 'premised on the idea that individuals have equal moral worth and rational capacity'. In this respect liberalism and the human rights tradition are grounded in similar assumptions and are 'rooted in identical premises'. On the other hand, they argue, liberal and human rights assumptions can differ in important ways that have significant consequences for peoples' understanding of justice and fairness and for practices and institutions. For example, referencing the work of Michael Kammen, Blau and Moncada note that liberalism 'prioritizes the independence of each person from the other and the independence of each from attachments, be they cultural, traditional, or communal'.[3] Further, the American brand of liberalism, they contend, prioritizes the claims of economic interests over many societal needs such that property rights and market freedoms come before the needs of individuals to develop their capacities.

Blau and Moncada go on to suggest that in liberal ideology the notion of freedom tends to operate negatively. That is, from the liberalist perspective, freedom is conceptualized as *freedom from* something else. As David Cochran observed, liberalism 'rests on a moral dedication to individual freedom. It stresses individual agency and places individual autonomy at the center of its project'; yet its notion of freedom is a negative one, 'centering on the individual unrestrained by interference'.[4] From this vantage point, 'once the basic guarantees of citizenship are secure, the state should let social and economic life unfold in a private sphere, without interference'.[5] The freedom embraced by the American liberal ethos thus centres on freedom as autonomy.

The discourse on freedom as autonomy is strongly tied to other values, such as political liberties, economic freedoms, and social independence. Liberalism-as-autonomy thus serves to shape American practices in profound ways. For example, achievement is seen as the accomplishment of each individual who must 'pull himself up by his bootstraps'. It embodies attitudes that make it difficult for Americans to see the potentially positive benefits of structures, processes, institutions and systems that aid in the development and well-being of the masses. Such projects are commonly seen as 'socialist' and antithetical to the American way of life.

Liberalism as a guiding ethos developed, not only out of philosophical documents that established America's political independence, but also in ways that were intertwined with meritocratic values that established boundaries between a growing, secure middle class of European immigrants in the late nineteenth and early twentieth centuries and the non-white Native American and negro poor who could not so easily enter and exit class boundaries. As a doctrine, liberalism was committed philosophically to the equality of all people and so it inspired resistance to any effort to leverage the power of government to overcome gross inequalities in wealth and opportunity that were the product of centuries of racial exclusion, exploitation and discrimination. And while 'affirmative action' efforts have, in various places and at various times, opened educational doors that would have remained sealed against those presumed to be 'less qualified', these efforts have met with consistent, widespread, and often well-meaning resistance.

American liberalism is tied to the formation of the liberal state, which has its origins in an unshakable commitment to absolute territorial sovereignty. Liberal states exist in a geopolitical domain in which each conceives that its duty is to maximize self-interests while safeguarding state autonomy within a precarious 'balance of power' vis-à-vis the claims and self-interests of other states. Since each state must pursue its own self-interest above all else, the liberal doctrine, when expressed in the international political arena, renders it difficult for nations to work together to address problems that are global in scope. If it is to be more than the statement of lofty ideals, the campaign to secure human rights for all requires interstate institutions with real power and workable mechanisms of cooperation.

Blau and Moncada note that although few cross-cultural or transnational empirical studies have examined liberal values, the contention that Americans value individualism, autonomy, and independence to a greater degree than others has been substantiated by a few polls. For example, when the Pew Research Center asked in its 2002 Global Attitudes survey: 'Should everyone be free to pursue their own life goals without interference from government?', Americans were about two and a half times more likely to agree with this statement than people from other Western and Eastern European countries. Further, while only 34 per cent of Americans agree that the state should 'play an active role so as to guarantee that nobody is in need',[6] nearly twice as many people in France and the United Kingdom agree with this statement – 62 per cent; and 71 per cent of Italians agreed. The authors conclude: 'the Americans conceive of the individual-state relationship primarily as a political one whereas others consider this relationship in more organic terms, as involving citizens, society, and the state, and view people's economic well-being as part of this organic relationship.'[7]

Charles Taylor has suggested that American liberalism is merely a reflection, a particular embodiment, of the more pervasive conception of the moral order of society that flows out of Western modernity. Reflecting on the penetrating influence of Western modernity, Taylor wrote: 'At first this moral order was just an idea in the minds of influential thinkers, but later came to shape the social imaginary of large strata, and then eventually whole societies.'[8] The moral order undergirding modernity tells us how we ought to live together as members of society. Modernity stresses the rights and obligations that rational beings have in regard to one another and tends to regard those rights as existing prior to or outside of any particular political bond. From the modernist perspective, political obligations are seen as an extension or application of the more fundamental moral ties that link human beings together in particular ways and for particular purposes. The pre-existent rights of those who share in modernism justifies limited government insofar as rights can be adduced against the imposition of government power. In Western modernisms, the defence of rights which are seen as 'natural', and thus independent of the government's power to bestow or take away, takes on great importance.

The relationship between liberalism as a worldview and the political economy is especially noteworthy in light of the disparities in wealth and opportunity that tend to become manifest when free, largely unregulated markets empower those who already have a great deal to continue to increase their share of a community's resources, while those who do not have are deprived of opportunities to acquire even the most basic necessities of life – such as access to a livable wage or stable employment. The threats imposed upon the human spirit as a consequence of exposure to poverty and unemployment in lands of great prosperity are substantial. Indeed, a great deal of research reveals that the harm done when people are exposed to gross economic inequalities may not be simply physical.

For example, in 2009 Kate Pickett and Richard Wilkinson published *The Spirit Level: Why More Equal Societies Almost Always Do Better*. The book highlights the many pernicious effects that inequality tends to have on societies. For example, significant inequality tends to erode trust, increase anxiety and illness, and encourage excessive consumption. In point of fact, the authors' meticulous research revealed that for each of eleven different health and social problems – physical health, mental health, drug abuse, education, imprisonment, obesity, social mobility, trust and community life, violence, teenage pregnancies, and child well-being – the outcomes are significantly worse in rich countries that are more unequal. These data suggest that the well-being of society would be better secured were there greater support for a living wage, the adoption of measures that would reduce taxation imposed upon citizens who are at the bottom of the economic ladder, and the implementation of policies that would limit excessive pay for citizens working at the very highest levels of compensation. As a worldview, liberalism tends to promote resistance to socially motivated efforts of this kind, as they impose limits on freedom.

It could be argued, however, that any approach to ethical government should render it possible for citizens to satisfy their basic needs through a life of fairly compensated, dignity-conferring work; should seek to advance those institutional systems that make it possible for people to cooperate with one another in the governance of human affairs; should protect security by limiting the need for the use of force and instruments of violence in the service of public order; and should institute laws and policies that enable citizens to participate in democratic processes that are fair, transparent, and accessible to all. Inasmuch as significant amounts of inequality threaten the achievement of these goals, and insofar as securing these outcomes depends upon the motivation and vision of local, national, and international leaders, the political economy will require profound rethinking and transformation over the course of the decades and centuries ahead.

The Bahá'í teachings invite humanity to regard material goods not merely as ends in themselves, but rather as means for cultivating and refining the limitless potentialities of the human spirit. Such an aspiration requires the harmonious interplay of material pursuits with spiritual values. When spiritual values guide processes of decision-making, a context for the healthy use of material resources is created. Let me provide one simple example by calling upon the condition of the United States.

It would be no exaggeration to affirm that from the perspective of material achievements, the United States is the wealthiest nation on earth. But the wealth of the country is distributed in very lopsided ways. For example, according to recent federal data, the top 1% of Americans have a combined net worth of US$34 trillion, while the bottom 50% of the population holds just $2.1 trillion combined – or only 1.9% of all wealth. The federal government estimates that the wealthiest 10% of Americans hold more than 88% of all available equity in corporations and mutual fund shares.[9] In addition, a recent report announced that white men hold 90% more wealth than black women.[10] What is the effect of these disparities on the quality of life in the United States?

Although the United States boasts a GDP that is many magnitudes higher than most industrialized nations, and notwithstanding the fact that it is the world's most dominant economic and military power, the country grapples with one of the highest rates of violence anywhere in the world. At many times during its recent history, it has proven safer to live in a country ravaged by war than to live in many of America's residential neighbourhoods. When evaluating the best countries to raise children, eight attributes are generally evaluated: caring about human rights, being considered family friendly, being concerned about gender equality, being seen as happy, having income equality, being safe, and having a well-developed public education and health care system. Along these dimensions, the United States ranked 18th – behind Portugal, Italy, Spain, France, Germany, Luxembourg, the United Kingdom, Austria, Australia, New Zealand, Switzerland, Finland, the Netherlands, Canada, Norway, Sweden, and Denmark. Part of the challenge in the United States has to do with how it chooses to invest its resources.

For several years I served on a ballistic missile submarine for the US Navy. The submarine was one of the most sophisticated objects ever designed and built by human beings. It had the capacity to launch a missile and hit a three-metre-wide target three thousand miles away, and it could do this no matter what the weather conditions happened to be between the submarine and its target destination. Also, because the multi-million dollar missiles that we carried were many times more powerful than the atom bombs that we dropped on Hiroshima and Nagasaki, once launched, the Polaris missile could destroy a city the size of New York in a matter of minutes. Each submarine in the fleet that I served carried 16 or 24 of these missiles and there were hundreds of them patrolling around the world at cost of at least a million dollars a day. Thus, one of the most sophisticated machines that humans have ever built was designed never to be used and continues to cost billions of dollars a year to keep in operation. What is more, in addition to the United States, many democratic industrialized nations have also built these machines, and they too are investing billions of dollars each year to keep them afloat beneath the sea. The submarine is, of course, but one of the vehicles of war into which trillions of dollars are being poured on an annual basis.

All of this is occurring in a context where the nations of the world complain of being incapable of providing for people's basic needs. Our democratic and humanitarian values thus appear to be misaligned with the ways that we deploy our intellectual and material resources. As our noble values are brought into closer harmony with our political economy, the vision of liberal democracy will have greater latitude to flourish.

PART IV

CARE OF THE SPIRIT

10

THE INNER LIFE

One of my favourite pieces of literature appears in *The Muses Among Us* by Kim Stafford. Although written with other themes in mind, it causes me to think of the dynamics of the spirit of the age in which we live:

> There was once a physicist who also played the violin. One morning he took his fiddle to the lab, wrapped it green with felt, clamped it gently in a vise, and trained the electron microscope close on the spruce belly, just beside the sound-hole, where a steel peg was set humming at a high frequency. Through the microscope, once he got it focused just right, he saw the molecular surface of the wood begin to pucker and ripple outward like rings on a pond, the ripples rising gradually into waves, and the steel peg a blur at the heart of play.
>
> When he drew the peg away, the ripples did not stop. In twenty-four hours, the ripples had not stopped. He saw, still, a concentric tremor on the molecular quilt of the wood. The violin, in the firm embrace of the vise, had a song, a thing to say. But then, in another twelve hours, the ripples had flattened and the wood lay inert.[1]

In this vignette Stafford captures the idea that it is possible for energies to vibrate within the reality of things. For our purposes, we might call this vibration the spirit of a thing. Every age, every cycle and stage of life is animated by a spirit. Thus, it is possible to speak of the spirit of the age in which one lives.

For example, in 1963, when Alabama Governor George Wallace said in response to the civil rights movement, 'segregation now, segregation tomorrow, segregation forever',[2] he was out of harmony with the spirit of the times. His thinking belonged to an era that had already passed. In this way it is possible for the spirit of any particular individual or group to vibrate in harmony or discord with the times. This is perhaps what Victor Hugo meant when he wrote: 'Nothing else in the world . . . not all the armies . . . is so powerful as an idea whose time has come.' At their core the transformative agents of any historical period are effective because their words and deeds vibrate in harmony with the deep imperatives of the age in which they live.

The idea vibrating within the collective life of humankind today is the truth that humanity, in all its diversity, is one; and so the enduring accomplishments in this age in governance, economics, technology, and the arts and entertainment will tend to derive their inspiration and vitality from their relationship to this fundamental truth. The point that I am attempting to make here can be somewhat clarified by drawing upon an analogy that centres on the distinction that psychologists make between moods and emotions.

While emotions are relatively unstable and arise in response to what we believe, or what is happening to or around us, a mood is a more stable tendency or readiness to experience a particular kind of emotion. For example, when people are in a relaxed and generally happy mood, it is more difficult to provoke them to anger. When, by contrast, they are anxious, tensed, worried, or otherwise disturbed, relatively minor slights can send them into rage. In this way can the spirit of an age be conceptualized as a kind of mood. The mood, which arises out of long-term exposure to certain kinds of experience, begins to steer human perceptions, aspirations and values in particular directions; they thus cause certain states of consciousness, certain desires or tendencies, to be more 'ready to hand' than others.

Like a mood, the spirit of an age can coalesce as people are forced to reflect on patterns of functioning and ways of thinking and being in the world that have begun to demonstrate, in profound ways, their ineffectiveness. If the species is to survive it must become increasingly clear to large numbers of people that we must somehow change. Karl Jaspers said of such periods that humanity is sometimes forced to 'think itself free'. But here I wish to say more than this. I wish to affirm that, periodically, the *capacities* that animate the human spirit – the capacity to know, to love, and to will – must themselves undergo transformation. And thus, the *way* that we think, the things that we most love and value, and the objects of aspiration that animate the exercise of will must somehow be transformed.

At such times the people of an era are restless and resistant to stability and stasis; to the contrary, social, political, and economic life are punctuated by upheaval, breakdown, and turmoil. Paradoxically, these periods are also typically characterized by creative dynamism, vision making, and social, political, and spiritual heroism. In this way is an old pattern of life discarded as the human spirit begins to dress itself in new conceptual garments. These changes in the inner life are inevitably reflected in the life of society. Indeed, because of the comprehensiveness of the transformation, such a stage may be properly called an 'Axial Age'.

During axial periods, technical forms of knowledge, though necessary, prove to be insufficient. Chronic exposure to stress compels us to draw upon the skills and insights that are embodied in the wisdom/enlightenment traditions of knowledge. These traditions are concerned with knowledge, mastery, and refinement of the self. Their primary aim has been to protect, cultivate, and deepen the inner life.

Where the wisdom traditions have been pursued with sincerity of purpose, purity of motive, and a desire to achieve spiritual excellence, they have resulted in the development of human beings that are as worthy of admiration as the great men and women that have distinguished themselves in the sciences and arts. Mother Teresa, Fred Rogers, Thich Nat Hanh, St Francis of Assisi are among those whose names come easily to mind. But there are millions more, unknown to most of us, who have traversed the spiritual paths and gathered along the way a harvest of beautiful qualities that befit and adorn human life. Given the role that they have played in shaping humanity's moral and spiritual development, we reflect here on what the wisdom traditions have had to say about the nature of those gem-like capacities that animate and adorn the human spirit. The sense is that the social, economic, and technological forces that have made of us a deeply interconnected species will require that the spiritual capacities that empower human beings to abide well with others can no longer be confined to the few, but must come to characterize the way of the masses.

In *Ancient Wisdom, Modern World*, the Dalai Lama wrote: 'Spirituality I take to be concerned with those qualities of the human spirit – such as love and compassion, a sense of responsibility, a sense of harmony – which bring happiness to both self and others.'[3] In this way does the Dalai Lama place the development of humanity's capacity for moral responsiveness at the heart of a well-functioning community and society.

Reflecting on the inherent moral capacities that animate the human spirit, the German philosopher Immanuel Kant suggested that all the good qualities that are traditionally associated with mind and intellect are necessarily conditional upon a good will:

Nothing can possibly be conceived in the world, or even out of it, which can be called good, without qualification, except a good will. Intelligence, wit, judgement, and the talents of the mind, however they may be named, or courage, resolution, perseverance, as qualities of temperament, are undoubtedly good and desirable in many respects; but these gifts of nature may also become extremely bad and mischievous if the will which is to make use of them, and which, therefore, constitutes character, is not good. It is the same with the gift of fortune. Power, riches, honour, even health, and the general well-being and contentment with one's condition which is called happiness, inspire pride, and often presumption, if there is not a good will to correct the influence of these on the mind, and with which this also to rectify the whole principle of acting and adapt it to its end. The sight of a being who is not adorned with a single feature of a pure and good will, enjoying unbroken prosperity, can never give pleasure to an impartial rational spectator. Thus a good will appears to constitute the indispensable condition even of being worthy of happiness.[4]

Amplifying the intrinsic and long-term value of good and noble intentions, the Native American sage Black Elk speaks of an early encounter with a 'sacred woman' who illumined the understanding of the Sioux and empowered them to distinguish between that which is foolish and that which is wise; between that which would harm the people and that which would be of benefit. They learned of these things in the manner of her coming: '. . . she came, very beautiful and singing . . . With visible breath I am walking. A voice I am sending as I walk. In a sacred manner I am walking. With visible tracks I am walking. In a sacred manner I walk.'[5] In this way are the Sioux awakened to a consciousness of the sacred. To nurture this awareness, they taught themselves to pray:

Grandfather, Great Spirit . . . lean close to the earth that you may hear the voice I send . . . Give me the strength to walk the soft earth, a relative to all that is! Give me the eyes to see and the strength to understand, that I may be like you. With your power only can I face the winds . . . Great Spirit, Great Spirit, my Grandfather, all over the earth the faces of living things are all alike. With tenderness have these come up out of the ground. Look upon these faces of children without number and with children in their arms, that they may face the winds and walk the good road to the day of quiet. This is my prayer; hear me! The voice I have sent is weak, yet with earnestness I have sent it. Hear me![6]

Might not such reflections of the spirit serve as an antidote to the brazen arrogance that seeks to exalt one race or nation or culture or class over all others?

In the far east Hsün Tzu spoke of the 'rectification of names'. In this way he drew attention to the importance of linking our words to reality. In this way our words 'transcend the murmur of syllables and sounds' as they bear relationship to that which is authentic and real. The writer of Corinthians speaks of the rectification of names when he affirms: 'If I speak in the tongues of men or of angels, but do not have love, I am only a resounding gong or a clanging cymbal.' When the meditations of the heart and the sentiments expressed by the tongue are in harmony, we are free of the stain of hypocrisy.

The human tongue is not the only force in nature with the power to deceive, distort, dissimilate or confuse – but its power to achieve this is unmatched by any other phenomenon. When names are no longer connected to real processes, they are dead letters. 'Democracy', for example, requires a commitment to certain values and virtues. When there is no real commitment to these values, when there is no interest in the virtues that are required in order to endow democracy with life, democracy becomes empty and dead and the actions that are carried out in its name are mere performances. Bahá'u'lláh says: 'Let deeds, not words, be your adorning.'[7] Such counsel serves to remind us of the many ways that the human spirit can both lead and be led into a show, 'vain and empty . . . a mere nothing'.[8]

∽

In the preface to his seminal work *The Broken Covenant: American Civil Religion in Time of Trial*, Robert Bellah writes:

> It is one of the oldest sociological generalizations that any coherent and viable society rests on a common set of moral understandings about good and bad, right and wrong, in the realm of individual and social action. It is almost as widely

held that these common moral understandings must also in turn rest upon a common set of religious understandings that provide a picture of the universe in terms of which the moral understandings make sense. Such moral and religious understandings produce both a basic cultural legitimation for a society which is viewed as at least approximately in accord with them and a standard of judgment for the criticism of a society that is seen as deviating too far from them.[9]

Bellah observes that in the United States, 'a decline of belief in all forms of obligation: to one's occupation, one's family, and one's country' is by now statistically well documented, and that 'a tendency to rank personal gratification above obligations to others correlates with a deepening cynicism about the established social, economic, and political institutions of society'.[10] Bellah's observation, made more than forty years ago, appears even more profoundly true today. Indeed, it would appear that America, which had long been characterized as an optimistic nation, finds itself struggling to imagine for itself a future that is better than its past. This decline in faith in the 'American dream' seems to be due, in large part, to the loss of a sense that the spirit of the American people is animated and inspired by those qualities of character that make this nation – or any other nation – truly great. Bellah goes on to attribute this decline in hopefulness to the hyperemphasis that the American people have consistently placed on freedom – which, for many, is simply the freedom to pursue self-interest, the freedom to do one's own thing – without regard to social obligations or those 'wise restraints' that truly 'make men free'.

In *Why Religion Matters: The Fate of the Human Spirit in an Age of Disbelief,* Huston Smith recounts a story involving his wife, Kendra, and their young grandson, whom she took to the neighbourhood playground 'where they found two children already on the swings and slides – a girl about eight and a younger boy, presumably her brother'. Smith picks up the story:

With the briefest of preliminaries the girl asked Kendra, 'What are we?' Kendra squinted a bit and answered, 'Chinese?' 'No.' 'Vietnamese?' 'No,' with a touch of irritation entering. When Kendra ventured a third mistaken possibility, the irritation erupted. 'No!' What *are* we?' At that point Kendra (thinking that if she knew the answer she might better understand the question) said, 'I give up. What are you?' 'We are brother and sister' the girl replied, 'and so we love each other. And our grandmother tells us that if we love her, when we become grandparents our grandchildren will love us.'[11]

The child, Smith notes, got it right. The question is not so much *who* we are as *what* we are. To address *what we are* is to point to our basic essence and it is that essence that transcends all limits of race, class, culture, nationality and religion; that essence has the potential to bring us into relationship with our closest kin and with all the others who dwell on earth. We have suggested here that that essence is the *human spirit* and that the spirit that animates and sustains the human spirit is love. When we have lost touch with the human spirit, we have lost touch with love, with one another, and with our own selves. The spiritual disciplines nourish our innate capacity for love, respect for truth, and pursuit of that which is good. We reflect upon those disciplines in the next chapter.

11

THE LOGIC OF PRAYER AND MEDITATION

Of all spiritual disciplines – including yoga, meditation, Tai chi, or the martial arts – none appears to be more inimical to modern sensibilities than the notion of prayer. Many regard prayer as the ultimate opiate of the untutored masses; others consider it a useless and superstitious attempt to influence outcomes that are best pursued by the deployment of human reason and action. It is possible, however, to defend the practice of prayer in three ways: by conceptualizing it as a conscious act of humility that seeks to bring human aspiration into harmony with that which many believe is ultimately responsible for our coming into being; by describing prayer as a personal and/or communal act designed to metabolize destructive thoughts or disturbing emotions; and by thinking of prayer as a strategy that families, groups, and communities might deploy in order to nurture the spirit of compassion, hope, and goodwill that is necessary as we confront the challenges and vicissitudes of life. Let us examine each of these perspectives.

In the previous chapter we made a distinction between moods and emotions and suggested that while emotions are relatively unstable and arise in response to what we believe or what is happening to or around us, moods may be thought of as a more stable tendency or readiness to experience a particular kind of emotion. We noted that when people are in a relaxed and generally happy mood, it is more difficult to provoke them to anger. When, by contrast, they are anxious, tensed, worried, or otherwise disturbed, relatively minor slights can send them into rage. One purpose of daily prayer is thus to nourish, with healthy thoughts and values, the kind of deep consciousness which steers us into directions that promote inner and interpersonal harmony, unity and peace. An example of such a prayer appears below:

> O God! Refresh and gladden my spirit. Purify my heart. Illumine my powers. I lay all my affairs in Thy hand. Thou art my Guide and my Refuge. I will no longer be sorrowful and grieved; I will be a happy and joyful being. O God! I will no longer be full of anxiety, nor will I let trouble harass me. I will not dwell on the unpleasant things of life.
>
> O God! Thou art more friend to me than I am to myself. I dedicate myself to Thee, O Lord.[1]

In addition to helping to regulate our own inner states, the thoughts that are typically encouraged by prayer serve to reduce our tendency to compete with others for socially conferred status or to see others as sources of social threat. This well-known prayer by the eighth-century Buddhist monk Shantideva captures a sense of the benevolent spirit that one seeks to cultivate in the practice of prayer:

> May I become at all times, both now and forever
> A protector of those without protection
> A guide for those who have lost their way
> A ship for those with oceans to cross
> A bridge for those with rivers to cross
> A sanctuary for those in danger
> A lamp for those without light
> A place of refuge for those who lack shelter
> And a servant to all in need
> For as long as space endures,
> And for as long as living beings remain,
> Until then may I, too, abide
> To dispel the misery of the world.[2]

This well-known Native American prayer functions in a similar way:

> Oh, Great Spirit, whose voice I hear in the wind, whose breath gives life to all the world.
> Hear me; I need your strength and wisdom.
> Let me walk in beauty, and make my eyes ever behold the red and purple sunset.
> Make my hands respect the things you have made and my ears sharp to hear your voice.
> Make me wise so that I may understand the things you have taught my people.
> Help me to remain calm and strong in the face of all that comes towards me.
> Let me learn the lessons you have hidden in every leaf and rock.
> Help me seek pure thoughts and act with the intention of helping others.
> Help me find compassion without empathy overwhelming me.
> I seek strength, not to be greater than my brother, but to fight my greatest enemy, Myself.
> Make me always ready to come to you with clean hands and straight eyes.
> So when life fades, as the fading sunset, my spirit may come to you without shame.[3]

Prayers are also often said as we seek to envision what we might become or what we might achieve if we are able to function from the place of our higher selves. Indeed, there is a prayer that I often recite, both for myself and for my students, as I seek to achieve higher levels of excellence in my professional work and community service:

> O God, O Thou Who hast cast Thy splendour over the luminous realities of men, shedding upon them the resplendent

lights of knowledge and guidance, and hast chosen them out of all created things for this supernal grace, and hast caused them to encompass all things, to understand their inmost essence, and to disclose their mysteries, bringing them forth out of darkness into the visible world! 'He verily showeth His special mercy to whomsoever He will.'

O Lord, help Thou Thy loved ones to acquire knowledge and the sciences and arts, and to unravel the secrets that are treasured up in the inmost reality of all created beings. Make them to hear the hidden truths that are written and embedded in the heart of all that is. Make them to be ensigns of guidance amongst all creatures, and piercing rays of the mind shedding forth their light in this, the 'first life'. Make them to be leaders unto Thee, guides unto Thy path, runners urging men on to Thy Kingdom.

Thou verily art the Powerful, the Protector, the Potent, the Defender, the Mighty, the Most Generous.[4]

The communal practice of prayer may serve to nurture in a population a set of shared values, and may cultivate a consciousness of that which is most noble in each of us, remind us of the respect and kindness that should animate our attitude toward others, and help us to reflect upon themes that may have enduring importance to our collective life rather than what is relatively superficial and trivial. Lastly, communal prayer may help us to visualize a future that is more beautiful, more harmonious, and more just than the present. Such reminders can, in turn, help to sustain hope for the future and faith in the destiny of humankind. This well-known prayer of Christ seems to serve some of these important functions:

Our Father which art in heaven, Hallowed be thy name.
Thy kingdom come, Thy will be done on earth, as it is in heaven.
Give us this day our daily bread.
And forgive us our debts, as we forgive our debtors.

And lead us not into temptation, but deliver us from evil: For thine is the kingdom, and the power, and the glory, forever. Amen.[5]

Meditation

We have suggested that the development of the human spirit during periods of sociocultural transformation requires cultivation of the capacity for reflection, self-awareness, and self-control. To reflect is to be aware of what one is doing, intending, and becoming. It is the opposite of mindlessness. Meditation is one of the ways in which the capacity to reflect can be enhanced and greater degrees of mindfulness and self-mastery can be achieved. The section that follows, which was written in collaboration with my former student Jingyi Gu, provides a brief history of meditation and reflects upon the role that meditation might play in the development and refinement of the human spirit.

The use of the word 'meditation' first appeared in the thirteenth century. Yet a variety of practices that involve contemplation and concentration, or what is known as *Dhyana* in Buddhist and Hindu traditions, animated human communities for thousands of years before the word 'meditation' emerged. What we refer to as meditation today usually includes a variety of attentional practices designed to train the mind in order to gain some enduring physical, psychological, or spiritual benefit. The benefits sought vary from tranquillity and physical relaxation, to insight, the cultivation of compassion for self and others, a deeper understanding of the truths that undergird reality, and the realization of union with that which is sacred or divine. And although meditative practices have arisen out of a diversity of traditions and worldviews, they all have as a focus the desire to reduce suffering and to achieve greater mastery over one's own mind and body.

The oldest meditative traditions can be traced back to Hinduism. Indeed, one of the earliest known documents that refer to meditative practices was contained on a seal found in the ruins of the pre-Aryan civilization on the Indian subcontinent from 1500 BCE.[6] The seal shows a figure sitting in a traditional meditative posture known as the lotus position. The lotus posture is part of the yoga practices that are integral to Hinduism.

'Yoga' literally means to join, to unite. The ultimate goal of the practice of yoga was long thought to be *Samadhi*, the union of one's true self with the Omnipresent. According to Sri Ramana Maharshi, the mind forms the conscious link between the human soul, the natural world, and the world of God.[7] According to Hinduism, when the mind is restless, one is unable to detect the presence of God. A restless mind is also prone to rumination, worry, and the development of unwholesome thoughts. Meditation, then, began as a practice that sought to bring the mind into union with God and to thereby induce states of inner tranquillity and peace.

Around the sixth century BC, Gautama Buddha articulated one of the most comprehensive systems designed to end existential suffering.[8] This system he referred to as the 'Eightfold Path' which is grounded in the Four Noble Truths. These truths include knowledge of the cause of suffering and a 'way' that promises to lead to the cessation of suffering.[9] The earnest seeker who follows the Path is assured of reaching nirvana, which is described as 'the supreme, eternally blissful abode'. The practice of meditation is an integral part of that path.

Basic Buddhist teachings suggest that all human suffering has its roots in craving. From this point of view, the mind, or human spirit, can be clouded and disturbed by desire, fear, pain, anger, and moral defilement. When accompanied by right living, meditation serves to purify the mind and spirit as practitioners seek to cultivate virtue, gain wisdom and attain single-minded devotion to the sacred teachings of the Enlightened One.[10]

Buddhism has articulated a clear concept of health. It suggests that physical, emotional and mental health are inseparable and that it is impossible to single out the concept of mental health from other forms of health. Much emphasis is placed, therefore, on the role of mental activity in the maintenance of health: 'All phenomena originate in the mind, and when the mind is fully known all phenomena are fully known. For by the mind the world is led.'[11]

Buddhist meditation is based on a profound, complete, and systematic theory of psychology and is perhaps the best representative of Eastern psychology. The Buddhist theory of the mind–body relationship differs widely from the Western Cartesian model. And while the mind and body in Buddhist ontology are said to be dependent on each other, neither the mind nor the body alone or together are adequate for understanding the nature of the self.[12] In Buddhism, as in many religions, the mind is not a thing, but is produced as a consequence of the union of the human essence with the body. Thus, the mind is the meeting point of heaven (the spiritual realm) and earth (the realm of nature).

Buddhist psychology has greatly influenced both later religious practices such as Taoism and Zen, and the cultures of many Asian countries. In Taoism and Zen, meditators strive to overcome critical and dichotomous thinking; and by strengthening the powers of intuition they seek to cultivate capacity for experience which is untainted by ego, craving, attachments, and fear. The Taoist 'Way' is thus to relinquish attachments in order to live in greater clarity, stillness, and freedom.

Taoists have introduced the concept of 'chi', which consists of the invisible flow of energy that is responsible for life and health within the mind and body. Through practices such as Qigong and Tai chi, meditators seek to gain conscious access to subtle, spiritual energies that aid in the maintenance of a delicate balance between tranquillity and movement. The literature on meditation suggests that the human spirit is illumined and refreshed by such practices.

Zen has its roots in early Chinese Taoism and Buddhism.

Yet the main emphasis of Zen shifts from the importance of Buddhist doctrine to understanding and mastery of self. Zen acknowledges the Buddha nature in every human being. According to Zen, personal enlightenment requires introspection: Zen practitioners were often required to meditate on a *kōan*, which consists of a perplexing question or a pithy phrase from a story. The effort to penetrate the inner reality or esoteric meaning of the kōan served to cultivate the mind. The ultimate goal of Zen practice is realization of the nature of things that arises from an opening of the mind's eye.

The doctrines outlined above identify craving, attachment, false perceptions and faulty beliefs as obstacles to sound mental health. They have each prescribed meditation as a means to achieve true knowledge of the self and greater detachment from that which is often trivial and fleeting. What unites these ancient systems of thought with the practice of Western psychology and medicine are the insights that have emerged out of stress-related research over the last four decades.

Meditation in the West

The first great milestone in the movement of meditation into the Western world occurred as a consequence of the first Parliament of World Religions held in 1893 in the city of Chicago. This historic gathering served to initiate a dialogue among and between the religions of the world and provided the first opportunity for many Eastern religious figures to visit the United States. Among the attendees were Swami Vivekananda, Zen master Soyen Shaku, and Jainism preacher Virchand Gandhi.[13] The parliament provided the first opportunity for a large number of Americans to learn about Asian meditation practices from these masters.

Another milestone in the meeting of Eastern and Western philosophy occurred in 1927 with the publication of *Essays in Zen Buddhism* by D.T. Suzuki. Suzuki's writings on Zen, Buddhism, and Shintoism were complemented by an extensive lecture tour to American universities in 1951. Because Suzuki was familiar with Western philosophy, his detraditionalized explanation of Zen was easy for Western audiences to accept.[14] His writings and lectures received tremendous attention from both scholars and the general population. He was profiled in the *New York Times* and settled in New York City as a professor at Columbia University until 1957.[15]

In 1941, because of the effort by Heinrich Zimmer, an Indologist and close friend of Carl Jung, English translations of Jung's collected works as well as numerous books by Zimmer himself were finally published.[16] Among them, the Bollingen edition of *I Ching*, or *Book of Changes*, a Taoist oracle and one of the six Confucian classics, was one of the most influential publications, still regarded as the best English edition. The book offers a comprehensive and profound Chinese worldview, and inspires the world in areas such as philosophy, psychology, mathematics, astronomy, music, and literature. Zimmer also introduced Jung to the world of Eastern meditation. Jung published a series of works on I Ching, Zen Buddhism, Eastern psychology and Hinduism.[17]

In the 1960s, America's young generation faced an age of spiritual famine. This is when the trend of Transcendental Meditation (TM) began to emerge. Transcendental Meditation is a secular form of Hindu meditation, introduced to India by Maharishi Mahesh Yogi in the mid-1950s. He translated terms in Hindu ideology into more universal, even westernized and Christianized language so as to be easier accepted by the Western population. It was an effort to adapt Eastern meditation to the Western context. And people bought it. Meditation was no longer necessarily associated with ascetic monks or yogis. It became mainstream, an accessible and practical exercise for simply everyone. TM gained tremendous popularity in America and worldwide during the 1960s. The Beatles, for example, were committed practitioners of TM. It is still the most widely practised form of meditation in the United States.

Because of popular attraction to Transcendental Meditation,

along with many scientific studies that tried to explain the mechanism at work in meditation, a surge of Western interest in meditation took place. Of particular interest to Western psychologists and physiologists is that meditation can induce a quantitatively measurable, altered state of consciousness. Meditators claimed that practising meditation changed their physiological state, a claim that attracted attention from both scientists and secularists. Instead of focusing on spiritual growth, secularists put emphasis on the physical changes brought by meditation, using meditation for tension reduction, relaxation and self-improvement. In particular, studies led by Herbert Benson at Harvard Medical School and his colleagues suggested that meditative practices could be used clinically to relieve stress-related illness. Therefore, the effort to interpret the mechanism of meditation with objective, scientific methods made the effect of meditation more credible for Western society.

Herbert Benson and relaxation response

For the first time, forms of meditation which were often perceived to be exotic and unscientific were brought into closer examination by practitioners of Western medicine. Benson at Harvard Medical School used the term 'relaxation response' to describe an integrated system of physiological and psychological changes elicited by various techniques of relaxation, including meditation. Using a simple pre-test/post-test experimental design, he investigated many physical indicators of the impact of Transcendental Meditation. Surprisingly, he found that a sudden drop of metabolic rate tended to occur a few minutes after meditation began, even though the practitioners displayed no other signs of change in posture, gaze, or any other visible features. Although the metabolic rate was lower than the resting state, the degree of hypometabolism achieved did not resemble sleep or a hibernation state. This observation inspired Benson to launch a forty-year study of the impact of meditation on physical and psychological health.

Effects of the relaxation response on physical measures often include decreased oxygen consumption, declined respiration rate, lowered blood pressure for hypertensive individuals, reduced pupillary sensitivity to topical phenylephrine, and reduced perception of pain, which correspond with the general decrease in sympathetic nervous system responsivity.[18] Regularly inducing the relaxation response also improved self-reported results on several psychological scales in both clinical and non-clinical populations. Therefore, the relaxation response has been found useful to treat or prevent a wide range of physical and psychological illnesses, such as hypertension, insomnia, depression, PMS, anxiety disorders, and stress-related somatic disorders, and practising eliciting the relaxation response is useful to ease tension. Benson believed that the relaxation response was the counterpart of the fight-or-flight response of our sympathetic nervous system, as an innate mechanism for self-recovery. When acute stress occurs, the body tends to recover naturally. However, when stress becomes chronic, implementation of the relaxation response might be induced in order to help the autonomic nervous system return to normal functioning.

According to Benson, techniques eliciting the relaxation response often include four fundamental elements: muscle relaxation, a quiet environment, a repetitive stimulus or 'an object to dwell upon', and a passive attitude toward relaxation. Although a secularist, Benson also mentioned the importance of the 'faith factor', a firm belief which is not necessarily religious, in the impact of the relaxation response. Accordingly, he outlined a simple relaxation response exercise using the four elements:

1. Sit quietly with eyes closed. Allow the body to remain still in a comfortable position.
2. Let the muscles of the body relax from bottom to top.
3. Direct the attention to breathing. Be aware of the movement of the nostrils or the chest and abdomen. Repeat the word 'one' silently when breathing out.
4. Continue the practice for 10 to 20 minutes. Do not worry

about entering a deep relaxing mode. When mind wanders, direct attention back to breathing passively by letting go any distracting thoughts. Allow relaxation to take place at its own pace. Do not use an alarm clock but leave a clock at sight to check the time.[19]

In further investigation of Benson's proposal, Jacobs and Lubar noted that focusing on a repetitive stimulus is a 'key element' in autogenic training. They carefully controlled for three of Benson's four elements in two groups of participants so that these only differed in whether they focused on a repetitive, internal stimulus. They found significant differences in participants' central nervous system activity.[20]

The sharpened attention may also enhance perception and thus induce greater insight and clearer thinking. Indeed, brain mapping revealed significantly enhanced signal activity in parts of the brain that are involved in attention and arousal, as well as autonomic control – despite decreases in cardiorespiratory activity.[21] It would thus appear that meditative practices confer a range of benefits that extend from neurological to cardiovascular, to cognitive, and perceptual. Indeed, in a talk delivered in Paris in 1911 'Abdu'l-Bahá suggested that the benefits of meditation extend well beyond the physical dimensions of human life. The capacity for meditation, he noted, is an essential human capacity and ought to be exercised if we wish to enjoy the full range of cognitive potential that has been brought within the reach of the human spirit:

> It is an axiomatic fact that while you meditate you are speaking with your own spirit. In that state of mind you put certain questions to your spirit and the spirit answers: the light breaks forth and the reality is revealed.
>
> You cannot apply the name 'man' to any being void of this faculty of meditation; without it he would be a mere animal . . .
>
> The spirit of man is itself informed and strengthened

during meditation; through it affairs of which man knew nothing are unfolded before his view. Through it he receives Divine inspiration, through it he receives heavenly food.[22]

'Abdu'l-Bahá goes further to affirm that 'meditation is the key for opening the doors of mysteries. In that state man abstracts himself: in that state man withdraws himself from all outside objects; in that subjective mood he is immersed in the ocean of spiritual life and can unfold the secrets of things-in-themselves.' In illustration of this, 'Abdu'l-Bahá invites us to think of human beings as being endowed with two kinds of sight: 'when the power of insight is being used the outward power of vision does not see'. The fruits of the exercise of the faculty of meditation are the sciences and arts: 'This faculty brings forth from the invisible plane the sciences and arts. Through the meditative faculty inventions are made possible, colossal undertakings are carried out; through it governments can run smoothly. Through this faculty man enters into the very Kingdom of God.'[23]

In expounding on the meditative faculty 'Abdu'l-Bahá said that it is

akin to the mirror; if you put it before earthly objects it will reflect them. Therefore if the spirit of man is contemplating earthly subjects he will be informed of these. But if you turn the mirror of your spirits heavenwards, the heavenly constellations and the rays of the Sun of Reality will be reflected in your hearts, and the virtues of the Kingdom will be obtained.

He closes his discourse on this weighty theme by expressing the hope that each of us might 'become mirrors reflecting the heavenly realities, and . . . become so pure as to reflect the stars of heaven'.[24]

In the chapter that follows, we propose that mindfulness and prayerful states achieve their greatest influence when they illumine the dialogue and social action of those who are serving together in order to create diverse and yet unified communities, wherein the capacities of the human spirit are most likely to flourish.

12

CONSULTATION: AN INSTRUMENT OF PERSONAL AND SOCIAL TRANSFORMATION

The preservation of all forms of life requires the movement of energy and information within, between, and among living systems. When energy and information are exchanged in various ways, organisms are both using and exercising power. There are four kinds of power: constructive power, destructive power, powers of nature, and powers of consciousness.[1]

Violence, for example, is a form of destructive power. Violence tends to be high in energy but low in information; and so, while it may be effective in killing and destroying things, it is not very effective if the desire is to make something useful or to create something new. For example, it takes a lot of energy but very little information to destroy a beautiful building, but a great deal of energy and a lot of information to create one. The Second Law of Thermodynamics explains why this is so.

In simple living systems, the exchange of energy and information tends to be sufficient to sustain life. As living systems become more complex and develop capacity for conscious awareness of the environment, *knowledge* must be added to information if the information is to be useful. One might think of knowledge as some degree of awareness of how to use information in order to achieve a goal. Primates, for example, must transmit forms of knowledge to their offspring if the community of primates is to survive.

At the most complex level of life, if the organisms that

constitute a community are to survive and function well it is necessary that they communicate not only information and knowledge, but also various forms of *wisdom* and *understanding*. Wisdom and understanding are necessary in order to sustain complex human cultures.

One might say that wisdom and understanding are the highest expressions of power available to living systems. When these powers are cultivated and deployed broadly and effectively, there is far less need for the use of more destructive, less effective forms of power, such as violence, manipulation, deceit, cruelty, and so forth. Indeed, the most effective human communities tend to transmit high levels of knowledge and rich resources of wisdom while also combining in their schemes of development various forms of instruction in the exercise of compassion, courtesy, goodwill, and kindness – each of which is a reflection of the capacity to love. In the aggregate, the deployment of these higher forms of power provides the spiritual foundation upon which great civilizations rest.

In this chapter we explore a method of collective decision-making that seeks to deploy these higher forms of power in the building of just, loving, and aesthetically beautiful communities. The development of such communities provides a kind of second womb within which the capacities of the human spirit can most effectively flourish. While this method of decision-making is known as *consultation*, we are not referring here to methods of discourse that are, at present, either widely used or understood.

In the most basic sense, consultation is a form of discourse that is designed to give those who are seeking to solve problems access to information, knowledge, and whatever wisdom and understanding may be accessible to a group, while at the same time nurturing among those who participate in it a spirit of compassion, courtesy, and goodwill – each of which is inimical to the tendency to use power to dominate, exploit, or belittle the perspectives and contributions of others. The nature and benefits of consultation are explored here because the practice of it provides an ideal method for empowering individuals to develop the best within themselves as they also labour alongside others in service to the community. The ultimate fruit of consultation is thought to be the further refinement of the powers that define and animate the human spirit, as well as the bringing into being of a more just and compassionate social order. What, then, is meant by *consultation*?

Consultation seeks to draw upon the enhanced powers of mind that are generated when minds work cooperatively together in pursuit of insights into the best way to proceed given the challenges that are before us. Its purpose is first to create a kind of moral or ethical space that empowers those who participate in it to bring to the discourse their best and highest selves. Thus, to enter into consultation, each participant must seek to purify their motives and elevate their aspirations. The hope of each participant must be to transcend the limits of their own subjectivity so that it is possible to perceive the reality of a situation through a diversity of perspectives. In a sense one could say that in the early stages of consultation, the 'seekers after truth' are endeavouring to render themselves capable of hearing the voice of truth from whomever it might appear. By *truth* in this context is meant that course of action that would be best for us given our current situation.

Consultation thus requires the effort to deploy states of consciousness that are akin to the states of prayer and mindfulness that were described in the previous chapter. But these states are sought, not so much in service to the individual's contentment and well-being, but in order to enhance the individual's ability to serve the development and well-being of the community.

Consultation thus begins by orienting those involved to the high ethical standards that must be pursued if the endeavour is to prove successful. In the Bahá'í context, consultation generally begins with the participants calling to mind certain moral and spiritual conditions: 'The prime requisites for them that take counsel together are purity of motive, radiance of spirit, detachment . . . humility . . . patience and long-suffering in difficulties . . .'[2]

It is thus clear that in addition to an approach to problem-solving, the practice of consultation seeks to cultivate within each member of the community the qualities of character that would enable them to participate more effectively as agents of social transformation. As we seek to transform society in ways that respect our dignity and the dignity of others, a transformed social order will, in turn, make it possible for us to discover, in greater measure, the capacities of consciousness that define the human spirit. In this way, the maturation of the individual and the development of society unfold in symbiosis.

In describing the mode of functioning that should animate the behaviour of those who consult together, the Bahá'í writings suggest that

> They must . . . proceed with the utmost devotion, courtesy, dignity, care and moderation to express their views. They must in every matter search out the truth and not insist upon their own opinion, for stubbornness and persistence in one's views will lead ultimately to discord and wrangling and the truth will remain hidden. The honoured members must with all freedom express their own thoughts, and it is in no wise permissible for one to belittle the thought of another, nay, he must with moderation set forth the truth, and should differences of opinion arise a majority of voices must prevail, and all must obey and submit to the majority. It is again not permitted that any one of the honoured members object to or censure, whether in or out of the meeting, any decision arrived at previously, though that decision be not right, for such criticism would prevent any decision from being enforced. In short, whatsoever thing is arranged in harmony and with love and purity of motive, its result is light . . .[3]

To be an effective agent of social change is difficult, in part because we do not yet have the qualities of character that make it possible for us to work well with a diverse range of others in pursuit of long-term, important, life-sustaining goals. The acquisition of the capacities necessary for consultation will require practice over long periods of time and, perhaps, across many generations. As we become better at it, we transform cultures of contest and conflict into cultures of unity and cooperation. Unity then becomes a power that we can draw upon as we pursue higher and higher levels of civilization-making.

As a method of decision-making, consultation takes into consideration the ethics of social change. Thus, in addition to drawing upon humanity's collective use of its rational faculties, consultation concerns itself with what might be called the human heart. What do I mean by the human heart?

I sometimes think of human beings as the most sensitive receptors in the natural world. Our very delicate perceptual systems empower us to detect all kinds of signals – some of which are physical phenomena – like sights and sounds, and others of which are phenomena that speak to our moral and spiritual sensibilities. One could say that the kinds of signals that stimulate our moral and spiritual sensibilities are detected in our hearts. Let me provide an example.

There is a great deal of research that suggests that human beings are capable of sensing the intention or motivation of a speaker; and while this capacity is never perfect, it is a capacity that appears to be present within us from very early stages of development. In early stages these perceptions are connected to the pitch, tone, volume, and cadence of speech. At later stages of development, they are also related to the discursive communities that have shaped the words that we use and the ways that we put those words together when we are in discourse with others. One group of researchers at the Swiss Centre for Affective Sciences at the University of Geneva has written about this phenomenon as *the capacity to be moved*.

In their paper published in *Philosophical Studies: An International Journal for Philosophy in the Analytic Tradition*, Florian Cova and Julien Deonna note that a unique emotional phenomenon is captured by the expression *being moved*: 'We often say of things (sights, scenes, events, or even works of art) that they "move us". . .' Their work, they note, seeks to describe 'the affective phenomenon that we refer to when we use this expression'.[4]

We are moved when we encounter phenomena that share some common features: 'an unexpectedly kind gesture, a reconciliation between two estranged friends, a long hoped for victory, a hopeful sign of the end of hostilities, an impossible love . . .'[5] A common feature of each of these cases, they point out, is that positive values have appeared in the presence of negative ones; light is revealed in a time of darkness.

We are moved most, they go further to note, by the *emergence* of positive values in circumstances that are unfavourable; that is, 'in cases in which these values are not only present but also succeed in making a stand, rather than, say, being ruined or swept away'.[6]

Recently, I have been reflecting on the life of 'Abdu'l-Bahá, who visited America from the Middle East in 1912. I have been reading about his intense interest in helping the Americans overcome racial prejudice and noticed how the words and gestures that he used in discourse embodied a kind of generosity of spirit that served as an antidote to the strife, bigotries, and inhumanity that were very much a part of the fabric of American life.

Addressing, for example, the opportunities available for overcoming racial prejudice at a time when racially motivated lynch mobs symbolized the state of race relations, 'Abdu'l-Bahá invited the blacks and whites assembled at a gathering to ponder in their hearts what they could become: 'In the clustered jewels of the races', He said, 'may the blacks be as sapphires and rubies and the whites as diamonds and pearls. The composite beauty of humanity will be witnessed in their unity and blending.'[7]

He used words such as these to transform the image of blacks and whites together from that grotesque picture painted by separatists to an image of beauty inspired by the recognition of the aesthetic and social power inherent in harmonious human relationships. When He spoke, He thus appealed both to our capacity to 'think ourselves free' as well as to the heart's natural attraction to that which is beautiful and good. In this way He brought to consciousness the wondrous potential for change within each human person, and invited these qualities to reveal themselves so that each person in the struggle for racial justice might become a source of inspiration to the hearts of others.

Indeed, as a social activist, 'Abdu'l-Bahá sought, most especially, to move the heart – not by appealing to superficial emotions but by rendering salient humanity's most precious and significant values, and by reminding us of our duty to revive, protect, and advance these values as a strategy for promoting social change and as a way of showing gratitude for the gift of life.

As an instrument of inner, interpersonal and social transformation, consultation invites awareness of the delicate nature of the human heart and of our power to influence the heart by speaking in ways that bring out the very best, rather than the worst, in others. I think that this is why many of the sacred traditions tell us to be careful about the words that we use and the ways that we use them. We are advised to use words 'as mild as milk'[8] so that they may have an edifying influence in the human heart. Thus, a focus on the aesthetic, ethical, and compassion-related dimensions of speech are an integral part of the process of consultation.

Consultation is also a method for arriving at a shared vision of what we might achieve together to improve our community in meaningful and enduring ways. Recently, for example, several youths between the ages of 11 and 15, living in Cambodia, used the tool of consultation to explore what they might be able to do to address the needs of their community as a group. Their consultation led them to concern about the road that leads to their neighbourhood – which many had observed was both very long and very hot.

In consultation about this problem, the youth decided that they would plant trees all along the way. The trees would provide shade. But what is more, these young people had decided that the trees should be both beautiful and fruit bearing. In this way the trees would provide shade for travellers, fruit that could be sold at market, and an aesthetically pleasing path into their community. The adult leaders of the community were stunned by the wisdom of these decisions. In addition, when such youth are able to see the impact of their cooperative efforts, they quite naturally wish to continue to work together to promote that which is good. There are, at present, thousands of projects unfolding around the world as a result of folks of various cultures and backgrounds using consultation as a method of personal and social transformation.

We might say, then, that consultation promotes an approach to the exercise of power that is productive. Rather than pursuing *power over others*, human beings are encouraged by its use to consecrate their intellectual, moral, and physical capacities to achieve outcomes that redound to the good of humankind.

13

A FINAL WORD: HUMANITY'S SPIRITUAL HERITAGE

In these brief pages, I have drawn upon the meagre resources of understanding that are available to me in order to describe some of the powers and capacities that animate and adorn the human spirit. My purpose has been to encourage further reflection on this universally shared reservoir in the hope that we might draw more richly from it as we labour to bring into being the kind of world that we both long for and deserve.

One realizes that a project of this sort will, of necessity, suffer many deficiencies, the most significant of which stems from the nature of the subject itself. Even a moment's reflection would reveal the vast distance that separates our understanding of the human spirit from its reality. Indeed, were we to contemplate, as our colleagues in physics do, the mysteries that are enshrined within a single atom, we would realize that even an atom exceeds in mystery the reach of our understanding. When we attempt to extend this reach into the mystery that lies within ourselves, we are doubly confounded. It is, indeed, as the mystic wrote: 'O Brother, if we ponder each created thing, we shall witness a myriad perfect wisdoms and learn a myriad new and wondrous truths . . . Dost thou reckon thyself only a puny form when within thee the universe is folded?'

A little more than a half-century ago, the German philosopher Ernst Cassirer captured well some of the unique powers that place human beings in a realm of existence that is shrouded in mystery. He wrote:

. . . this world [the human world] forms no exception to those biological rules which govern the life of all the other organisms. Yet in the human world we find a new characteristic which appears to be the distinctive mark of human life. The functional circle of man is not only quantitatively enlarged; it has also undergone a qualitative change. Man has, as it were, discovered a new method of adapting himself to his environment. Between the receptor system and the effector system, which are to be found in all animal species, we find in man a third link which we may describe as the *symbolic system.* This new acquisition transforms the whole of human life. As compared with the other animals man lives not merely in a broader reality; he lives, so to speak, in a new *dimension* of reality.[1]

Cassirer's keen observation invites reflection on one final conundrum that has to do with the mysteries that may well link the human spirit with that transcendent realm traditionally associated with God. For as is well known, some of our wisest have asked whether the powers of the human spirit are the highest powers from which we might draw as we labour in service to the needs of the world. This question has been on the minds of philosophers, mystics, and even great scientists such as Newton, Descartes, Einstein, Francis Collins, and many others, across the ages.

In this closing chapter, we approach this question by drawing upon some of the responses to this question that have been given by the founders of the world's religions. We turn to these souls with a mixture of caution and anticipation. The anticipation is derived from an awareness of the many wisdoms that have been enshrined in what some writers have aptly called the 'spiritual heritage' of humankind;[2] and on the other hand, we approach this material with caution because we are aware of the ways in which religious dogmas have been invoked to justify suppression of ideas, gender-based violence, terrorism, innumerable wars, and interminable conflict in nearly every place on earth.

Notwithstanding these reservations, fair-minded observers are also apt to recognize how the founders of the world's religions have given birth to insights that have served to guide and refresh the development of the human spirit over many millennia. And while the benevolent spirit embodied in these traditions has been so often transformed into ideologies that justify oppression, fanaticism, and strife – like fire, which can be used either for good or for harm – the gifts of religion have also enriched the language of love, humility, and compassion with which we need urgently to think.

Furthermore, although they have appeared to particular cultures and have tended to speak in the idiom of that culture, the teachings of the world's religions have tended to transcend socially constructed boundaries of race, class, culture, and nationality. In this sense, they have proven capable of speaking into the city of the human heart. For these reasons, then, we pause in this closing chapter to consider the relevance of this spiritual heritage to the challenges that are within and before us.

In the Bhagavad Gita a shared mission is described for the founders of the world's religions: 'When goodness grows weak, when evil increases, I make myself a body. In every age I come back to deliver the holy, to destroy the sin of the sinner, to establish the righteous.'³ Similarly, in his discourse with Ananda, the Buddha affirmed:

> I am not the first Buddha who came upon the earth, nor shall I be the last. In due time another Buddha will arise in the world, a Holy One, a supremely enlightened One, endowed with wisdom in conduct, auspicious, knowing the universe, an incomparable leader of men, a master of angels and mortals. He will reveal to you the same eternal truths which I have taught you. He will preach his religion, glorious in its origin, glorious at the climax, and glorious at the

goal, in the spirit and in the letter. He will proclaim a religious life, wholly perfect and pure; such as I now proclaim.[4]

Jesus advanced a similar perspective when he said to his disciples, 'I have yet many things to say unto you, but ye cannot bear them now. Howbeit when he, the Spirit of Truth, is come, he will guide you into all truth . . .'[5]

The Bahá'í writings describe the Enlightened Ones that have established the world's religions as divinely inspired educators whose teachings have ever widened the scope of human understanding and extended the reach of the bonds of love that link and harmonize conflicting members of the human race. In addition, when they appear in the world, their inspiration and teachings provide the pattern for the emergence of a new way of life. 'He was in the world,' says the Bible, 'and the world was made by him, and the world knew him not.'[6]

'Abdu'l-Bahá wrote that these divine educators

> so educate human minds and thoughts that they may become capable of substantive progress; that science and knowledge may expand; that the realities of things, the mysteries of the universe, and the properties of all that exists may be revealed; that learning, discoveries, and major undertakings may day by day increase; and that matters of the intellect may be deduced from and conveyed through the sensible.[7]

These Great Ones, 'Abdu'l-Bahá goes further to note, function in the realm of consciousness as sunlight functions in nature.

Indeed, sunlight is both the cause of the eye and the means by which the eye sees. Sunlight confers life, endows living beings with the energies necessary to transform intrinsic capacities into capabilities, and thus stimulates the development of nature's hidden potential. Similarly, the development of human consciousness depends, 'Abdu'l-Bahá notes, upon a divine power that reaches us through the influence of these supremely Enlightened Ones:

Behold! One sanctified Soul revives the world of humanity
. . . delivers man from the realm of baseness and deficiency,
and exhorts and encourages him to develop his innate and
acquired perfections. Certainly nothing short of a divine
power could accomplish this feat! One must examine this
matter fairly . . .[8]

~

Hinduism is among the earliest of the world religions and its
influence has reached into every sphere of life across the ages.
In *Ancient Hindu Science: Its Transmission and Impact on World
Cultures* (2019), Professor Alok Kumar writes:

The accomplishments of the ancient Hindus span many
fields. In mathematics, they invented our base-ten number
system and zero that are now used globally, carefully mapped
the sky and assigned motion to the earth in their astronomy,
developed a sophisticated system of medicine with its mind-
body approach known as Ayurveda, mastered metallurgical
methods of extraction and purification of metals . . . and
developed the science of self-improvement that is popu-
larly known as yoga. Their scientific contributions made
impact on noted scholars from all over the world, Aristotle,
Megasthenes, and Appolonius of Tyana among the Greeks;
Al-Biruni, Al-Khwarizmi, Ibn Labban, and Al-Uqlidisi,
Al-Jahiz among the Islamic scholars; Fa-Hien, Hiuen Tsang,
and I'tsing among the Chinese; and Leonardo Fibbonacci,
Pope Sylvester II, Roger Bacon, Voltaire, and Copernicus
from Europe . . . In the modern era, thinkers and scientists as diverse as Ralph Waldo Emerson, Johann Wolfgang
von Goethe, Johann Gottfried Herder, Carl Jung, Max
Müller, Robert Oppenheimer, Erwin Schrödinger, Arthur
Schopenhauer, and Henry David Thoreau have acknowl-
edged their debt to ancient Hindu achievements in science,
technology, and philosophy.[9]

Thus, far from being concerned with matters solely related to philosophy, theology, and metaphysics, Hindu thinkers and texts have contributed in profound and enduring ways to the development of both technology and the natural sciences.

As noted above, the base 10 notation system that is used to represent numbers throughout the world is Hindu in origin. And while many cultures, including the Greeks, Romans, Egyptians, Babylonians, Mayans and Chinese had all invented their own unique number system, the Hindu base 10 system replaced them all because that system rendered it possible to represent and manipulate large numbers more precisely and efficiently. Indeed, in his classic work *On the Revolutions of the Celestial Spheres*, Nicolaus Copernicus (1473–1543) employed the approach to numbering articulated by Hindu scholars for the calculations made to argue for a heliocentric model of the solar system. Furthermore, approximately three hundred years before Copernicus, the Italian mathematician Leonardo Fibonacci (1170–1250) introduced the Hindu system of numeration and computation to the West in his work *Liber Abaci*.[10]

Many millennia before the Big Bang theory was to earn scientific credibility, the ancient Hindu texts had fixed the age of the universe in billions of years. Noting this, the late astrophysicist Carl Sagan wrote:

> The Hindu dharma is the only one of the world's great faiths dedicated to the idea that the Cosmos itself undergoes an immense, indeed, an infinite, number of deaths and rebirths. It is the only dharma in which time scales correspond to those of modern scientific cosmology. Its cycles run from ordinary day and night to a day and night of the Brahma, 8.64 billion years long, longer than the age of the Earth or the Sun and about half the time since the Big Bang.[11]

The scientific disciplines that emerged out of, or were greatly influenced by, Hinduism were considered sacred disciplines. That is, the acquisition of knowledge of the natural world was thought to be intimately linked to the practice of a moral life, the observance of periods of prayer, and the study of sacred literature. Far from perceiving a chasm between science and religion, the early Hindus considered the use of reason and the acquisition of secular knowledge to be critical to the achievement of spiritual insight and wisdom. Knowledge of the creation, they believed, led inevitably to knowledge of the Creator: 'Said the God of fire: Now I shall describe the system of veins and arteries that are to be found in the human body. A knowledge of these leads to a knowledge of the divine Hari.'[12]

Five centuries before Christ, Buddhism begins with Siddhartha Gautama, who was born of the Sakya family around 563 BCE near the border of India in what is now Nepal. His father was a king and his early upbringing was one of luxurious comfort. 'I wore garments of silk and my attendants held a white umbrella over me. My unguents were always from Banaras.'[13] Historians tell us that Siddhartha Gautama was exceptionally beautiful and that at sixteen he married princess Yasodhara who is described as 'majestic as a queen of heaven, constant, ever cheerful night and day, full of dignity and exceeding grace'.[14] Together they had a son whom they named Rahula.

But Gautama's life was not to be spent in ease and comfort. He would, at twenty-nine years of age, abandon it all and set out from his home in order to pursue his own enlightenment and awaken others to a new approach to life that was to revolutionize human thought and aspiration. The Buddha's teachings were among the first attempts to articulate the essential causes of what Western psychologists would later come to call 'existential suffering'.

Existential suffering is a special kind of suffering that only humans face because of the complex inner world that is made possible by the reach of human consciousness. Unlike other animals, we may stress over events that have never occurred and will never occur; we may stress over the things that we have done or failed to do; or we may stress over the kind of person that we have become, or the kind of person that we wish we were. When the Buddha identified suffering as the first of the Four Noble Truths and prescribed the Eightfold Path – right effort, right conduct, right livelihood, right mindfulness, right speech, and so forth – as its remedy, he provided a prescription for living that has enriched the quality of life for billions of people for hundreds of years. In this sense, one could say that the Buddha was not just the author of a new religion, but was the progenitor of a way of thinking that was to evolve into one of the most powerful psychological and moral sciences of the East.

Buddha promised that He was not the last of the Great Messengers. He said that another Buddha, the Buddha of Universal Fellowship, would arise in the fullness of time. He told His followers:

> The Tathagata, God's messenger, recreates the whole world like a cloud shedding its waters without distinction. He has the same sentiments for the high as for the low, for the wise as for the ignorant, for the noble minded as for the immoral. He is the same to all, and yet, knowing the requirements of every single being does not reveal himself to all alike.[15]

In the land of Persia, in the seventh century before Christ, there appeared the saintly person of Zoroaster. Zoroaster gave birth to a new religion that raised consciousness of the power of human beings to create a more desirable existence for themselves and others by pursuing good and forsaking evil. He thus taught that humans hold within their grasp their own destiny and that, to a considerable degree, our lives are not the result of arbitrary forces. Rather, the universe, He insisted, has a moral purpose and we must strive to bring our lives into harmony with the moral principles that animate it.

Unlike many philosophers, Zoroaster not only taught lofty principles, but he also lived them to a superlative degree. Even in his childhood Zoroaster manifested exceptional qualities of mind, heart, and foresight – qualities that would attract the wonder of those who beheld his innate beauty. By the time he was a youth, he was already renowned for his profound wisdom, his lofty virtues, and his devotion to truth.

He gave generously to the poor, was modest and gentle. His meekness, it is said, was combined with lion-like courage, and he pursued with vigour that which was right and true. The traditions foretold that Zoroaster would become a great prophet who would reveal a new faith that would replace the existing one which was centred in the practice of magic. The role of religion, he taught, was not to dazzle the senses with 'miracles', but to edify and illumine the human heart and thus bring virtue into the human world. Inasmuch as the profoundly moral teachings of Zoroaster proved to be a threat to the corrupt religious leaders of his time, there were many attempts on his life.

At about the age of thirty, in a series of visions Zoroaster became aware that he would lead his country to a higher religion than it had ever known before. At its heart, his religion taught purity of mind. So great was its vitality, and so appealing to the human soul, that many of its conceptions and precepts lived on in the religions of Israel. Indeed, the Magi, or wise men, who visited the child Jesus as mentioned in the New Testament, were Zoroastrian priests.

Zoroaster foretold of a period of 3,000 years of conflict and contention, which must precede the advent of the World Saviour – the 'Shah Bahram', who would usher in an era of blessedness and peace. In His Holy Book, the Zend Avesta, are found the following words: 'Hath the religions of mankind no common ground? Broad indeed is the carpet God hath spread and many are the colors He has given. Whatever road I take, joins the highway that leads to Him.'[16]

≈

Abraham is generally recognized as the father of Judaism. His most essential teaching centred on monotheism, the claim that there is only one God. To affirm the oneness of God is to affirm that the idols that are produced, either by human hands or human imagination, have no enduring power or authority. They are as the dew that vanishes with the rising sun. Furthermore, monotheism embodies the idea that the universe is not under the influence of a diversity of metaphysical forces that reign according to their whims and proclivities – as the polytheists of a variety of cultures tended to believe. Rather, monotheism nourishes the conviction that reality is coherent and intelligible as it flows from the Mind and Will of a single, all-informed, all-powerful and benevolent God. Commenting on this theme, the religious studies scholar Huston Smith writes: 'For the Egyptians, Babylonians, Syrians, and lesser Mediterranean peoples of the day, each major power of nature was a distinct deity. The storm was the storm-god, the sun, the sun-god, the rain, the rain-god. When we turn to the Hebrew Bible, we find ourselves in a completely different atmosphere. Nature here is an expression of a single Lord of all being.'[17]

In addition to affirming the oneness of God, Abraham's teachings stress the importance of human virtues. The scriptures and historical records reveal that Abraham was exiled from His home in Ur (Mesopotamia) by King Nimrod in the hope that no trace of Him might be left in His own country. A promise, however, had been given to Abraham that a great blessing would descend upon Him and all His descendants: 'I will make thee a great nation, and I will bless thee and magnify thy name and in thee shall all the kindreds of the earth be blessed.'[18]

As is well known, Abraham had three wives. First there was Sarah who, at first, proved unable to bear a child. Sarah insisted that Abraham take another wife so that their home would be blessed by a son. His second wife, Hagar, gave birth to a lovely boy whose name was Ishmael. In her old age, Sarah eventually had a son whom they named Isaac. After Sarah's death, Abraham married his third wife, whose name was Katurah, who bore him six children. From the three wives of Abraham were to come three religions.

The progeny of Isaac, Sarah's son, would result in the line that led to the birth of Christ; Muhammad and the Báb descended from Ishmael, the son of Hagar; and Katurah's offspring would lead to Bahá'u'lláh, founder of the Bahá'í Faith. There is no religion that bears the name of Abraham, but Abraham established the spiritual principles and social teachings that would emerge into Judaism under the influence of Moses.

Moses embodied a deeply spiritual nature and had great compassion for the oppressed. He longed, ardently, for the well-being of His people and became increasingly aware of the cruelty of slavery and the brutality with which the Egyptians treated the Israelites. On Mount Sinai Moses experienced the sacred encounter known as the burning bush, and this inspired him to liberate his people and lead them out of Egypt into Canaan – formerly known as Palestine and part of present-day Israel.

The teachings of Abraham and Moses were to spread through their descendants across the world. Indeed, the chief contributions of Judaism to civilization are in the realm of ideas. Since ideas are among the most precious of all gifts, the blessings bestowed upon humanity by the teachings of Abraham and His descendants are incalculable. For example, the notion of God bequeathed to humanity by Judaism is a God that has created a universe that is, at its very foundation, essentially good. Furthermore, human history, from the point of view of Judaism, is not simply 'one damn thing after another'. Rather, history has a direction and it is possible for humanity to make progress in realizing the inherent potentiality of historical processes. The ultimate goal of history, Judaism teaches, is the achievement of justice and peace. Judaism thus fertilizes the human mind with a vision of the future that is noble and good.

Moses elevated the consciousness of the people of Israel to such a degree that they became among the most literate people on earth. He laid the basis of a moral order that has inspired the creation of civil laws around the world. Before he passed away,

Moses, as did Buddha and Zoroaster, promised his followers that another great Teacher would also come: 'And the Lord, thy God, shall raise up from the midst of thee a Prophet, like unto Me . . . I will raise them up a prophet out of the midst of their brethren like unto Thee (Moses) and I will put my words in His mouth and He shall speak to them all that I shall command Him.'[19] And from the Torah, a promise of universal peace is found:

> And it shall come to pass in the end of days that the mountain of the Lord's House shall be established at the top of the mountain and shall be exalted above the hills. And all people shall flow into it. And many people shall go and say, 'Come ye and let us go up to the House of the God of Jacob and He will teach us His ways; we will walk in His path for out of Zion shall go forth the law and the word of the Lord from Jerusalem. And He shall judge among the nations and shall decide for many peoples. And they shall beat their swords into plowshares and their spears into pruning hooks; nation shall not lift up sword against nation, nor shall they learn war anymore.[20]

Jesus's short life and ministry have had a greater impact on the Western world than almost any other figure. We are told that he was born poor in a manger in Palestine in the days of Herod. His teachings were simple; those which are contained in the New Testament could be recited in their entirety in just a few hours. In describing his approach, it is said that 'he went about doing good'; that he spoke in parables that were designed to stimulate deep reflection; that he told the people of his day that the kingdom of God is 'within'; and that he urged men, women, and children to 'seek the truth' as 'truth shall make you free'. When asked about the qualities that should adorn the righteous, he told a story about the 'good Samaritan' who placed himself in danger in order to render service to a man who had been beaten and robbed along a dangerous stretch of road. The parable serves to illustrate the self-sacrificing compassion that should characterize the life of a follower of Christ.

The truths of religion, like the truths of science, are exposed to human consciousness in a gradual and progressive way; indeed, each of the world's religions have acquainted humanity with those social, moral, and spiritual teachings that it could bear at the time and which were necessary in order for the human family to be able to realize a greater share of its limitless potential. Each of them recognized that if humanity was to develop in safety, we would have to be periodically reminded of the moral and spiritual truths that are the pillars upon which all forms of social cohesion rest. Jesus alludes to these truths when he declares that 'Man shall not live by bread alone, but by every word that proceedeth out of the mouth of God.'[21]

Jesus spoke to simple people in simple language about the essential teachings of religion. He taught that God was the great Spirit and motivating Power behind the movement of history; that God was love and light and compassion and mercy; and that we were all made in the image of God and should also strive to love one another. Christ referred to Himself as having been sent by God, His 'Father'.

The transforming influence of Christ attracted fierce opposition from many who objected to His teachings. He was cruelly abused, and at the age of thirty-three, He was crucified. His last words would ring across the earth: 'Father, forgive them, for they know not what they do.' Over the course of the centuries following his execution, the simple teachings of Christ would unite many peoples across the world under the light of his commandment to love. The Bahá'í teachings tell us that

> The deepest wisdom which the sages have uttered, the profoundest learning which any mind hath unfolded, the arts which the ablest hands have produced, the influence exerted by the most potent of rulers, are but manifestations of the

quickening power released by His transcendent, His all-pervasive and resplendent spirit.[22]

And in another place: 'He it is Who purified the world. Blessed is the man who, with a face beaming with light, hath turned towards Him.'[23]

The teachings of Christ provided mankind with a great spiritual rebirth and awakened in the human community moral aspirations that exceeded those that had preceded Him. He inaugurated a 'spiritual springtime', as had the Prophets and Manifestations of God before Him. From a small following of disciples, His teachings spread throughout the civilized world. Great nations were built upon the profound but simple teachings of the carpenter of Nazareth. Speaking of the unity of these Holy Ones, Jesus said:

Verily, verily I say unto you, before Abraham was, I am.[24]

Had ye believed in Moses you would have believed in Me, for He spoke of Me.[25]

He that believeth on Me, believeth not on Me, but on Him that sent Me . . . I am come as a light unto the world that he that believeth on me shall not abide in darkness.[26]

And other sheep I have which are not of this fold: them also must I bring, and they shall hear my voice, and there shall be one fold and one shepherd.[27]

Jesus foretold that another would come in the 'fullness of time'. He sometimes referred to this as His return. It was to be a return of the eternal Spirit of God. He referred to this promised age as the 'time of the end'. He promised that this One to come would be the Comforter and would be the Spirit of Truth who would guide men 'into all truth'. He was to be the Lord of the Vineyard who would return in the Glory of the Father; in the clouds of heaven, with power and great glory: 'I have yet many things to say unto you, but ye cannot bear them now. Howbeit, when He, the Spirit of Truth is come, He will guide you into all truth. What He shall speak, He shall not speak of Himself, but whatsoever He shall hear, that He shall speak, and He will show you things to come.'[28] Jesus left His followers with a prayer that was also a promise: 'Thy kingdom come, Thy will be done, on earth, as it is in Heaven.'[29]

~

The Prophet Muhammad established the religion of Islam in 622 AD. He was born in Mecca in the then barren land of Arabia.

Muhammad is a title which means 'Highly Praised One'. He was renowned for His kindness and the nobility of His life, characterized by love, modesty, compassion, and generosity. His manners were refined and courteous, and He showed great benevolence not only to human beings, but also to animals. It was said of Him that He had such sweetness in His face that when one was on His presence, one would dread having to leave.

The people of His time had many barbaric practices – such as burying the female newborn alive as they wished most often to have boys. The tribes also engaged in constant bloody battles which destroyed many homes and families. Idolatry was also widespread. These oppressive conditions led Muhammad to withdraw into a cave on Mount Hira, where He prayed and meditated.

One night, in a vision of light, the Angel Gabriel appeared to Him and told Him that He should speak in the Name of God. The angel said: 'Arise, you are the Prophet of God. Go about the world and speak in the Name of the Lord.'[30] Muhammad was at that time forty years of age. He immediately proclaimed the oneness of almighty God ('Allah' in Arabic) and He arose to denounce the many gods of the pagan religions, as they were sources of constant conflict.

Submission to the will of God became the central basis of

His teachings. Diversity of colour, He taught, was a sign of God. Thus, all men were equal before their Creator. In this way would the Holy Book of Muhammad – the Qur'án – create a society that stretched from Baghdad to Spain that was, for a time, free of racial prejudice.

Muhammad and His followers suffered severe persecution. Many of them were tortured and killed. When He learned of the plan to assassinate Him, He fled from Mecca to the city of Medina on the night of 16 July, 622 AD. That date is considered the beginning of the Muhammadan Era.

In Medina Muhammad was enthusiastically received, and His success mounted the throne of many great achievements. He encouraged science, learning, and reading; and under His influence His followers were to preserve the profound Greek texts and translate them into Arabic; they would pioneer many new arts, philosophies, and sciences; they would become renowned in the practice of medicine and surgery. What is more, Muhammad taught that both Christians and Jews should be treated with respect and that their rights as human beings should be honoured. Under the teachings of Muhammad, the Arabians rose to great heights of culture and the contributions of the people of Islam to the process of civilization-building is beyond telling. Indeed, Islam became the epicentre of the most advanced civilization that the world had ever known.

The golden rule of Islam is: 'Let no one treat his brother in a way he himself would dislike to be treated.'[31]

Muhammad, like His prophetic forerunners, told of a time of great troubles, and of another who would come after Him. He taught that God will send to His people, at the beginning of each new age, Him who will renew religion. There is a prophecy in Islam that two divinely guided messianic personages will succeed one another in the latter days. The first of these two is the Mihdi or the Qá'im. These two great Beings, when they come, would cause the earth to shine with the Light of its Lord.

≈

Further to the East, the great thinkers of China were among the first to reflect deeply upon the capacities that might distinguish humans from other life forms. For example, Mencius (372–289 BCE), who was the most distinguished intellectual offspring of the Chinese sage Confucius, spoke of *hsing*. *Hsing*, Mencius noted, 'is that in man which, though slight, makes him different from animals'[32] and is, in regard to mind, common to all men. In this way does Mencius affirm that *hsing* consists of those capacities of consciousness that define our common humanity and that set us apart from the minerals, plants, and animals to whom we are also related.

Mencius noted further that when circumstances permit it to develop in the directions to which it is naturally inclined, human consciousness is naturally attracted towards that which is good. However, these impulsions can be interfered with by bad conditions. Bad government, for example, can frustrate and curtail its natural development – so also can exposure to famine, drought, and other environmental threats. That which is common in all of us thus requires a healthy environment and community if its development is to be fully realized.

The powers and capacities that characterize *hsing*, Mencius taught, are universal promptings towards pity, shame, reverence, and a sense of right and wrong. These moral sentiments, Mencius noted, do not arise as a result of social pressures – and so they are not equivalent to what the Freudians might regard as the superego. Rather, they were believed to be innate and native to the human person. Thus, while each person embodies a *mind* which is particular and unique to them, each, according to Mencius, also embodies *hsing*, which is a collection of universal powers and capacities that become evident, to varying degrees, in all human beings according to their degree of cultivation and refinement. In the language of classical Chinese philosophy, *hsing* is the phenomenon that best corresponds to the notion of the *human spirit* that we have been seeking to describe in this volume.

The moral promptings associated with pity, shame, respect,

and a sensitivity to truth (or right and wrong) are said to be 'the first and lowliest signs of the *virtues* which under favorable conditions . . .'[33] are the powers associated with the human spirit. All people, according to Mencius, are attracted to the virtues by universal inheritance. This innate attraction appears in childhood, but must be nurtured if it is to remain active and grow strong.

Contemporary empirical research by J. Kiley Hamlin, Karen Wynn, and Paul Bloom has provided some support for such a claim. Their research has shown that 6-month-olds are attracted to prosocial individuals and avoid individuals who manifest antisocial characteristics. For example, 6- and 10-month-old infants tend to approach those who have helped another achieve a goal, and avoid those who have hindered another from achieving a goal.[34] The researchers note that the infants who participated in these studies were passive observers who had been neither helped nor hindered themselves; further, they had no previous experience with the individuals involved. This suggests that the simple observation of social behaviour is sufficient to motivate social evaluation and that this faculty may not require social priming or instruction as a precondition of its activation. Other research by the same scholars has shown that even 3-month-old infants evaluate others based on the moral qualities of their behaviour towards others and that they prefer people who demonstrate positive virtues over those who manifest negative ones.[35]

Associated with the virtues that are intrinsic to *hsing* are other qualities such as *jen*, *yi*, *li*, and *ch'i*. *Jen* can be rendered as *humanity* or *love* (if we are careful to exclude romantic, passionate, and sexual associations). According to I. A. Richards, 'humaneness, reciprocity in desirable acts, and fellow-feeling, all come near it'.[36] But more than an emotion, *jen* may be thought of as a form of activity or a general tendency to act in certain ways. *Jen* is the 'heart of man' and is associated with being in such a way that one's presence is edifying – that is, one teaches others without trying. To embody *jen* is to be a source of honour, while its absence is the cause of humiliation and self-abasement.

'Its first sign', noted Richards, 'is the shame and dislike'[37] of having done wrong in one's relationship and duties to others.

Jen is related to a second virtue, *li*, which is concerned with propriety and good manners – such as courtesy (which Bahá'u'lláh refers to as 'the prince of virtues'). According to Mencius, all are capable of manifesting courtesy and good manners; and the presence of courtesy warms and enriches a community or culture.

Whenever a concern for *li* slips from consciousness people begin to treat one another as though they were merely objects that are being moved from here to there to facilitate commerce and exchange. In this way is the sense of 'humanity' lost. Furthermore, where prejudice exists, the courtesy that is the inevitable result of recognizing the humanity of others is regarded as unnecessary and undeserved. Under such conditions, we see forms of disregard for *li* that stains relations and creates the kind of inhumanity that spills blood. What the early Chinese philosophers sought to teach is that *li*, a capacity of the human spirit, is not a luxury that we can just as well do without.

Hsing is also associated with *ch'i*, as *ch'i* is inseparable from *jen* and *li*. *Ch'i* is the breath, the subtle life force, the vital energy, upon which the body depends. *Ch'i* may be thought of as not only an energy but as a form of innate intelligence (or even wisdom) that makes possible the human potential to discern, and thus to contribute to the moral development of self and others. The will, Mencius noted, is *ch'i's* commander. In controlling the *ch'i*, the will 'must do it no violence'.[38] In this way does Mencius appear to disapprove of what might be called repression. The function of will is to 'make few the desires' and to steer desire in profitable directions. Since it is in the nature of the mind to seek its own development, the will is thought to be, by nature, in harmony with one's *ch'i*. From this perspective, 'skill in maintaining and managing one's vast *ch'i* would consist, not in repressing it, but in distributing it so that the leadership of the will is not imperiled'.[39] In such a state, one has what the Greeks thought of as 'command over one's self'.

The tendency towards self-development, the longing to cultivate one's own personhood, is what renders *hsing* essentially good.

It was possible in the days of Mencius to begin to speak
about these things because thought and language had evolved
to a point where we were capable of taking our inner selves as
objects of reflection. We could ask questions about the factors
that made us, at once, different from other human beings and
yet also the same. In Western discourse, the study of human
beings has tended to focus on what makes us unique and different; the focus has thus been on 'personality'. In the East, the
focus has been on what we have in common – and so the focus
has tended to be on the human spirit.

∾

The great Seneca chief and orator Red Jacket once said: 'We also
have a religion which has been handed down to us children. It
teaches us to be thankful, to be united, and to love one another!
We never quarrel about religion.'[40]

The first inhabitants of the lands of North America were in
the past sometimes referred to as American Indians. In their
speech, the Native American tribes embodied a quality of reverence for the 'Great Mystery' that evokes a sense of wonder in
those with ears to hear and hearts to understand. In *The Soul
of the Indian*, which records the words of Charles Alexander
Eastman – known in the language of his people as Ohiyesa – we
read:

> Long before I ever heard of Christ, or saw a white man, I had
> learned from an untutored woman the essence of morality.
> With the help of dear Nature herself, she taught me things
> simple but of mighty import. I knew God. I perceived
> what goodness is. I saw and loved what is really beautiful.
> Civilization has not taught me anything better!
>
> As a child, I understood how to give; I have forgotten
> that grace since I became civilized. I lived the natural life,

whereas I now live the artificial. Any pretty pebble was valuable to me then; every growing tree an object of reverence. Now I worship with the white man before a painted landscape whose value is estimated in dollars! Thus the Indian is reconstructed, as the natural rocks are ground to powder, and made into artificial blocks which may be built into the walls of modern society.

The first American mingled with his pride a singular humility. Spiritual arrogance was foreign to his nature and teachings. He never claimed that the power of articulate speech was proof of superiority over the dumb creation; on the other hand, it is to him a perilous gift. He believes profoundly in silence – the sign of a perfect equilibrium. Silence is the absolute poise or balance of body, mind, and spirit. The man who preserves his selfhood ever calm and unshaken by the storms of existence – not a leaf, as it were, astir on the tree; not a ripple upon the surface of shining pool – his, in the mind of the unlettered sage, is the ideal attitude and conduct of life.[41]

We call to mind the great wisdom of the Native Americans because these peoples, in their many varieties of colours, languages and traditions, have provided the world with much that can be called upon to reawaken and nourish the starving soul. In their ways they offered a model, an attitude and respect for nature, that the planet can no longer live without.

On 23 May 1844, in a small room in the city of Shiraz, the noble and youthful figure of the Báb proclaimed to a student of religion that He was as a herald of the dawn of a new age in the collective life of mankind. The Báb claimed to be the inaugurator of that age and the Manifestation of God that would prepare the way for the coming of the Promised One of all ages.

Like many of the Manifestations of God before Him, the

Báb and His followers were to face unimaginable cruelty and eventual death for such a claim. At the age of 31, after six brief years of ministry, the Báb was executed in the Persian city of Tabriz, along with a young companion who refused to leave His side. His last words, uttered as He gazed upon a crowd that had gathered in the town square to witness His execution were these: 'Had you believed in Me, O wayward generation, every one of you would have followed the example of this youth, who stood in rank above most of you, and willingly would have sacrificed himself in My path. The day will come when you will have recognized Me; that day I shall have ceased to be with you.'[42]

The founders of the great religions appear in the world in order to make it possible for the human heart to recognize those truths that are fundamental to achieving a successful human life; they nurture the capacity to perceive that 'ancient beauty' which illuminates the universe; their words inspire attraction to that which is good and noble. Thus, what the Báb lamented on the day of His execution was not the loss of His own life, but the lack of receptivity to these spiritual forces upon which the life and vitality of the human soul depends.

The Báb taught that the deepest aspiration of every living being is to realize its potential; to uncover its hidden excellence; to become everything that it is capable of becoming; to manifest its God-given endowments. He appeared in Persia at a time when lawlessness, corruption, superstition, prejudice and cruelty were the way of life.

Muhammad Shah ruled Iran during the early days of the ministry of the Báb, but real power, we are told by historians of the period, rested in his Grand Vizier, Hájí Mírzá Áqásí – who has been described as 'a man ignorant and devoid of all graces':

He was cruel and treacherous, proud and over-bearing, although he affected humility . . . The religious character which he had assumed made him intolerant and bigoted, and he was known to be a fanatical hater of Christians. He had been the Shah's tutor and instructor in the Koran, and had acquired a great influence over his pupil, who had raised him to the lofty position which he then held . . . His misgovernment, and the corruption and general oppression which everywhere existed had brought Persia to the verge of ruin. Distress, misery, and discontent prevailed to an extent previously unknown.[43]

In addition to the vicious qualities manifested by the Prime Minister, the religious leaders of Persia were, by and large, equally cruel, self-serving, proud and corrupt. Writing of this sad state of affairs, one chronicler of the period noted that: 'Corruption, fanaticism, and cruelty gather against the cause of the reformation to destroy it . . .'[44] This was the society into which the Báb was born – but He was to say that this condition was not confined to the people of Persia. Rather, the spirit of humanity, in general, had exhausted its most vital spiritual resources and needed desperately to be encouraged, uplifted, and inspired by that One Power which, periodically, gives birth to new life. That Power, as we have noted, is embodied in the Messengers of God who are the founders of the world's great religions, and who breathe into the human heart the spirit of love and compassion when it has nearly died.

The Báb's teachings sought to liberate religion from the darkness of superstition by emphasizing the metaphorical nature of many of the truths that are articulated in the world's scriptures. In His final address to those disciples who were the first to recognize His divinely ordained station, the Báb reiterated the principle of the unity of the Prophets that had appeared in the world before Him. To these disciples He said:

Heed not your weaknesses and frailty; fix your gaze upon the invincible power of the Lord, your God, the Almighty. Has He not, in past days, caused Abraham, in spite of His seeming helplessness, to triumph over the forces of Nimrod? Has He not enabled Moses, whose staff was His only companion, to vanquish Pharaoh and his hosts? Has

He not established the ascendancy of Jesus, poor and lowly as He was in the eyes of men, over the combined forces of the Jewish people? Has He not subjected the barbarous and militant tribes of Arabia to the holy and transforming discipline of Muḥammad, His Prophet? Arise in His name, put your trust wholly in Him, and be assured of ultimate victory.[45]

In addition, the Báb's purpose was to prepare humanity for the coming of the One foretold in all the sacred scriptures of the past. That One the Báb referred to in His many tablets, epistles, commentaries, and books as: 'Him Whom God Shall Make Manifest'. The Bahá'ís of the world know that Promised One to be Mirzá Ḥusayn 'Alí, who is known to the world today by the title Bahá'u'lláh.

Bahá'ís believe that Bahá'u'lláh's and the Báb's appearance inaugurates a new age. Bahá'u'lláh's purpose was to reveal forces, principles, and laws that are necessary for the rehabilitation of the entire planet and the inauguration of that long-anticipated era of global peace. It insists upon the equality of women and men; it abrogates the priesthood and invites all to become independent seekers after truth; it stresses that the pursuit of knowledge and learning is the moral obligation of those who thirst after God; and it restores awareness of the unique power that animates the deeds of those who are oriented toward service to the entire human race. In addition to the works of Bahá'u'lláh and the Báb, the writings of the Bahá'í Faith include those penned by Bahá'u'lláh's eldest son, 'Abdu'l-Bahá, as well as his great-grandson, Shoghi Effendi. We close this volume by sampling from just a few of those writings of the Bahá'í Faith that address the transformation of the world by transforming the city of the human heart, and by recreating the social institutions that form the basis of humanity's civilized life.[46]

≈

In calling humanity to the respect that should be shown to people of different philosophies, faiths, and ways of life, Bahá'u'lláh offered this counsel:

> Consort with all men, O people of Bahá, in a spirit of friendliness and fellowship. If ye be aware of a certain truth, if ye possess a jewel, of which others are deprived, share it with them in a language of utmost kindliness and goodwill. If it be accepted, if it fulfil its purpose, your object is attained. If any one should refuse it, leave him unto himself, and beseech God to guide him. Beware lest ye deal unkindly with him. A kindly tongue is the lodestone of the hearts of men. It is the bread of the spirit, it clotheth the words with meaning, it is the fountain of the light of wisdom and understanding . . .[47]

And when addressing the spiritual attitude that would aid in overcoming various forms of prejudice, 'Abdu'l-Bahá once said:

> Necessarily there will be some who are defective amongst men, but it is our duty to enable them by kind methods of guidance and teaching to become perfected. Some will be found who are morally sick; they should be treated in order that they may be healed. Others are immature and like children; they must be trained and educated so that they may become wise and mature. Those who are asleep must be awakened; the indifferent must become mindful and attentive. But all this must be accomplished in the spirit of kindness and love and not by strife, antagonism nor in a spirit of hostility and hatred, for this is contrary to the good pleasure of God. Love is, in reality, the first effulgence of Divinity and the greatest splendor of God.[48]

But also realizing the systemic and institutionalized nature of many types of bigotry, in 1931 Shoghi Effendi wrote:

Let there be no mistake. The principle of the Oneness of Mankind – the pivot round which all the teachings of Bahá'u'lláh revolve – is no mere outburst of ignorant emotionalism or an expression of vague and pious hope. Its appeal is not to be merely identified with a reawakening of the spirit of brotherhood and good-will among men, nor does it aim solely at the fostering of harmonious cooperation among individual peoples and nations. Its implications are deeper, its claims greater than any which the Prophets of old were allowed to advance. Its message is applicable not only to the individual, but concerns itself primarily with the nature of those essential relationships that must bind all the states and nations as members of one human family. It does not constitute merely the enunciation of an ideal, but stands inseparably associated with an institution adequate to embody its truth, demonstrate its validity, and perpetuate its influence. It implies an organic change in the structure of present-day society, a change such as the world has not yet experienced. It constitutes a challenge, at once bold and universal, to outworn shibboleths of national creeds – creeds that have had their day and which must, in the ordinary course of events as shaped and controlled by Providence, give way to a new gospel, fundamentally different from, and infinitely superior to, what the world has already conceived. It calls for no less than the reconstruction and the demilitarization of the whole civilized world – a world organically unified in all the essential aspects of its life, its political machinery, its spiritual aspiration, its trade and finance, its script and language, and yet infinite in the diversity of the national characteristics of its federated units.[49]

While walking along the banks of the Tigris river, Bahá'u'lláh summarized some of the spiritual teachings that had been articulated by the Prophets of God across the ages. In the brief introduction to this outpouring of divine guidance, which is contained in a series of short spiritual aphorisms that He titled *Hidden Words*, He wrote:

> This is that which hath descended from the realm of glory, uttered by the tongue of power and might, and revealed unto the Prophets of old. We have taken the inner essence thereof and clothed it in the garment of brevity, as a token of grace unto the righteous, that they may stand faithful unto the Covenant of God, may fulfil in their lives His trust, and in the realm of spirit obtain the gem of divine virtue.[50]

The first of these spiritual aphorisms reads:

> O Son of Spirit! My first counsel is this: Possess a pure, kindly and radiant heart, that thine may be a sovereignty ancient, imperishable and everlasting.[51]

And in the second He proclaimed:

> O Son of Spirit! The best beloved of all things in My sight is Justice; turn not away therefrom if thou desirest Me, and neglect it not that I may confide in thee. By its aid thou shalt see with thine own eyes and not through the eyes of others, and shalt know of thine own knowledge and not through the knowledge of thy neighbour. Ponder this in thy heart; how it behooveth thee to be. Verily justice is My gift to thee and the sign of My loving-kindness. Set it then before thine eyes.[52]

When He sought to address the immortality of the human soul He wrote:

> O Son of Man! Thou art My dominion and My dominion perisheth not; wherefore fearest thou thy perishing? Thou art My light and My light shall never be extinguished; why dost thou dread extinction? Thou art My glory and My glory fadeth not; thou art My robe and My robe shall never be

outworn. Abide then in thy love for Me, that thou mayest find Me in the realm of glory.[53]

And in a voice that sounds to my ear much like the mystical teachings that animate many of the world's faiths, He proclaimed:

O Son of Man! The light hath shone on thee from the horizon of the sacred Mount and the spirit of enlightenment hath breathed in the Sinai of thy heart. Wherefore, free thyself from the veils of idle fancies and enter into My court, that thou mayest be fit for everlasting life and worthy to meet Me. Thus may death not come upon thee, neither weariness nor trouble.[54]

In addressing the truth that is at the heart of the principle of the oneness of humankind He asked:

Know ye not why We created you all from the same dust? That no one should exalt himself over the other. Ponder at all times in your hearts how ye were created. Since We have created you all from one same substance it is incumbent on you to be even as one soul, to walk with the same feet, eat with the same mouth and dwell in the same land, that from your inmost being, by your deeds and actions, the signs of oneness and the essence of detachment may be made manifest. Such is My counsel to you, O concourse of light! Heed ye this counsel that ye may obtain the fruit of holiness from the tree of wondrous glory.[55]

And in letters to the rulers of His day, all of which He wrote as a prisoner and exile, He drew attention to the moral and ethical foundations of good governance.

O ye friends of God in His cities and His loved ones in His lands! This Wronged One enjoineth on you honesty and

214

piety. Blessed the city that shineth by their light. Through them man is exalted, and the door of security is unlocked before the face of all creation. Happy the man that cleaveth fast unto them, and recognizeth their virtue, and woe betide him that denieth their station.[56]

There is no force on earth that can equal in its conquering power the forces of justice and wisdom. I, verily, affirm that there is not, and hath never been, a host more mighty than that of justice and wisdom . . . There can be no doubt whatever that if the daystar of justice, which the clouds of tyranny have obscured, were to shed its light upon men, the face of the earth would be completely transformed.[57]

His son, 'Abdu'l-Bahá, drew attention to these same values when he wrote a treatise to the rulers of Persia in the hope of helping them to reflect on what was necessary if they wished to be successful in their efforts to rehabilitate the nation.

The second attribute of perfection is justice and impartiality. This means to have no regard for one's own personal benefits and selfish advantages, and to carry out the laws of God without the slightest concern for anything else. It means to see one's self as only one of the servants of God, the All-Possessing, and except for aspiring to spiritual distinction, never attempting to be singled out from the others. It means to consider the welfare of the community as one's own. It means, in brief, to regard humanity as a single individual, and one's own self as a member of that corporeal form, and to know of a certainty that if pain or injury afflicts any member of that body, it must inevitably result in suffering for all the rest.[58]

And while writing of the impact of the decline of true religion on the social order, Shoghi Effendi noted:

The perversion of human nature, the degradation of human conduct, the corruption and dissolution of human institutions, reveal themselves, under such circumstances, in their worst and most revolting aspects. Human character is debased, confidence is shaken, the nerves of discipline are relaxed, the voice of human conscience is stilled, the sense of decency and shame is obscured, conceptions of duty, of solidarity, of reciprocity and loyalty are distorted, and the very feeling of peacefulness, of joy and of hope is gradually extinguished.[59]

Expatiating on the indispensability of science, 'Abdu'l-Bahá affirmed:

The priests are attached to ancient superstitions and when these are not in keeping with science, the priests denounce science. When religion is upheld by science and reason we can believe with assurance and act with conviction, for this rational faculty is the greatest power in the world. Through it industries are established, the past and present are laid bare and the underlying realities are brought to light. Let us make nature our captive, break through all laws of limitation and with deep penetration bring to light that which is hidden. The power to do this is the greatest of divine benefits. Why treat with indifference such a divine spark? Why ignore a faculty so beneficial, a sun so powerful?[60]

The Bahá'í writings invite all of humanity to rethink relationships; to see human society from an evolutionary and developmental perspective. It offers a hopeful perspective on human history, and observes that the crucial need is to draw upon the limitless potentialities of the human spirit and to find a unifying vision of the future of society:

History has thus far recorded principally the experience of tribes, cultures, classes, and nations. With the physical unification of the planet in this century and acknowledgement of the interdependence of all who live on it, the history of humanity as one people is now beginning. The long, slow civilizing of human character has been a sporadic development, uneven and admittedly inequitable in the material advantages it has conferred. Nevertheless, endowed with the wealth of all the genetic and cultural diversity that has evolved through past ages, the earth's inhabitants are now challenged to draw on their collective inheritance to take up, consciously and systematically, the responsibility for the design of their future . . .[61]

The writings of the Bahá'í Faith are an invitation to seize the opportunities that have been placed at our disposal as a result of millions of years of social, cultural, technological, philosophical, and religious evolution and development:

> Throughout the world, immense intellectual and spiritual energies are seeking expression . . . Everywhere the signs multiply that the earth's peoples yearn for an end to conflict and to the suffering and ruin from which no land is any longer immune. These rising impulses for change must be seized upon and channeled . . . The effort of will required . . . cannot be summoned up merely by appeals for action against the countless ills afflicting society. It must be galvanized by a vision of human prosperity in the fullest sense of the term – an awakening to the possibilities of the spiritual and material well-being now brought within grasp.[62]

On 29 May 1892 Bahá'u'lláh passed away. The community that He established has since spread to every nation on earth. By working to build diverse communities that promote individual and collective growth and empowerment, by applying spiritual principles to social and economic life, and by contributing to the transformation of society through engagement in important discourses, the Bahá'í community is seeking to learn alongside others what it can do to promote the development and well-being of the human spirit. The hope is that the current volume will contribute to this ongoing endeavour.

BIBLIOGRAPHY

'Abdu'l-Bahá. Online sources of the following works by 'Abdu'l-Bahá are available at https://www.bahai.org/library.

— *Abdul Baha on Divine Philosophy.* Comp. I. F. Chamberlain. Boston: The Tudor Press, 1918.

— *Paris Talks: Addresses given by 'Abdu'l-Bahá in 1911* (1912). London: Bahá'í Publishing Trust, 12th ed. 1995.

— *The Promulgation of Universal Peace: Talks Delivered by 'Abdu'l-Bahá During His Visit to the United States and Canada in 1912* (1922, 1925). Comp. H. MacNutt. Wilmette, IL: Bahá'í Publishing Trust, 2nd ed. 1982.

— *The Secret of Divine Civilization.* Trans. M. Gail. Wilmette, IL: Bahá'í Publishing Trust, 1957.

— *Selections from the Writings of 'Abdu'l-Bahá.* Comp. Research Department of the Universal House of Justice. Haifa: Bahá'í World Centre, 1978.

— *Some Answered Questions* (1908). Comp. and trans. Laura Clifford Barney. Haifa: Bahá'í World Centre, rev. ed. 2014.

— *Tablets of Abdul-Baha Abbas.* 3 vols. Chicago: Bahá'í Publishing Society (1909–1916). Wilmette, IL: National Spiritual Assembly of the Bahá'ís of the United States, 1980.

— Tablet to August Forel. https://www.bahai.org/library/authoritative-texts/search#q=is%20the%20power%20of%20the%20human%20spirit.

Allen, Michael. *Politics of Global Industries: Toward New Images of World Politics and World Society* (In progress, under review).

Anderson, F. (ed). *Bacon: The New Organon.* New York: Macmillan, 1960.

Arbab, Farzam. 'Promoting a Discourse on Science, Religion, and Development', in Sharon Harper (ed), *The Lab, the Temple and the Market: Reflections at the Intersection of Science, Religion and Development.* Ottawa, CA: International Development Research Centre, 2000.

Aristotle. *Nicomachean Ethics.* Trans. and ed. Roger Crisp. Cambridge University Press, 2000.

Bahá'í International Community. *Century of Light.* Wilmette, IL: Bahá'í Publishing Trust, 2000.

— *The Prosperity of Humankind* (1995). https://www.bic.org/statements/prosperity-humankind.

— 'Religious Values and the Measurement of Poverty and Prosperity', paper prepared for the workshop 'Values, Norms and Poverty: A Consultation on the World Development Report 2000', Johannesburg, South Africa, 12 January 1999. This workshop was co-sponsored by the World Bank, the World Faiths Development Dialogue, Cornell University, the MacArthur Foundation, the Swedish International Development Cooperation Agency, and the Swiss Development Corporation.

Bahá'u'lláh. Online sources of the following works by Bahá'u'lláh are available at https://www.bahai.org/library.

— *Epistle to the Son of the Wolf.* Trans. Shoghi Effendi. Wilmette, IL: Bahá'í Publishing Trust, rev. ed. 1976.

— *Gleanings from the Writings of Bahá'u'lláh.* Trans. Shoghi Effendi. Wilmette, IL: Bahá'í Publishing Trust, 2nd ed. 1976.

— *The Hidden Words of Bahá'u'lláh.* Trans. Shoghi Effendi. Wilmette, IL: Bahá'í Publishing Trust, 1970; New Delhi: Bahá'í Publishing Trust, 1987.

— *Tablets of Bahá'u'lláh Revealed after the Kitáb-i-Aqdas.* Comp. Research Department of the Universal House of Justice. Haifa: Bahá'í World Centre, 1978.

Balyuzi, H. M. *The Báb: The Herald of the Day of Days.* Oxford: George Ronald, 1973.

Bean, R. B. 'Some Racial Peculiarities of the Negro Brain', in *American Journal of Anatomy,* vol. 5 (1906), pp. 353–415.

Beer, Tommy. 'Top 1% of U.S. Households Hold 15 Times More Wealth than Bottom 50% Combined', in *Forbes,* 8 October 2020.

Bellah, Robert. *The Broken Covenant: American Civil Religion in Time of Trial.* New York: Seabury Press, 1975.

—; Joas, Hans (eds). *The Axial Age and Its Consequences.* New York: Belknap/Harvard, 2012.

Benson, H. *The Relaxation Response.* New York: Avon Books, 1975.

Beras, Erika. 'Goldman Sachs to Invest Billions in Black Women', in *Marketplace*, 12 March 2021.

Bergner, Raymond. 'Love and Barriers to Love', in *American Journal of Psychotherapy*, vol. 54, no. 1 (Winter 2000), p. 3.

Berkowitz, Leonard. *Aggression: Its Causes, Consequences, and Control.* New York: McGraw, 1993.

Bethencourt, Francisco. *Racisms: From the Crusades to the Twentieth Century.* Princeton, NJ: Princeton University Press, 2013.

Blau, Judith; Moncada, Alberto. *Human Rights: Beyond the Liberal Vision.* Lanham, MD: Rowman and Littlefield, 2005.

Boghossian, Paul A. *Fear of Knowledge: Against Relativism and Constructivism.* Oxford: Clarendon Press, 2006.

Brenner, Charles. *An Elementary Textbook of Psychoanalysis.* New York: Anchor Doubleday, 1974.

Brinkmann, Svend. 'The Typology of Moral Ecology', in *Theory & Psychology*, vol. 14 (2001), no. 1, p. 59.

Bushrui, S.; Massoudi, M. *The Spiritual Heritage of the Human Race: An Introduction to the World's Religions.* Oxford: OneWorld, 2010.

Callahan, David. *Between Two Worlds: Realism, Idealism and American Foreign Policy After the Cold War.* New York: Harper, 1994.

Carus, Paul. *The Gospel of Buddha* (1894). London and Chicago: Open Court, 2015.

Cassirer, E. *An Essay on Man: An Introduction to a Philosophy of Human Culture.* New Haven, CT: Yale University Press, 1944.

Cochran, David C. *The Color of Freedom: Race and Contemporary American Liberalism.* Albany, NY: State University of New York Press, 1999.

Confucius. *The Great Learning.* http://classics.mit.edu/Confucius/learning.html.

Conway, Moncure Daniel. *The Sacred Anthology.* New York: Henry Holt,

1874. https://quod.lib.umich.edu/m/moa/AJF2747.0001.001?rgn=main;view=fulltext.

Copernicus, Nikolaus. *On the Revolutions in the Celestial Spheres* (De revolutionibus orbium coelestium, 1543). https://www.wdl.org/en/item/3164/.

Cova, F.; Deonna, J. A. 'Being Moved', in *Philosophical Studies: An International Journal for Philosophy in the Analytic Tradition*, vol. 169, no. 3 (July 2014), pp. 447–66.

Dalai Lama, *Ancient Wisdom, Modern World: Ethics for the New Millennium*. London: Abacus, 2001.

Danesh, Hossain B. *The Psychology of Spirituality*. Victoria, Canada: Paradigm Publishing and Ottawa, Canada: Nine Pines Publishing, 1994.

— *The Psychology of Spirituality: From Divided Self to Integrated Self*. Sterling Publications, 2004.

Dawkins, Richard. *The Selfish Gene* (1976). 40th Anniversary Edition, Oxford: Oxford University Press, 2016.

De Bary, W. T. *The Buddhist Tradition in India, China and Japan*. New York: Vintage, 1972.

Everly, G. S.; Lating, J. M. *A Clinical Guide to the Treatment of Human Stress Response*. New York: Kluwer Academic, 2002.

Fancher, Raymond. *Psychoanalytic Psychology: The Development of Freud's Thought*. New York: Norton, 1973.

Fitts, Dudley; Fitzgerald, Robert. *Sophocles: The Oedipus Cycle*. Trans. 1939. New York: Harcourt Brace, 1977.

Frankfurt, H. G. 'Freedom of the Will and the Concept of a Person', in *Journal of Philosophy*, vol. 68, no. 1 (14 January 1971). www.jstor.org/stable/2024717.

Franklin, C. L. *Sermons and Hymns*. Atlanta International Records, 2005.

Freire, Paolo. *Education for Critical Consciousness*. New York: Continuum, 2005.

Gay, Peter. *The Enlightenment: An Interpretation*. 2 vols. New York: Knopf, 1966, 1969.

Guignon, Charles (ed). *The Good Life: Readings in Philosophy*. Indianapolis: Hackett, 1999.

Haeckel, Ernst. *The Evolution of Man: A Popular Exposition*. New York: Appleton, 1897.

Haidt, J. *The Happiness Hypothesis: Finding Modern Truth in Ancient Wisdom*. New York: Basic Books, 2006.

Hall, A. H.; Gow, K. M.; Penn, M. L. 'Do Chronic Moral Emotions Mediate between Value Congruence and Psychological Health in University Students?', in K. M. Gow and M. J. Celinski (eds), *Wayfinding through Life's Challenges: Coping and Survival*, pp. 519–531. New York: Nova Science, 2011.

Hamlin, J. Kiley; Wynn, Karen; Bloom, Paul. 'Social Evaluation by Preverbal Infants', in *Nature*, vol. 450 (22 November 2007), pp. 557–9.

—;—;—. 'Three-Months-Olds Show a Negativity Bias in their Social Evaluations', in *Developmental Science*, vol. 13 (2010), no. 6, pp. 923–9.

Harari, Yuval. *Sapiens: A Brief History of Humankind*. New York: Harper, 2015.

Hatcher, John S. *The Purpose of Physical Reality*. Wilmette, IL: Bahá'í Publishing Trust, 1987.

—; Hatcher, William S. (eds). *The Law of Love Enshrined*. Oxford: George Ronald, 1996.

Hatcher, William S. *Love, Power, and Justice: The Dynamics of Authentic Morality*. Wilmette, IL: Bahá'í Publishing Trust, 1998, 2002.

—. *Minimalism: A Bridge Between Classical Philosophy and the Bahá'í Revelation*. Hong Kong: Juxta Publishing, 2004.

Henry, William A. 'Beyond the Melting Pot', in *Time*, 9 April 1990.

Herman, Judith L. *Trauma and Recovery: The Aftermath of Violence from Domestic Abuse to Political Terror*. New York: Basic Books, 1992.

Herrick, C. J. *Brains of Rats and Man*. Chicago: University of Chicago Press, 1928.

Higgins, Tracy. 'Anti-Essentialism, Relativism, and Human Rights', in *Harvard Women's Law Journal*, vol. 89 (1996), pp. 111–15.

Hoffmann, J. W.; Benson, H.; Arns, P. A.; Stainbrook, G. L.; Landsberg, L.; Young, J. B.; Gill, A. 'Reduced Sympathetic Nervous System Responsivity Associated with the Relaxation Response', in *Science*, vol. 215 (1982), no. 4529, pp. 190–92.

Hume, David. *Essays, Moral, Political and Literary* (1772, 1777). Ed. Eugene. G. Miller, 1986. https://www.econlib.org/library/LFBooks/ Hume/hmMPL.html.

Hunt, Lynn. *Inventing Human Rights: A History*. New York: W.W. Norton, 2007.

Institute for Studies in Global Prosperity. 'Science, Religion and Development: Some Initial Considerations', 2 November 2008. https://www.globalprosperity.org/resources/.

Internet Encyclopedia of Philosophy. www.iep.utm.edu/s/sophists.htm.

Jacobs, G. D.; Lubar, J. F. 'Spectral Analysis of the Central Nervous System Effects of the Relaxation Response Elicited by Autogenic Training', in *Behavioral Medicine,* vol. 15 (1989), pp. 125–132.

James, William. *The Varieties of Religious Experience: A Study in Human Nature*. London: Longmans, Green, 1902.

Jung, Carl. *The Undiscovered Self.* New York: American Library, 1957.

Kant, Immanuel (1785). *Fundamental Principles of the Metaphysics of Morals.* Trans. Thomas Kingsmill Abbott. http://www.gutenberg.org/ files/5682/5682-h/5682-h.htm#link2H_4_0002.

Kluge, Ian. 'The Aristotelian Substratum of the Bahá'í Writings', in *Lights of 'Irfán: Papers Presented at 'Irfán Colloquia and Seminars,* vol. 10, pp. 17–78. Wilmette, IL: Bahá'í Publishing Trust, 2003.

Koltko-Rivera, M. 'The Psychology of Worldviews', in *Review of General Psychology,* vol. 8 (2004), pp. 3–58.

Kroll, Jerome; Egan, Elizabeth; Erickson, Paul; Carey, Kathleen; Johnson, Myles. 'Moral Conflict, Religiosity and Neuroticism in an Outpatient Sample', in *Journal of Nervous and Mental Disease,* vol. 192 (2004), no. 10, pp. 682–88.

Kumar, Alok. *Ancient Hindu Science: Its Transmission and Impact on World Cultures*. Morgan & Claypool, 2019.

Kumarajiva. *Sutra on the Concentration of Sitting Meditation.* Trans. N.Yamabe and F. Sueki. Berkeley, CA: Numata Center for Buddhist Translation and Research, 2009.

Lao-Tzu. *Tao Te Ching.* Trans. Jonathan Star. Tarcher Cornerstone Editions, 2001.

Lazar, S.W.; Bush, G.; Gollub, R. L.; Fricchione, G. L.; Khalsa, G.; Benson, H. 'Functional Brain Mapping of the Relaxation Response and Meditation', in *NeuroReport*, vol. 11, no. 7 (May 2000).

Lee, H. J.; Pak, M.; Song, H.; Lee, H.; Kim, S.; Jeong, H. 'Mysterious Coherence in Several-megasparsec Scales between Galaxy Rotation and Neighbor Motion', in *The Astrophysical Journal*, vol. 884, no. 2 (20 October 2019). https://iopscience.iop.org/article/10.3847/1538-4357/ab3fa3.

Lewis, Thomas; Amini, Fari; Lannon, Richard. *A General Theory of Love*. New York: Vintage, 2000.

Livingston, R. B. 'How Man Looks at His Own Brain: An Adventure Shared by Psychology and Neurology', in S. Koch (ed), *Biologically Oriented Fields. Psychology: A Study of Science*, New York: McGraw Hill, 1967.

Maharshi, R. *The Collected Works of Ramana Maharshi*. Ed. A. Osborne. York Beach, ME: Red Wheel Weiser, 1997.

Margulis, Lynn; Sagan, Dorion. *What is Life?* University of California Press, 2000.

Markus, H.; Nurius, P. (1986). 'Possible Selves', in *American Psychologist*, vol. 41 (1986), no. 9, pp. 954–69.

McMahan, D. *The Making of Buddhist Modernism*. Oxford: Oxford University Press, 2008.

Nabíl-i-A'zam (Muḥammad-i-Zarandí). *The Dawn-Breakers: Nabíl's Narrative of the Early Days of the Bahá'í Revelation*. Trans. Shoghi Effendi. Wilmette, IL: Bahá'í Publishing Trust, 1932.

Nasseri, A.; Penn, M. *Moral Trauma: An Analysis of Akrasia and Mental Health*. Verlag Academic, 2015.

Neihardt, J. *Black Elk Speaks: Being the Life Story of a Holy Man of the Oglala Sioux*. Albany, NY: State University of New York Press, 2008.

New York Times. 'Fear, and Discord, among Asian Americans over Attacks in San Francisco', 18 July 2021.

Noguchi, L.; Hanson, H.; Lample, P. *Exploring a Framework for Moral Education*. West Palm Beach, FL: Palabra Publications, 1992.

O'Hear, Anthony. *Beyond Evolution: Human Nature and the Limits of Evolutionary Explanation*. Oxford: Oxford University Press, 1997.

Otto, Rudolf. *The Idea of the Holy* (1917). Trans. John W. Harvey. Oxford: Oxford University Press, 1968.

'Pañcavaggi Sutta: Five Brethren' (SN 22.59). Trans. Thanissaro Bhikkhu. In *Access to Insight*, 29 June 2010. http://www.accesstoinsight.org/tipitaka/sn/sn22/sn22.059.than.html .

Paul, R.; Elder, L. *Critical Thinking: Concepts and Tools*. Foundation for Critical Thinking Press, 2009. www.criticalthinking.org.

Penn, M. L. 'Values and Human Rights: Implications of an Emerging Discourse on Virtue Ethics', in H. Mahmoudi, A. Brysk, and K. Seaman (eds), *The Changing Ethos of Human Rights*. Cheltenham, UK: Edward Elgar, 2020.

—; Malik, A. 'The Protection and Development of the Human Spirit: An Expanded Focus for Human Rights Discourse', in *Human Rights Quarterly*, vol. 32 (2010), pp. 666–90.

—; Pharaon, A. (2007). 'Biological, Psychological, and Social Factors in the Pathogenesis of Psychopathy', in G. Walker (ed), *The Science of Morality*, pp. 105–16. London: Royal College of Physicians, 2007.

—; Wilson, L. 'Mind, Medicine and Metaphysics: Reflections on the Reclamation of the Human Spirit', in *American Journal of Psychotherapy*, vol. 57 (2003), pp. 18–31.

Pickett, Kate; Wilkinson, Richard. *The Spirit Level: Why More Equal Societies Almost Always Do Better*. London: Allen Lane; New York: Bloomsbury, 2009.

Pinker, Steven. *The Better Angels of Our Nature: Why Violence Has Declined*. New York: Penguin, 2011.

Popkin, Richard. 'The Philosophical Bases of Modern Racism', in R. A. Watson and J. E. Force (eds), *The High Road to Pyrrhonism: Studies in Hume and Scottish Philosophy* (San Diego: Austin Hill, 1980), vol. 2, pp. 79–102. The article first appeared in E. Pagliaro, *Racism in the Eighteenth Century* (Cleveland: Case Western Reserve University Press, 1973), pp. 254–62.

Popper, Karl. *The Poverty of Historicism*. Boston: Beacon Press, 1957.

Porges, S. (2011). *The Polyvagal Theory: Neurophysiological Foundations of Emotions, Attachment, Communication, Self-Regulation*. New York: Norton, 2011.

Pretorius, P. J. 'A Foundation for Physiology', in *Medical Hypotheses*, vol. 31, no. 2 (February 1990).

Rana, Zat. 'The Invisible Strings: How to See the World Like Nobody Else', online article in *Medium*, 11 February 2020, at: https://medium.com/personal-growth/the-invisible-strings-how-to-see-the-world-like-nobody-else-1b7ede14baeb.

Regier, Willis G. (ed). *Masterpieces of American Indian Literature*. New York: MJF Books, 1993.

Richards, I. A. *Mencius on the Mind*. The International Library of Psychology, Philosophy and Scientific Method. London: Routledge & Kegan Paul, 1932.

Savi, Julio. *The Eternal Quest for God*. Oxford: George Ronald, 1989.

Schrag, Calvin O. 'The Topology of Hope', in *Humanitas*, vol. 13 (1977).

Schulz, W. F. *In Our Best Interest: How Defending Human Rights Benefits Us All*. Boston, MA: Beacon Press, 2002.

Shantideva. This prayer is available in many translations. https://wexnermedical.osu.edu/-/media/files/wexnermedical/patient-care/patient-and-visitor-guide/patient-support-services/spiritual-and-pastoral-care/faith-specific-prayers/buddhism/shantideva-prayer.pdf?la=en&hash=F923D9653029AE6F78966589CEC84F2D50201776.

Sherif, M. *In Common Predicament*. Boston, MA: Houghton Mifflin, 1966.

Shoghi Effendi. *The Advent of Divine Justice* (1939). Wilmette, IL: Bahá'í Publishing Trust, 1984.

— *Arohanui: Letters from Shoghi Effendi to New Zealand*. Suva, Fiji: Bahá'í Publishing Trust, 1982.

— *Bahá'í Administration: Selected Messages 1922–1932*. Wilmette, IL: Bahá'í Publishing Trust, 1980.

— *The World Order of Bahá'u'lláh: Selected Letters by Shoghi Effendi* (1938). Wilmette, IL: Bahá'í Publishing Trust, 2nd rev. ed. 1974.

Smith, Huston. *The World's Religions*. New York: HarperOne, 1991.

— *Why Religion Matters: The Fate of the Human Spirit in an Age of Disbelief*. New York: HarperCollins, 2001.

Spykman, Nicholas. *America's Strategy in World Politics: The United States as the Balance of Power.* New York: Harcourt, 1942.

Stafford, Kim. *The Muses Among Us: Eloquent Listening and Other Pleasures of the Writer's Craft.* Athens, GA: The University of Georgia Press, 2003.

Stanton, W. *The Leopard's Spots: Scientific Attitudes Towards Race in America, 1815–1859.* Chicago: University of Chicago Press, 1960.

Star of the West: The Bahai Magazine. Periodical, 25 vols. 1910–1935. Vols. 1–14 RP Oxford: George Ronald, 1978. Complete CD-ROM version: Talisman Educational Software/Special Ideas, 2001.

Statman, D. *Virtue Ethics: A Critical Reader.* Washington, DC: Georgetown University Press, 2007.

Sunrise Projects. *Truth is One* (2011). Available at: http://www.1844sunrise projects.com.

Swaab, Dick F. *We Are Our Brains: A Neurobiography of the Brain from the Womb to Alzheimer's.* Trans. Jane Hedley-Prole. New York: Random House, 2014.

Szasz, Thomas. *The Myth of Mental Illness: Foundations of a Theory of Personal Conduct.* New York: Harper, 1974.

Taylor, Charles. 'Modern Social Imaginaries', in *Public Culture*, vol. 14, no. 1 (Winter 2002).

Taylor, E. 'Introduction', in S. Donovan and M. Murphy, *The Physical and Psychological Effects of Meditation: A Review of Contemporary Research with a Comprehensive Bibliography, 1931–1996*, 2nd ed., pp. 1–23. Sausalito, CA: Institute of Noetic Sciences, 1997.

Taylor, G. *Pride, Shame, and Guilt: Emotions of Self-Assessment.* Oxford: Clarendon Press, 1985.

Thomas, Alexander; Sillen, Samuel. *Racism & Psychiatry.* Secaucus, NJ: Citadel Press, 1979.

Toynbee, Arnold J. *A Study of History.* 12 vols. Oxford: Oxford University Press, 1934–1961.

Universal House of Justice, The. *The Constitution of the Universal House of Justice.* Haifa: Bahá'í World Centre, 1972.

— *Framework for Action: Selected Messages of the Universal House of Justice and Supplementary Material, 2006–2016.* West Palm Beach, FL: Palabra Publications, 2017.

— *Our Common Humanity.* https://reference.bahai.org/en/t/b/.

Wallace, A. *Mind in the Balance: Meditation in Science, Buddhism and Christianity.* New York: Columbia University Press, 2009.

Wilson, Edward O. *On Human Nature.* Cambridge, MA: Harvard University Press, 1978.

Wolfe, Tom. *The Kingdom of Speech.* New York: Little, Brown, 2016.

Zajonc, A. *Catching the Light: The Entwined History of Light and Mind.* Oxford: Oxford University Press, 1993.

Zarqání, Mírzá Maḥmúd. *Maḥmúd's Diary: The Diary of Mírzá Maḥmud-i-Zarqání Chronicling 'Abdu'l-Bahá's Journey to America.* Trans. Mohi Sobhani with the assistance of Shirley Macias. Oxford: George Ronald, 1998.

NOTES AND REFERENCES

Preface

1 Freire, *Education for Critical Consciousness*, pp. 4–5.
2 See Penn and Malik, 'The Protection and Development of the Human Spirit: An Expanded Focus for Human Rights Discourse.'
3 See Penn and Pharaon, 'Biological, Psychological, and Social Factors in the Pathogenesis of Psychopathy.'
4 See Penn and Wilson, 'Mind, Medicine and Metaphysics: Reflections on the Reclamation of the Human Spirit.'

Introduction

1 See William Hatcher, *Love, Power, and Justice: The Dynamics of Authentic Morality* (2002).
2 Danesh, *The Psychology of Spirituality: From Divided Self to Integrated Self* (2000).
3 Savi, *The Eternal Quest for God* (1989).
4 William Hatcher, *Love, Power, and Justice: The Dynamics of Authentic Morality* (2002).
5 See Tom Wolfe's engaging discussion of the enigma of human language in *The Kingdom of Speech* (2016).
6 Bahá'u'lláh, *Gleanings from the Writings of Bahá'u'lláh*, LXXXII, p. 158.
7 Bahá'u'lláh, the Founder of the Bahá'í Faith, has written, 'Verily I say, the human soul is, in its essence, one of the signs of God, a mystery among His mysteries. It is one of the mighty signs of the Almighty, the harbinger that proclaimeth the reality of all the worlds of God. Within it lieth concealed that which the world is now utterly incapable of apprehending' (ibid. p. 160).
8 Zajonc, *Catching the Light: The Entwined History of Light and Mind*, pp. 2–3.
9 It is interesting to note that gravitational waves, which are

disturbances in the curvature of space/time, and which were hypothesized to exist in 1916 by Albert Einstein, were only actually observed and measured a century later in February 2016. Confidence in the existence of such waves was thus not a result of physical observation of the senses, but of a kind of reasoning that is achieved only by human beings. Here, and in a chapter that follows, we suggest that this type of reasoning is, itself, evidence of the unique powers of the human spirit.

10 'Abdu'l-Bahá, *Some Answered Questions,* ch. 55, p. 242.

11 ibid.

12 'Abdu'l-Bahá, Tablet to August Forel.

13 Bahá'u'lláh, *Gleanings from the Writings of Bahá'u'lláh,* LXXX, pp. 153–4.

14 'Abdu'l-Bahá, quoted in Zarqání, *Maḥmúd's Diary,* p. 195.

15 'Abdu'l-Bahá, *Selections from the Writings of 'Abdu'l-Bahá,* no. 143, p. 167.

16 'Abdu'l-Bahá, quoted in *Star of the West,* vol. 7, no. 19 (2 March 1917), p. 190.

17 Shoghi Effendi, *Arohanui: Letters from Shoghi Effendi to New Zealand,* p. 89.

18 See Kluge, 'The Aristotelian Substratum of the Bahá'í Writings', in *Lights of 'Irfán,* vol. 10, no. 4, pp. 17–78.

19 According to Carnot's principle, order is improbable while disorder is probable. This is the case because order represents a limited number of stable configurations (e.g. a brick house), whereas any possible configuration represents disorder (e.g. a pile of bricks).

20 'Abdu'l-Bahá, *Selections from the Writings of 'Abdu'l-Bahá,* no. 163, pp. 193–4.

21 From a Bahá'í perspective, there are at least three expressions of the 'good'. The first is revealed in the attributes of God. These attributes are reflected both in nature and in human behaviour; when manifested in human behaviour they are called 'virtues'. In the same way that we are attracted to nature because of its intrinsic beauty, the human heart is attracted to virtues because of their beauty. A second way that the good is conceptualized relates to the transcendent spiritual teachings that animate the lives of the founders of the world's religions and that are left in the form of the sacred texts and writings that express the love, knowledge, and will of God to humanity and around which a great civilization forms. Last, in the Bahá'í view, the good is expressed by social institutions

whose policies and practices seek to protect and advance social justice.

22 Noguchi, Hanson, and Lample (1992), *Exploring a Framework for Moral Education*, p. 5.
23 'Abdu'l-Bahá, *The Promulgation of Universal Peace*, p. 448.
24 ibid. pp. 175–6.
25 ibid. p. 239.
26 'Abdu'l-Bahá, *Paris Talks*, no. 29, p. 88.
27 ibid. p. 57.

1 The Capacity to Know

1 Noguchi, Hanson, and Lample, *Exploring a Framework for Moral Education*, p. 5.
2 'Abdu'l-Bahá, *Some Answered Questions,* ch. 55, pp. 241–2.
3 From Bahá'u'lláh, 'Lawḥ-i-Hikmat', in *Tablets of Bahá'u'lláh*, pp. 146–7.
4 See: *A Brief History of the Idea of Critical Thinking*, at www.criticalthinking.org.
5 ibid.
6 'Abdu'l-Bahá, *Paris Talks,* no. 40, p. 131.
7 From the *Internet Encyclopedia of Philosophy*, at www.iep.utm.edu/s/sophists.htm.
8 Bahá'u'lláh, *Gleanings from the Writings of Bahá'u'lláh.* CXXXIX, p. 304.
9 Matt. 5:8.
10 See: http://plato.stanford.edu/entries/aquinas.
11 'Abdu'l-Bahá, *The Promulgation of Universal Peace*, p. 231.
12 'Abdu'l-Bahá, *Paris Talks,* no. 44, pp. 148–9.
13 'Abdu'l-Bahá, *Abdul Baha on Divine Philosophy*, p. 102.
14 See Arbab, 'Promoting a Discourse on Science, Religion, and Development' (2000) for a discussion of this theme.
15 See: 'Abdu'l-Bahá, 'Intelligible Realities and Their Expression Through Sensible Forms', in *Some Answered Questions*, ch. 16, p. 94.
16 Anderson, *Bacon: The New Organon*, p. viii.
17 William Hatcher, *Minimalism: A Bridge Between Classical Philosophy and the Bahá'í Revelation* (2004), p. 9.
18 See Gay, *The Enlightenment: An Interpretation* (2 vols. 1966, 1969).
19 'Abdu'l-Bahá, *Paris Talks*, no. 44, pp. 147–8.
20 See Boghossian, *Fear of Knowledge: Against Relativism and Constructivism* (2006) for a thoughtful discussion of this perspective.

21 'Abdu'l-Bahá, *The Secret of Divine Civilization*, pp. 2–3.
22 Paul and Elder, *Critical Thinking: Concepts and Tools* (2009), pp. 14–15.
23 Confucius, *The Great Learning*.

2 The Capacity to Love

1 'Abdu'l-Bahá, *Selections from the Writings of 'Abdu'l-Bahá*, no. 12, p. 27.
2 For a discussion see Margulis and Sagan, *What is Life?* (2000).
3 Lewis, Amini, and Lannon, *A General Theory of Love* (2000), p. 23.
4 ibid. pp. 25–6.
5 ibid. p. 26.
6 As quoted in Bergner, 'Love and Barriers to Love', in *American Journal of Psychotherapy*, vol. 54, no. 1 (Winter, 2000), p. 3.
7 ibid. p. 3.
8 William S. Hatcher, *Love, Power, and Justice: The Dynamics of Authentic Morality*.
9 'Abdu'l-Bahá, *Selections from the Writings of 'Abdu'l-Bahá*, no. 236, p. 318.
10 William S. Hatcher, *Love, Power, and Justice: The Dynamics of Authentic Morality*, p. 69.
11 'Abdu'l-Bahá, *Selections from the Writings of 'Abdu'l-Bahá*, no. 34, p. 69.
12 Lao-Tzu, *Tao Te Ching*, verse 4, p. 5.
13 ibid. verse 34, p. 45.
14 ibid. verse 9, p. 10.
15 Brinkmann, 'The Typology of Moral Ecology', in *Theory & Psychology*, vol. 14, no. 1 (2001), p. 59.
16 Institute for Studies in Global Prosperity, *Science, Religion and Development: Some Initial Considerations*, p. 1.
17 Bahá'í International Community, 'Religious Values and the Measurement of Poverty and Prosperity' (1999).
18 The Universal House of Justice serves as a nine-member elected body that is responsible for guiding and protecting the development of the Bahá'í world community. In addition to serving the Bahá'ís of the world, its Constitution requires it to 'do its utmost for the realization of greater cordiality and comity amongst the nations and for the attainment of universal peace; and to foster that which is conducive to the enlightenment and illumination of the souls of men and the advancement and betterment of the world'.

19   The Universal House of Justice, *Century of Light*, pp. 135–6.
20   ibid. pp. 89–90.
21   Message from the Universal House of Justice to the Bahá'ís of Iran, 2 April 2010, authorized English translation in Bahá'í Reference Library (www.bahai.org).
22   Message from the Universal House of Justice to the Bahá'ís of Iran, 2 March 2013, in *Framework for Action*, no. 23, p. 152.
23   Hysteria was to later become a wide variety of trauma-related disorders, including dissociative states, PTSD, Borderline Personality Disorder, psychoneuro-immunological disorders, and so forth.
24   See Herman, *Trauma and Recovery: The Aftermath of Violence – from Domestic Abuse to Political Terror* (1992) for a thoughtful exploration of these themes.
25   'Abdu'l-Bahá, *Tablets of Abdul-Baha Abbas*, vol. II, p. 309.
26   Porges, *The Polyvagal Theory: Neurophysiological Foundations of Emotions, Attachment, Communication, Self-Regulation* (2011), p. 11.
27   'Abdu'l-Bahá, *Paris Talks*, no. 15, pp. 46–6.

3 The Nature of Will

1   'Abdu'l-Bahá, *The Promulgation of Universal Peace*, p. 17.
2   Danesh, *The Psychology of Spirituality*, pp. 45–6.
3   See for example Higgins, 'Anti-Essentialism, Relativism, and Human Rights', in *Harvard Women's Law Journal* (1996), pp. 89–105, 111–15.
4   William Hatcher, 'The Kitáb-i-Aqdas: The Causality Principle', in Hatcher and Hatcher (eds), *The Law of Love Enshrined* (1996), p. 117.
5   Herrick, *Brains of Rats and Man* (1928), quoted in Livingston, 'How Man Looks at His Own Brain: An Adventure Shared by Psychology and Neurology' (1967).
6   See Statman, *Virtue Ethics: A Critical Reader* (2007); Penn, 'Values and Human Rights: Implications of an Emerging Discourse on Virtue Ethics', in Mahmoudi, Brysk, and Seaman (eds), *The Changing Ethos of Human Rights* (2020).
7   Aristotle, *Nicomachean Ethics*, p. 30.
8   Penn and Malik, 'The Protection and Development of the Human Spirit: An Expanded Focus for Human Rights Discourse', in *Human Rights Quarterly*, vol. 32 (2010), pp. 668–9.

9 While freedom consists in the liberty to choose among options, autonomy is the capacity to choose from among options that which would most contribute to one's well-being, development, and long-term interests.

10 Bahá'u'lláh, *Gleanings from the Writings of Bahá'u'lláh*, XCVI, p. 196.

11 Bahá'u'lláh, *Tablets of Bahá'u'lláh*, p. 125.

12 Bahá'u'lláh, *Hidden Words*, Arabic no. 2.

13 Bahá'u'lláh, *Tablets of Bahá'u'lláh*, p. 67.

14 'Abdu'l-Bahá, *Paris Talks*, no. 23, p. 68.

15 Letter on behalf of the Universal House of Justice, 5 June 1993.

16 For a discussion of the Axial Age, see Bellah and Joas (eds), *The Axial Age and Its Consequences* (2012).

17 Aristotle, *Nicomachean Ethics*.

18 See Nasseri and Penn, *Moral Trauma: An Analysis of Akrasia and Mental Health* (2015); Hall, Gow, and Penn, 'Do Chronic Moral Emotions Mediate between Value Congruence and Psychological Health in University Students?' (2011).

19 Kroll et al., 'Moral Conflict, Religiosity and Neuroticism in an Outpatient Sample', in *Journal of Nervous and Mental Disease*, vol. 192, no. 10 (2004), pp. 682–8.

20 See Taylor, *Pride, Shame, and Guilt: Emotions of Self-Assessment* (1985).

21 As quoted in Haidt, *The Happiness Hypothesis: Finding Modern Truth in Ancient Wisdom* (2006).

22 Markus and Nurius, 'Possible Selves', in *American Psychologist*, vol. 41, no. 9 (1986), pp. 954–69.

23 One might also note that these emotions are simply feedback about a condition of internal conflict, and are thus neither good nor bad in themselves, but rather information that can be utilized to achieve desired objectives.

24 Frankfurt, 'Freedom of the Will and the Concept of a Person', in *Journal of Philosophy*, vol. 68, no. 1, p. 12.

4 The Psychoanalytic Perspective

1 Fitts and Fitzgerald, *Sophocles: The Oedipus Cycle* (1977).

2 Fancher, *Psychoanalytic Psychology: The Development of Freud's Thought* (1973).

3 Herman, *Trauma and Recovery* (1992), p. 11.

4 As quoted ibid. p. 13.

5   Herman observes that within a year of the publication of his work, Freud had reluctantly repudiated the traumatic theory of the origins of hysteria: 'His correspondence makes clear that he was increasingly troubled by the radical social implications of this hypothesis. Hysteria was so common among women that if his patients' stories were true, and if his theory were correct, he would be forced to conclude that what he called "perverted acts against children" were endemic, not only among the proletariat of Paris, where he first studied hysteria, but also among the respectable bourgeois families of Vienna . . . This idea was simply unacceptable. It was beyond credibility' (p. 14).

6   See Penn and Wilson, 'Mind, Medicine and Metaphysics: Reflections on the Reclamation of the Human Spirit', pp. 18–31.

7   In his hugely popular work *An Elementary Textbook of Psychoanalysis* (1974), Charles Brenner renders this point sufficiently clear: 'Two . . . fundamental hypotheses which have been abundantly confirmed are the principle of psychic determinism, or causality, and the proposition that consciousness is an exceptional rather than a regular attribute of psychic processes. Let us start with the principle of psychic determinism. The sense of this principle is that in the mind, as in physical nature about us, nothing happens by chance, or in a random way. Each psychic event is determined by the ones which preceded it . . . In fact, mental phenomena are no more capable of . . . a lack of causal connection with what preceded them than are physical ones. Discontinuity in this sense does not exist in mental life' (p. 2). Commenting on this assumption, the noted psychiatrist and philosopher Thomas Szasz observed: 'It is obvious . . . that not only psychoanalysis but also much of traditional modern psychiatry theory assumes that personal conduct is determined by prior personal historical events. All these theories downgrade and even negate explanations of behavior in terms of freedom, choice, and responsibility' (*The Myth of Mental Illness: Foundations of a Theory of Personal Conduct* (1974), p. 5).

8   Popper, *The Poverty of Historicism* (1957).

9   Schrag, 'The Topology of Hope', in *Humanitas*, vol. 13 (1977), p. 269.

10 ibid.

11 Fitts and Fitzgerald, *Sophocles: The Oedipus Cycle*, p. 4.

12 Indeed, in this trilogy Sophocles has brilliantly chosen to hide from the reader much important information about Oedipus's

family history in order to show us that there are many things about ourselves that impact our lives but are hidden from us. Sophocles achieves this by telling us a great deal about Oedipus's father and about the House of Cadmos from which he comes, not in the Oedipus trilogy itself, but in another work.

13 Fitts and Fitzgerald, *Sophocles: The Oedipus Cycle*, p. 43.
14 ibid. pp. 90–91.
15 ibid. p. 190.

5 The View of Evolutionary Psychology and Neuroscience

1 Dawkins, *The Selfish Gene* (1976), p. 2.
2 ibid.
3 See Koltko-Rivera, 'The Psychology of Worldviews', in *Review of General Psychology*, vol. 8 (2004), pp. 3–58.
4 O'Hear, *Beyond Evolution: Human Nature and the Limits of Evolutionary Explanation* (1997), p. 3.
5 ibid.
6 ibid.
7 Harari, *Sapiens: A Brief History of Humankind* (2015), p. 24.

6 Discourses on the Problem of Evil

1 See Franklin, *Sermons and Hymns* (2005).
2 Guignon (ed), *The Good Life: Readings in Philosophy* (1999), p. 19.
3 ibid. p. 18.
4 'Abdu'l-Bahá, *The Secret of Divine Civilization*, pp. 59–60.
5 Sherif, *In Common Predicament* (1966), p. 90.
6 Henry, 'Beyond the Melting Pot', in *Time,* 9 April 1990, p. 28.

7 The Journey Out of the Racial Divide

1 See Popkin, 'The Philosophical Bases of Modern Racism' (1973), in Watson and Force (eds), *The High Road to Pyrrhonism: Studies in Hume and Scottish Philosophy*, vol. 2, pp. 79–102.
2 ibid.
3 Bethencourt, *Racism: From the Crusades to the Twentieth Century* (2013).
4 Thomas and Sillen, *Racism and Psychiatry* (1979), pp. 1–2.
5 As quoted in Popkin, 'The Philosophical Bases of Modern Racism', p. 93.
6 Hume, *Essays, Moral, Political and Literary.*

7   See Stanton, *The Leopard's Spots: Scientific Attitudes Towards Race in America, 1815–1859* (1960).

8   Bean, 'Some Racial Peculiarities of the Negro Brain', in *American Journal of Anatomy*, vol. 5 (1906), pp. 353–415.

9   ibid.

10 *New York Times*, 'Fear, and Discord, among Asian Americans over Attacks in San Francisco', 18 July 2021.

11 Lee et al., 'Mysterious Coherence in Several-megasparsec Scales between Galaxy Rotation and Neighbor Motion', in *The Astrophysical Journal*, vol. 884, no. 2 (20 October 2019), p. 104.

12 Rana, 'The Invisible Strings: How to See the World Like Nobody Else', online article in *Medium*, 11 February 2020.

13 Shoghi Effendi, *The Advent of Divine Justice* (1939), pp. 33–4.

14 Letter on behalf of Shoghi Effendi to the Bahá'í Inter-Racial Teaching Committee, 27 May 1957, in *Lights of Guidance*, no. 1816, p. 534.

15 Bahá'í International Community, *The Prosperity of Humankind*.

16 Schulz, *In Our Best Interest: How Defending Human Rights Benefits Us All* (2002), p. 3.

8 Ideological Arguments that Seek to Justify and Sustain the Practice of War

1   Callahan, *Between Two Worlds: Realism, Idealism and American Foreign Policy After the Cold War* (1994).

2   Lippmann, as quoted in Callahan, ibid. p. 40.

3   ibid. p. 42.

4   Spykman, *America's Strategy in World Politics: The United States as the Balance of Power* (1942), p. 488.

5   Most notably Joseph Nye, Richard Falk, Robert Keohane, Zbigniew Brzezinski, and David Callahan, among others.

6   Henry Kissinger, quoted in Callahan, *Between Two Worlds*, pp. 188–9.

7   Allen, *Politics of Global Industries: Toward New Images of World Politics and World Society* (under review).

8   ibid.

9   Callahan, *Between Two Worlds*, p. 2.

10 Bahá'u'lláh, quoted in Shoghi Effendi, *The World Order of Bahá'u'lláh*, p. 40.

11 ibid. pp. 40–41.

12 Bahá'í International Community, *The Prosperity of Humankind*, para. 7.

13 Shoghi Effendi, *The World Order of Bahá'u'lláh*, p. 45.

14 For a review of literature on this subject, see Berkowitz, *Aggression: Its Causes, Consequences, and Control* (1993).

15 Pinker, *The Better Angels of Our Nature: Why Violence Has Declined* (2011), p. 69.

16 ibid. p. 72.

17 ibid. p. 83.

18 ibid. p. 133.

19 It should be noted that this concept of human development is not the same as the now discredited notion that 'ontogeny recapitulates phylogeny' first articulated by Ernst Haeckel in the late 1800s (in *The Evolution of Man: A Popular Exposition*). This view suggests not that individual biological development in the womb mirrors the phylogenetic evolution of the species but, rather, that the stages in humanity's collective psychosocial development are roughly analogous to the psychosocial development of an individual.

20 Bahá'í International Community, *The Prosperity of Humankind*, para. 7.

9 Neo-Liberal Obstacles to Addressing Universal Human Needs

1 Blau and Moncada, *Human Rights: Beyond the Liberal Vision* (2005), p. 1.

2 ibid.

3 ibid. p. 2.

4 Cochran, *The Color of Freedom: Race and Contemporary American Liberalism* (1999), p. 6.

5 ibid. p. 8.

6 Blau and Moncada, *Human Rights*, p. 16.

7 ibid.

8 Taylor, 'Modern Social Imaginaries', in *Public Culture*, vol. 14, no. 1 (Winter 2002), p. 92.

9 See Beer, 'Top 1% of U.S. Households Hold 15 Times More Wealth than Bottom 50% Combined', in *Forbes*, 8 October 2020.

10 Beras, 'Goldman Sachs to Invest Billions in Black Women', in *Marketplace*, 12 March 2021.

10 The Inner Life

1 Stafford, *The Muses Among Us: Eloquent Listening and Other Pleasures of the Writer's Craft* (2003), p. 1.

2 From George Wallace's Inaugural Address as Governor.

3   Dalai Lama, *Ancient Wisdom, Modern World: Ethics for the New Millennium* (2001). Boston, MA: Little Brown & Company, p. 23.

4   Kant, *Fundamental Principles of the Metaphysics of Morals* (1785), pp. 17–18.

5   Neihardt, *Black Elk Speaks: Being the Life Story of a Holy Man of the Oglala Sioux* (2008), pp. 5–6.

6   ibid.

7   Bahá'u'lláh, *Hidden Words*, Persian no. 5.

8   Bahá'u'lláh, *Gleanings from the Writings of Bahá'u'lláh,* CLIII, p. 328.

9   Bellah, *The Broken Covenant: American Civil Religion in Time of Trial* (1975), p. ix.

10   ibid. p. x.

11   Smith, *Why Religion Matters: The Fate of the Human Spirit in an Age of Disbelief* (2001), p. 52.

11 The Logic of Prayer and Meditation

1   'Abdu'l-Bahá, in most Bahá'í prayer books.

2   Shantideva.

3   Translated by Chief Yellow Lark, http://aktalakota.stjo.org/site/News2?page=NewsArticle&id=8580.

4   'Abdu'l-Bahá, in *Bahá'í Prayers* (section 'Mankind'.) Also available at Bahá'í Reference Library, and https://www.bahaiprayers.org/mankind5.htm.

5   Matt. 6: 9–13 (King James Version).

6   See Everly and Lating, *A Clinical Guide to the Treatment of Human Stress Response* (2002); Taylor, 'Introduction', in Donovan and Murphy, *The Physical and Psychological Effects of Meditation: A Review of Contemporary Research with a Comprehensive Bibliography, 1931–1996*, pp. 1–23.

7   See Maharshi, *The Collected Works of Ramana Maharshi* (1997).

8   Existential suffering is a special kind of suffering that only humans face because of the complex inner world that is made possible by the reach of human consciousness. Unlike other animals, we may stress over events that have never occurred and will never occur; we may stress over the things that we have done or failed to do; or we may stress over the kind of person that we have become, or the kind of person that we wish we were. Existential suffering thus emerges either from our 'way of being' in the world, or from the ways that we think. It is this form of suffering that the world's wisdom traditions have sought, most deeply, to address.

9   See Wallace, *Mind in the Balance: Meditation in Science, Buddhism and Christianity* (2009).

10   See Kumarajiva, *Sutra on the Concentration of Sitting Meditation* (2009).

11   As quoted in De Bary, *The Buddhist Tradition in India, China and Japan* (1972), p. 100.

12   'Pañcavaggi Sutta: Five Brethren'(SN 22.59), in *Access to Insight*, 29 June 2010.

13   Taylor, 'Introduction', op. cit.

14   See McMahan, *The Making of Buddhist Modernism* (2008).

15   Taylor, 'Introduction', op. cit.

16   ibid.

17   Jung, *The Undiscovered Self* (1957).

18   Hoffmann et al., 'Reduced Sympathetic Nervous System Responsivity Associated with the Relaxation Response', in *Science*, vol. 215 (1982), no. 4529, pp. 190–92.

19   Benson, *The Relaxation Response* (1975), pp. 114–15.

20   Jacobs and Lubar, 'Spectral Analysis of the Central Nervous System Effects of the Relaxation Response Elicited by Autogenic Training', in *Behavioral Medicine*, vol. 15 (1989), pp. 125–132.

21   Lazar et al., 'Functional Brain Mapping of the Relaxation Response and Meditation', in *NeuroReport*, vol. 11, no. 7 (May 2000).

22   'Abdu'l-Bahá, *Paris Talks*, no. 54, p. 187.

23   ibid. pp. 187–8.

24   ibid. p. 188.

12 Consultation: An Instrument of Personal and Social Transformation

1   The four fundamental powers of nature include the strong nuclear force, the weak nuclear force, electromagnetic energy, and gravity. All the other natural forces are believed to be derived from these; and as noted earlier, the three powers of consciousness include the power to know, love, and will.

2   'Abdu'l-Bahá, quoted in a letter from Shoghi Effendi to the Bahá'ís of the United States and Canada, 5 March 1922, in Shoghi Effendi, *Bahá'í Administration*, p. 21.

3   ibid. p. 22; also in 'Abdu'l-Bahá, *Selections from the Writings of 'Abdu'l-Bahá*, no. 45, p. 88.

4   Cova and Deonna, 'Being Moved', in *Philosophical Studies: An International Journal for Philosophy in the Analytic Tradition*, vol. 169, no. 3 (July 2014), pp. 447–66.

5   ibid. p. 450.
6   ibid. p. 451.
7   'Abdu'l-Bahá, *The Promulgation of Universal Peace*, p. 56.
8   Bahá'u'lláh, *Tablets of Bahá'u'lláh*, p. 173.

13 A Final Word: Humanity's Spiritual Heritage

1   Cassirer, *An Essay on Man: An Introduction to a Philosophy of Human Culture* (1944), pp. 42–3.
2   See for example Bushrui and Massoudi (eds), *The Spiritual Heritage of the Human Race: An Introduction to the World's Religions* (2010).
3   Ch. 4, verse 8, as quoted in Smith, *The World's Religions* (1991), p. 36.
4   Carus, *The Gospel of Buddha*, XCVI: 13, p. 245.
5   John 16: 12–13.
6   John 1:10.
7   'Abdu'l-Bahá, *Some Answered Questions*, ch. 3, p. 10.
8   ibid. p. 11.
9   Kumar, *Ancient Hindu Science: Its Transmission and Impact on World Cultures* (2019), p. 6.
10   ibid.
11   ibid. p. 7.
12   As quoted ibid. p. 15.
13   As quoted in Smith, *The World's Religions* (1991), p. 83.
14   ibid.
15   As quoted in Carus, *The Gospel of Buddha*, LV: 7, p. 164.
16   See Conway, *The Sacred Anthology* (1874).
17   Smith, *The World's Religions*, pp. 273–4.
18   Gen. 12:2.
19   Deut. 18:15.
20   Is. 2:2.
21   Matt. 4:4.
22   Bahá'u'lláh, *Gleanings from the Writings of Bahá'u'lláh*, XXXV, pp. 85–6.
23   ibid. XXXVI, p. 86.
24   John 8:58.
25   John 5:46.
26   John 12:44, 46.
27   John 10:16.
28   John 16:12–13.
29   Matt. 6:10.

30 For a discussion of the origins and teachings of Islam, see Bushrui and Massoudi (eds), *The Spiritual Heritage of the Human Race*.

31 Smith, *The World's Religions*, pp. 221–70.

32 Richards, *Mencius on the Mind* (1932), p. 66.

33 ibid. p. 68.

34 Hamlin, Wynn, and Bloom, 'Social Evaluation by Preverbal Infants', in *Nature*, vol. 450 (22 November 2007), pp. 557–9.

35 Hamlin, Wynn, and Bloom, 'Three-months-olds Show a Negativity Bias in their Social Evaluations', in *Developmental Science*, vol. 13 (2010), no. 6, pp. 923–9.

36 Richards, *Mencius on the Mind* (1932), p. 69.

37 ibid. p. 69.

38 ibid. p. 72.

39 ibid. p. 73.

40 As quoted in Regier (ed), *Masterpieces of American Indian Literature* (1993), p. 153.

41 ibid. pp. 172–3.

42 As recorded in Nabíl, *The Dawn-Breakers* (1932), p. 514.

43 Sir Henry Layard, quoted in Balyuzi, *The Báb* (1971), p. 11.

44 'Introduction' to Nabíl, *The Dawn-Breakers*, p. xxiii.

45 From the Báb's farewell address to the Letters of the Living, ibid. p. 94.

46 The quotations from the Bahá'í teachings cited in the following section may be found at https://www.bahai.org/library.

47 Bahá'u'lláh, *Gleanings from the Writings of Bahá'u'lláh*, CXXXII, p. 289.

48 'Abdu'l-Bahá, *The Promulgation of Universal Peace*, p. 397.

49 Shoghi Effendi, *The World Order of Bahá'u'lláh*, p. 50.

50 Bahá'u'lláh, *Hidden Words*, opening paragraph.

51 ibid. Arabic no. 1.

52 ibid. Arabic no. 2.

53 ibid. Arabic no. 14.

54 ibid. Arabic no. 63.

55 ibid. Arabic no. 68.

56 Bahá'u'lláh, *Epistle to the Son of the Wolf*, para. 38, p. 23.

57 Bahá'u'lláh, *Tablets of Bahá'u'lláh*, pp. 164–5.

58 'Abdu'l-Bahá, *The Secret of Divine Civilization*, p. 39.

59 Shoghi Effendi, 'The Unfoldment of World Civilization', in *The World Order of Bahá'u'lláh*, p. 187.

60 'Abdu'l-Bahá, *Abdul Baha on Divine Philosophy*, pp, 102–3.

61 Bahá'í International Community, *The Prosperity of Humankind*
(1995).
62 ibid.

INDEX

'Abdu'l-Bahá 6, 184-5, 210; teachings on:
diversity 59-60
divine educators 190
energy 11
existence 10
Holy Spirit 19
human spirit 6, 8, 9, 18, 32, 75, 176-7
justice 215
love 43, 46-7, 211
meditation 176-7
mind 6-7, 9, 12-13, 31
nature and man 63
opposing one's passions 109
prejudice 28, 184-5, 211
reason 31
science and art 177
science and religion 18, 36, 216
service to humanity 17, 48
sympathetic nervous system 58
truth 28
Abraham 25, 125, 196-7, 200, 209
abuse 58, 81, 136, 199
drug, substance abuse 76-7, 150
Adamites, pre-Adamites 122-3
addiction 72, 77-8
aesthetics 14, 16, 30, 101, 180, 184-6
Africa 115, 119, 122, 126, 130
akrasia 76
Allen, Michael 134-5
America, Americans xi, 13, 53, 59, 100-01, 115-16, 122, 125-6,
128-30, 132-4, 137-9, 141, 145-9, 151-2, 161, 162, 163, 172-3, 184, 206-7
African-Americans xi, 100, 115
Hispanic Americans 115
Native Americans 122, 138, 148, 161, 167, 206-7
Amini, Fari 44
Analects, The 41, 75
analogy 31-2, 158 see also metaphor
Anderson, Fulton 33
anger 158, 165, 170
animals 11, 24, 63-4, 66, 68, 78, 96, 108, 127, 142, 188, 193, 201, 203, 241
Antigone 83, 92-5
anxiety 8, 76, 150, 158, 165-6, 175
Áqásí, Ḥájí Mírzá 208-9
Aquinas, Thomas 30-33
Arabia, Arabic 201-2, 210
Aristotle 10-11, 28, 30-33, 67, 75, 142, 191
arms, armaments 136-7
nuclear 115, 152
arms race 134, 146
arrogance 38, 143, 162, 207
art(s), artists 3, 6, 10, 12, 16, 18, 25, 31, 37, 40, 46, 50, 63, 100, 124, 158, 159, 168, 177, 183, 199, 202
healing 56-7
martial 165
Asclepius 97
Asia, Asians 115, 126, 130, 171-2

astronomy 24-5, 173, 191
astrophysics 126-7, 192
autonomy 38-9, 66, 71-2, 147-8,
    176, 236
    of machines 62
Avicenna 33
Axial Age 75, 159
Ayurveda 191

Báb, the 25, 197, 207-10
Babylonians 131, 192, 196
Bacon, Francis 33-4
Bacon, Roger 191
Bahá'í community 6, 52, 217, 234
Bahá'í International Community 52
Bahá'í perspective, teachings see
    individual entries
Bahá'u'lláh 18, 25, 27, 197, 205,
    210-12, 217
    Writings 27, 73-4, 136-7, 162,
        211, 231
Bean, R. B. 124
Beatles, the 173
beauty 2, 12, 14, 15-18, 24, 29-30,
    48, 50, 59-60, 167, 180, 184-5,
    206, 208, 232
belief 1, 12, 18, 24-8, 31, 33-4,
    38-9, 46, 63, 71, 121, 139, 163,
    172, 175
Bellah, Robert 162-3
Benson, Herbert 174-6
Bethencourt, Francisco 121-2
Bhagavad Gita 189
Big Bang 192
biochemistry 9, 99
biology ix, 9-10, 25, 44, 51, 65, 71,
    77, 79, 87-9, 91, 92, 97, 99-101,
    119-23, 127, 136, 188, 240
Biosphere II 105
Black Elk 161
Blau, Judith 145-8
Bloom, Paul 204

body politic 73-4, 143
brain, human 4-9, 18, 44, 55, 59,
    74, 99, 124, 170
Brenner, Charles 237
Breuer, Joseph 87
Brinkmann, Svend 51
Buddha (Gautama) 25, 41, 125,
    170-72, 189, 193-4, 198
Buddhism, Buddhists 49, 75, 106,
    166, 169, 170-73, 193-4

California 115
Callahan, David 132-3, 135
Cambodia 185
Camus, Albert 66
capacities, human ix, 2-4, 6-8,
    13-19, 23-79 passim, 95, 99,
    103-4, 146-7, 159-60, 164, 169,
    171, 176, 178-80, 182-4, 186,
    190, 203-5, 208
capitalism 53
Carnot's theorem 11, 232
Cassirer, Ernst 187-8
Caucasians 115, 124
causality 4, 9, 10, 69, 74, 237
character, human 4, 16, 30, 40,
    65-6, 67, 78, 89, 101, 124, 139,
    143, 160, 163, 182, 188, 216,
    217
Charcot, Jean-Martin 86
chi (energy) 57, 171
childhood, children 13, 15, 44-5,
    46, 49, 62, 71, 84, 88, 91-2, 94,
    105, 115, 142-3, 150, 152, 161,
    163-4, 204, 206, 211, 237
    infants 13, 71, 142, 204
China, Chinese 41, 126, 164, 171,
    173, 191, 192, 203-5
choice 51, 62, 64, 68, 95, 98, 116,
    152, 237
    capacity to choose 61, 65, 66, 68,
        103, 236, 237

Christ *see* Jesus
Christianity, Christians 30, 75, 106,
    120-23, 173, 202, 208
Church, Christian 33, 36, 120-21
civilization(s) 3, 5, 6, 15, 18, 25, 31,
    37, 40-41, 43, 53, 106, 120, 170,
    180, 183, 197, 202, 206, 232
    global 138, 144
civil rights (movement) 52, 138,
    157-8
Cochran, David 147
cohort replacement 129
Cold War 134-5
collective development 1, 69, 73
collective security 133-4, 136-7
Collins, Francis 188
Columbus, Christopher 121-2
community 3, 42, 48, 72, 102, 108,
    128, 150, 167, 181-2, 186, 200,
    205
    global 52, 125, 132, 133
    role of 67, 160, 203
    sense of 2, 40, 181-2, 185, 215
compassion 15, 41, 52, 71, 76, 94,
    103, 128, 141, 160, 165, 167,
    169, 180-81, 185, 189, 197, 199,
    201, 209
competition 112-13, 127
composition, compositional pro-
    cesses 7-8, 10
community 3, 40, 42, 48, 67, 72,
    74, 102, 108, 125, 128, 150,
    160, 167, 179-81, 185-6, 200,
    203, 205, 215
    global 52, 125
    international 132-3
    sense of 2
concern for others 14-15, 47-8, 52,
    110, 185
conflict 54, 74, 83, 98, 102-5,
    110-14, 125, 127, 133, 138, 183,
    188, 190, 195, 201, 217, 236

Confucius 41, 75, 173, 203
consciousness
    in animals 78
    human 2-3, 10-14, 16, 19, 23,
        25, 29, 34, 38-40, 49, 53, 62,
        65, 71, 89, 90, 95, 135, 158,
        179, 181-2, 185, 190, 193,
        194, 197, 199, 203, 205, 237,
        241, 242
    of interdependence, oneness
        143-4
    in meditation, prayer 166, 168,
        174, 181
    moral and spiritual 53, 72, 166,
        168
    in organic systems 44
    of the sacred 16, 161, 166
    social 90
consumerism 54-5
controllability 69
cooperation 113-14, 132, 136-7,
    143, 148, 183, 212
Corinthians 162
corruption 41, 69, 115, 195, 208-9,
    216
courage 17, 38-9, 103, 107, 160,
    195
courtesy 128, 180, 182, 201, 205
Cova, Florian 183
COVID-19 114
critical thinking 24-35, 38-9, 42,
    171
culture(s) 1, 3, 25, 30, 36, 53, 54,
    59, 66, 73, 106, 110, 120, 125,
    130, 140-41, 146, 162, 164, 171,
    180, 183, 186, 189, 191, 192,
    196, 202, 205, 216

Dalai Lama 160
Danesh, Hossain B. 2, 64
Dart, Raymond 119
Darwinians 98

Dawkins, Richard 96
death 8, 45, 64, 83-4, 91, 97-8, 120,
    127, 192, 208, 214
decision-making 151, 180, 182-3
Declaration of Independence
    (American) 141-2
democracy 132, 151-3, 162
Deonna, Julien 183
Depression 8, 58, 76, 176
Descartes, René 34-5, 87, 188
desires, human 13, 15, 16, 23,
    41, 47-8, 52, 54, 76, 78-9, 99,
    109-10, 111, 158, 159, 169, 170,
    179, 205, 213
determinism 9, 84, 89-90, 95, 123,
    237
development, human 13-18, 40,
    74, 240
Diderot , Denis 35
dignity x, xi, 3, 66, 72, 76, 95, 97,
    116, 126, 130, 141, 142, 146,
    150, 182
discrimination 69, 121, 131, 148
diversity xi, 16, 23, 37, 59-60,
    119-20, 123-4, 127, 158, 181,
    202, 212, 217
dogma 28, 35-6, 42, 53, 55, 188
doubt 34
dreams 83

Eastman, Charles Alexander 206
education 10, 18, 40, 67, 71, 124,
    126, 130, 138, 142-3, 146, 148,
    150, §52, 190, 211
egocentricity 38-40
Egyptians, ancient 97, 192, 196-7
Einstein, Albert 188, 132
Elder, Linda 38
Elias, Norbert 140
empathy 38-9, 112, 167
emotion(s) 8, 13-14, 15, 16, 38,
    44-5, 71, 75-6, 99, 105, 141, 158,

165, 171, 183, 185, 204, 212
    moral 75
empiricism, empirical studies 3-5,
    33-6, 41, 54, 84, 90, 97, 148,
    204
    empirical sciences 3, 4, 5, 34-6,
        41, 54, 84, 148, 204
energy 6, 10-11, 46, 56-7, 63, 126,
    128, 157, 171, 179, 190, 205,
    217, 242
enlightenment, spiritual 30, 41,
    159, 170, 172, 189-90, 193, 214,
    234
Enlightenment, the European 35,
    37, 123, 132, 141
enslavement 108-9 see also slavery
entropy 41
environment 1, 11, 13, 44, 45, 53,
    89, 114-15, 119, 146, 179, 188,
    203
epidemics 53
epistemology 28-30, 33-4, 37-8, 42
ethics, ethical 3, 12, 14, 29-30, 33,
    38, 66-7, 71, 101, 150, 181, 183,
    185, 214
ethnicity 53, 115, 120-21, 126-8,
    131
ethnocentrism 120-21
Europe 13, 30, 53, 88-9, 115-16,
    120, 122, 126, 130-31, 140-41,
    148, 149, 191
European Community 134
evil 86, 93, 102-4, 110, 129, 169,
    189, 194
evolution 9-10, 17, 19, 25, 42, 44-5,
    66, 96-101, 119, 122, 125, 128,
    216-17, 240
evolutionary psychology 96-101
exegesis 26
existentialism 66-7
    existential suffering 170, 193,
        241

fairmindedness 38, 40
faith 17-31, 40, 126, 133, 143, 163, 168, 213
  faith factor 175
Fancher, Raymond 84
federal system 138, 212
fear 59, 69, 106, 125, 170, 171, 213
Finonacci, Leonardo 191-2
fictive kinship 125
fight or flight 59, 64, 175
Fitts, Dudley 83
Fitzgerald, Robert 83
foreign policy (American) 132-4
Foucault, Michel 36
France, French 66, 87, 149, 152
Francis, St, of Assisi 159
Franklin, Aretha 104
Franklin, C. L. 104
Frankfurt, Harry 78
freedom 4, 9, 11-12, 15, 28, 35, 61, 63, 66-7, 71-5, 79, 95, 116, 130, 142, 145-50, 159, 163, 171, 182, 184, 198, 214, 236, 237
Freire, Paulo ix, 36
Freud, Sigmund 56, 83-4, 86-90, 92, 95, 203, 237
Fromm, Erich 66
Functional Delta 85

Galileo 33
Gandhi, Mahatma 65
Gandhi, Virchand 172
Gay, Peter 35
genes 71, 96-8, 99
Genesis 133
Germany, Germans 66, 124, 140, 160, 187
God 4, 8, 9, 15, 17, 19, 24, 30, 31, 33, 34, 43, 74, 93, 170, 177, 188, 194, 195-202, 206, 207-15, 231, 232
  and theodicy 102-3

good, the 2, 14-18, 27, 29-30, 48-50, 61, 67, 75, 95, 99, 102-4, 110, 160-64, 185-6, 189, 194, 203, 206, 208, 232
Gorgias 29
governance 12, 122, 139, 150, 158, 214
  global 138
government, role of ix, 67, 137, 145, 148-50, 167, 181-2, 186, 200, 205
gravity 5, 11, 12, 43, 242
greed 52, 115
Greeks, ancient 26, 28-9, 32, 73, 76, 83, 116, 120, 191, 192, 202, 205
Gu, Jingyi 169
guilt 75-6

Haeckel, Ernst 240
Ham, son of Noah 122-3
Hamilton, Alexander 132
Hamlin, J. Kiley 204
Hammurabi 131
Hanson, H. 15-16, 23
happiness 14, 32, 37-8, 51, 54, 71, 74-6, 107, 109, 160-61
Harari, Yuval 98
Hatcher, John S. 7
Hatcher, William 2, 34, 46, 65
hatred 36, 46-8, 60, 142, 211, 208
health 9, 46, 58, 68, 76, 109, 115, 127, 142, 146, 150, 152, 160, 170-71, 174
  mental 30, 71-2, 75, 88, 115, 150, 170-72, 174 see also mental illness
  spiritual 8, 74
heart, human 15-16, 18, 30, 32, 41, 48, 59-60, 92, 94, 110, 129, 141, 162, 166, 177, 183-5, 189, 195, 204, 208-10, 211, 213-14, 232

Hebrews, ancient 120
Heidegger, Martin 66
Heisenberg, Werner 36
helplessness 68-9, 70, 142-3, 209
Henry III, William 115
Herman, Judith 86, 237
hermeneutics 25-6, 120
Herrick, C. J. 66
Hidden Words 213
history, historicism ix, x, 16, 25, 41,
    48-9, 65, 67, 75, 89-92, 98, 101,
    102, 112, 120, 125, 138-41, 143,
    145, 158, 197-8, 199, 216-7
Hitler, Adolf 131, 133
Hmong people 115
Holocaust, the 66-7, 140
Holy Spirit 17, 19
honour 3, 95, 160, 204
hope, hopefulness 1, 2, 52, 76, 90,
    97, 136, 163, 165, 168, 181,
    184, 212, 216
hsing 203-6
Hsün Tzu 162
Hugo, Victor 158
humanism 66-7, 106
human nature 82, 89, 97, 109,
    123-4, 132, 139, 142-3, 216
human rights ix, 35, 66-7, 81, 131,
    136, 138, 142-2, 145-8, 152
human spirit ix-xi, 2-3, 5-6, 10,
    12-13, 18-19, 23-7, 40, 52, 55-6,
    71-5, 83, 89-90, 94-5, 97, 120,
    130, 131, 146, 150-51, 159-60,
    162-4, 169-71, 176-8, 180-82,
    187-9, 203-6, 216-18, 232
Hume, David 35, 124
humility 16, 38, 41, 50, 71, 129,
    165, 181, 189, 207, 208
Hunt, Lynn 141-2
hypothetical constructs 5
hysteria 86-8, 235, 237

identity, human xi, 3-4, 9-10,, 42,
    81, 99, 122-3
ideology 1-2, 18, 81, 125, 131,
    132-5, 145-7, 173, 189
imagination 18, 28, 39, 66, 69, 71,
    84, 141, 163, 196
    social imaginaries 1, 149
India 126, 170, 173, 193
inequality 148, 150-51
infants 13, 71, 142, 204 *see also*
    childhood
injustice 56, 58, 68-9, 94-5, 106-8,
    125, 136
Inquisition, the 121
Institute for Studies in Global
    Prosperity 52
intellect, intellectuals ix, 7, 14, 24,
    27, 30, 35-6, 38-40, 48, 53, 61,
    66, 86, 88, 134, 153, 160, 186,
    190, 217
intelligence 5, 12, 13, 30, 63, 66,
    116, 160, 205
interdependence ix, 73, 126, 132,
    134, 136, 143, 217
international relations 138
intuition 5, 26, 35, 171
Isaac 196-7
Ishmael 196-7
Islam 73, 75, 106, 191, 201-2
Italy, Italians 121, 149, 152, 192

Jacobs, G. D. 176
Jainism 172
James, William 16
Janet, Pierre 86-7
Jaspers, Karl 66. 159
jen 204-5
Jesus Christ 25, 30, 41, 73, 121-2,
    125, 168, 190, 193, 194, 195,
    197, 198-201, 206, 210
Jews 32, 106, 120-22, 126, 127,
    140, 202, 210

jihad 106
Job (prophet) 95
Jordan, Daniel 81
Judaism, 73, 75, 196-7 *see also* Jews
Jung, Carl 173, 191
justice 15, 24, 64, 69, 70, 74, 94,
    105, 107, 128, 131, 132, 137,
    141, 143, 146-7, 185, 197, 213,
    215 *see also* injustice

Katurah 196-7
Kammen, Michael 147
Kant, Immanuel 36, 160
Kennan, George 134
kindness 47, 60, 168, 180, 201,
    211, 213
Kissinger, Henry 134
knowledge 2, 5, 10, 12-14, Ch.
    1 complete, 48-50, 61-9, 71,
    99-101, 103, 109, 121, 126,
    142, 159, 168, 170-72, 179-80,
    189-90, 192-3, 194, 210, 213,
    232, 242
Koltko-Rivera, Mark 36
Koran (Qu'rán) 106, 202, 208
Krishna 25 *see also* Hinduism
Kumar, Alok 191

Lample, Paul 15-16, 160
language, human 24, 35, 120, 123,
    173, 199, 206-7, 211, 212, 231
    universal auxiliary 138
Lannon, Richard 44
law 3, 4, 7, 9, 11, 12, 24, 35, 54, 62,
    63-4, 67, 69, 106, 109, 128, 131,
    133, 138, 141, 216
    civil 74, 151, 197
    human rights 66, 138
    sacred 74-5, 198, 210, 215
Lazarus, Emma 115-6 *see also* Statue
    of Liberty
Lewis, Thomas 44

liberalism 145-50
light (As metaphor) 4-6, 9, 19, 56-7,
    168, 190, 200, 211, 213-15
limbic system 44-5
Lippmann, Walter 133
logic 12, 24, 33-5, 38, 40
love 5, 13-4, 16, Ch. 2 complete,
    96, 103, 105, 128-9, 160, 162,
    164, 182, 189, 190, 199-201,
    204, 206, 209, 211, 214, 232,
    242
    capacity to 2, 13, 41-2, Ch. 2
        complete, 71, 103, 159, 164,
        180
loyalty 112, 138, 216
Lubar, J. F. 176

Magi, the 195
Mahan, Alfred 133
Maharishi Mahesh Yogi 173
Maharshi, Sri Ramana 170
Mahmoudi, Hoda x
Maier, David 68
Maimonides 32-3
Malik, Aditi ix
Mammals 44-5, 58, 89
Mandela, Nelson 95
Manifestations of God 19, 200, 207
    see also individual entries
Marxism 53
material cause 10-11
materialism 52-4, 73
    materialistic philosophy 3, 53-4
    materialistic psychology 73, 88
Mathnavi 110
May, Rollo 66
Mayan people 192
meditation 162, 165, 169-77
    Transcendental Meditation 173-4
Mencius 203-6
mental illness 3, 71-2, 89
meta-cognition 11-13, 24, 62

metaphor 6-7, 26, 29, 32, 49, 83, 84, 89-92, 108. 209 *see also* analogy
Middle Ages 30, 122, 140
Middle East 115, 126, 130, 184
Mihdi, the 202
mind, human 3, 6-10, 13-14, 18, 25-8, 31, 33-5, 37, 42, 56, 77-8, 83-9, 124, 160-61, 169-71, 176-7, 181, 190, 191, 195, 197, 203, 205, 207, 237
mindfulness 93, 169, 177, 181, 194, 211
modernism 149
postmodernism 23
Moncada, Alberto 145-8
monotheism 196
Montesquieu, Charles Louis 35
morality, moral ix-x, 1-2, 7, 14-15, 19, 25, 29, 42, 51, 53, 66-7, 75-6, 98, 99, 102, 103, 122, 125, 134, 136, 139, 140, 146, 147, 160, 162-3, 170, 181, 193-5, 199, 200, 203-4, 205, 206, 211, 214
    capacity 186
    ecology 51
    emotions 75-6
    imperatives 51
    legitimacy 2
    obligations, responsibility 72, 95, 210
    order 149, 197
    sensibilities 49, 109, 183, 203-4
    truth ix, 41, 199
Morgenthau, Hans 134
Morton, Samuel G. 124
Moses 125, 197-8, 200, 209
Mother Teresa 159
Muhammad 25, 41, 125, 197, 201-2, 210
Muhammad Shah 208

Muslims 32, 121, 126, 127 *see also* Islam
Myanmar 126

nationalism 2, 81, 103
natural sciences ix, 46, 56, 127, 192
nature, natural world 1, 2, 3-4, 6-7, 11, 16, 24-5, 32, 35, 37, 42, 46, 48-9, 55, 61-3, 65-6, 69, 71, 74, 79, 89, 92, 110, 128, 170, 171, 179, 183, 190, 192, 196, 206-7, 216, 242
nature-nurture 9-10, 89
Nazis 30, 66, 130
needs, human ix-xi, 23, 28, 35-40, 53, 70-71, 105, 128, 131, 145-7, 150, 167, 188, 216
Negro 124, 148
neo-liberalism 145
Nepal 193
nervous system 8, 30, 57-8, 99, 175-6
    autonomic 175
    sympathetic 57-8, 175
neuroanatomy 56
neuroception 58-9
neurochemistry 56
neurology 3, 56, 58, 84, 86-7, 176
neuroscience 92, 99
neurotransmitters 8, 57-8, 77
Newton, Isaac 188
New York, NY 17, 63, 115, 152, 173
Noah 123
Noguchi, L. 15-16, 23
nuclear
    arms 115, 152
    forces 11, 242
number systems 191-2

Oedipus, Oedipus trilogy 83-95
    Oedipus at Colonus 83, 92-5

Oedipus Rex 83-4, 89, 91-2
Antigone 83, 92-5
O'Hear, Anthony 97-8
oneness of humanity ix, 3, 73, 131,
    136, 144, 212, 214
oppression 56, 66, 70, 115, 126,
    146, 189, 197, 201, 209
omniscience 61, 102
order 3-4, 11, 16, 69, 74, 128, 133,
    232
    international, world 133, 135-7
    moral 149, 197
    public 151
    social 15, 18, 35, 41, 69, 108,
        128, 181-2, 215
Organization of Petroleum Export-
    ing Countries (OPEC) 134
Otto, Rudolph 16
Ovid 76

pain 13, 64, 72, 93-4, 126, 130-31,
    170, 175, 215
Paine, Thomas 35
Palestine, Palestinians 126, 197, 198
paradox 9, 29, 33
Parliament of World Religions 172
patience, impatience 76 128-9, 181
Paul, Apostle 95
Paul, Richard 38
peace 38, 132, 136, 139, 143, 195,
    197-8
    global, universal 17, 198, 210,
        234
    inner 14, 30, 109, 166, 170, 216
peace-keeping 136, 138
perseverance 38-9, 160
Persia 109, 194, 208-9, 215
personality disorders 72, 235
Pew Research Center 148
phenomenology 16
philosophical materialism 54
philosophy, philosophers xi, 2, 3,

10, 17, 23, 26-9, 33-7, 41-2, 52,
    54, 66-7, 90, 97, 100, 102, 106,
    121-4, 131, 136, 145, 147-8,
    160, 172-3, 1833, 187-8, 211,
    237
    Chinese 203-5
    Eastern 56, 172
    Hindu 191-2
Pickett, Kate 150
Pinker, Steven 140-42
Plato 26-9, 34, 48, 97, 106-9
pleasure 13, 16, 77, 109, 161
political economy 149, 151, 153
political science 67
polygenesis 122
Popkin, Richard 121, 123
Popper, Karl 90
Porges, Stephen 58-9
Portugal 121-2, 152
postmodernism 23, 37
powers, human 5, 7-9, 12-14, 19,
    25-6, 31, 36, 42, 55, 58, 62-64-
    5, 71, 73, 89, 103, 166, 177,
    179-81, 187-8, 203-4, 232, 242;
    also Chapters 1-3
prayer 93, 129, 161, 165-9, 177,
    181, 193, 201
prejudice 28, 38, 59, 73, 110-12,
    120, 122, 129, 184, 202, 205,
    208, 211
    racial *see* racism
progress 19, 70, 139, 190, 197, 199
prosperity 1, 42, 48, 52, 54, 74,
    121, 127, 130, 150, 161, 217
psyche, the 9, 56-7, 73, 87-9, 92,
    125, 129
psychiatry x, 3, 56, 83-5, 237
psychic determinism 84, 89-90, 237
psychoanalytic psychiatry 83, 85, 89
psychoneurobiological disorders 58
psychopathology 3, 68, 76
psychosomatic illness 57

Qá'im, the 202
Qigong 171
Qu'rán 106, 202, 208

race xi, 3, 48, 59-60, 73, 100,
    124-6, 128-30, 162, 164, 184,
    189
racialism, racism 2, 48, 59, 103,
    120-26, 129-31, 148, 184-5, 202
Rana, Zat 127
realism 132-6, 139, 143
    essential 135
    political 132-4
reality ix, 1, 4, 7, 9, 18, 23, 26, 32,
    34-7, 41, 48, 53, 61, 87, 102,
    135, 157, 162, 168, 169, 172,
    176-7, 181, 187-8, 196, 231
    Divine Reality 19, 177
reason 8, 18, 28-31, 37-40, 76, 123,
    165, 193, 216, 232
Red Jacket 206
regret 75-6, 109
relaxation response 174-5
religion 18, 28, 35-6, 42, 48, 73, 75,
    126, 162-4, 172, 189-90, 195,
    197, 199, 202, 206, 208-9
    and materialism 53
    and science 18, 36-7, 42, 193,
        199, 216
remorse 75-6
reptiles 44-5
responsibility 4, 11, 55, 62, 67, 72,
    73, 88-9, 95, 103, 105, 135, 142,
    146, 160, 165, 217, 237
reward 107
    centres 77
    and punishment 62, 69
rhetoric 27, 33-4
Richards, I. A. 204-5
rights revolution 140-42, 146
Robbers Cave 110-14
Rogers, Fred 66, 159

Romans, ancient 76, 192
Roosevelt, Theodore 133
Rousseau, Jean-Jacques 35
Rumi 110

sacred, the 2, 16-17, 71, 161, 169
Sagan, Carl 192
saints, saintliness 16, 194
Salpêtrière, La
Satan 102-3
Savi, Julio 2
Schrag, Calvin 90
Schulz, W. F. 131
science(s) 3, 6, 12, 18, 25, 27, 31,
    37, 40, 41-2, 46, 53, 63, 66, 99,
    124, 159, 168, 177, 190, 202
    affective 183-4
    clinical, medical 56, 85
    cognitive x
    empirical 3, 4, 5, 34-6, 41, 54,
        84, 148, 204
    Hindu 191
    moral 194 see also morality
    and philosophy 33-4, 42
    political 67, 134-5
    and religion 18, 36-7, 42, 193,
        199, 216
    see also neuroscience
scientific materialism 54
Secret of Divine Civilization, The 109
self (identity) 2, 4, 6, 16, 23, 34,
    40, 55-6, 64-6, 75-8, 99, 109,
    159-60, 169-72, 205, 215
self-centredness 48, 110
self-indulgence 52
self-interest 133, 135, 148, 163, 209
selfishness 15, 29, 37, 54, 96, 132,
    139, 215
self-mastery 106, 169, 205
self-sacrifice 14, 95, 199
self-transcendence 46, 95

Seligman, Martin 68
sexism 81
sexual exploitation 56
Shah Bahram 195
shame 75-6, 98, 109, 167, 203, 205, 216
Shantideva 166
Sherif, Muzafar 110-14
Shintoism 172
Shoghi Effendi 9, 137-8, 210, 211, 215-6
Sillen, Samuel 122-3
Singer, Peter 46
Sioux people 161
slavery 108, 122-3, 125, 197
    to nature 92, 94, 108
    see also enslavement
Smith, Huston 163-4, 196
social change, transformation 52, 182-6
social imaginaries 1, 149
social order 15, 18, 35, 41, 69, 108, 128, 181-2, 215
social planning 9
social processes 10, 88-9
socio-economic status 141
Sociologists without Borders 145
Socrates 27-9, 95, 97-8
somatoform disorders 57
Sophists, sophistry 29
Sophocles 83-4, 89, 91-2
South Africa 119
Soyen Shaku 172
Spain 32, 120-21, 152, 202
spirit of faith 17
spirituality 14-16, 160
Spykman, Nicholas 133
Stafford, Kim 157
Statue of Liberty 130 see also
    Lazarus, Emma
St Paul, Minnesota 115
subtle body 56-7

suicide 76
sun the 6, 19, 25, 37, 49, 62-3, 192, 196
Sun of Reality 177
suffering 30, 69, 71-2, 104, 106, 126, 130, 141, 169, 170, 194, 215, 217
    existential 193-4, 241
Sumner, William 36
superordinate tasks 114
superstition 3, 18, 28, 36-7, 42, 54-5, 89, 165, 208-9, 216
Suzuki, D. T. 172-3
Swaab, Dick 99
Swami Vivekananda 172
Swiss Centre for Affective Sciences 183
Szasz, Thomas 237

Tai chi 165, 171
Tao, Taoism 49-50, 171-3
Taylor, Charles 149
technology vii, 18, 31, 41-2, 53, 81, 90, 132, 143, 158, 160, 191-2, 217
terrorism 106, 115, 136, 188
theodicy 102-3 see also evil
theology 30-31, 102
thermodynamics, laws of 11, 128, 179
Thich Nat Hanh 159
Thomas, Alexander 122-3
Torah 198
Toynbee, Arnold 41
Transcendental Meditation 173-4
trauma-related disorders 56, 58, 72, 86-7, 235, 236
    post-traumatic stress disorder 57, 72
triadic design 68
trust, trustworthiness 15, 69, 128, 150

truth, truthfulness 15, 16, 18, 23-9,
    31, 33-41, 50, 60, 164, 168-9,
    170, 181-2, 187, 189, 190, 194,
    195, 198-201, 204, 208, 209,
    210-11, 212, 214
    moral ix
    ontological ix

understanding 7, 23, 25, 32, 40,
    56, 62, 67, 73, 81, 94, 110, 147,
    161-3, 167-9, 171-2, 180, 187,
    190, 206, 211
United Kingdom 126, 139, 152
United States xi, 115-16, 125-6,
    133-4, 137-8, 151-2, 163, 172-3
    see also America
unity 28, 65, 74, 123-4, 125, 127,
    137, 166, 170, 178, 183-4, 199-
    200, 206, 209
Universal Declaration of Human
    Rights 141-2
Universal House of Justice, The 54,
    75

Vagus nerve 58
value(s) ix, 1-2, 12, 14-15, 35, 36,
    38-9, 46, 51-3, 63, 67, 69, 72,
    76-9, 95, 98-100, 105, 120,
    128, 131, 139, 146-8, 151, 153,
    158-9, 161-2, 166, 168, 184-5,
    207, 215
Vienna, Austria 87, 237
Vietnamese 115, 164
violence 1-2, 29, 45, 53, 56, 72, 73,
    102, 106, 110-12, 115-16, 128,
    139-43, 150-51, 179-80, 188,
    205
virtue ethics 67
volition 77-8, 88-9 see also will

Voltaire 35, 191

Wallace, George 157-8
war 2, 72, 111, 115, 131, 132-7,
    143, 145, 152, 188, 198
    holy 106
well-being 14, 38, 46-7, 51, 71, 74,
    109, 116, 126, 130, 143, 147,
    150, 160, 181, 217, 236
Wilkinson, Richard 150
will, human 2, 13-14, 15, 17, 51,
    55, Ch. 3 complete, 95, 103-4,
    128, 129, 130, 159, 160-61, 166,
    205, 217, 232, 242
    paralysis of 69, 126
Will of God 17, 201, 232
Wilson, Woodrow 133-4
wisdom 2, 7, 14, 27, 30, 41, 42,
    93, 98, 107, 129, 130, 163, 167,
    170, 180, 186, 187, 193, 194,
    195, 199, 205, 211, 215
wisdom traditions 12, 55, 74-5,
    159-61, 167, 207, 241
    moral 67
women 86, 116, 127, 143, 151,
    159, 161, 198, 206, 210, 237
world order 136-7
world superstate 137
worldview 1, 14, 46, 97, 100, 145-6,
    149-50, 173
Wynn, Karen 204

yoga 56, 165, 170, 191

Zajonc, Arthur 4
Zen 49, 171-3
Zend Avesta 195
Zimmer, Heinrich 173
Zoroaster 25, 41, 125, 194-5, 198

ABOUT THE AUTHOR

Dr Michael Penn is a Clinical Psychologist and a Professor of Psychology at Franklin & Marshall College, Pennsylvania, United States, and is trained in the fields of clinical and experimental psychopathology. His research interests and publications explore trauma-related disorders, the application of psychological research and theory to human rights, the inter-penetration of psychology and philosophy, and the relationship between culture and mental health.

Professor Penn is a member of the US Council on Foreign Relations, and has lived and lectured widely around the world. For more than a decade, he served the UN Leaders Programme, which trains director-level United Nations officers in a variety of countries. He has also supported the Federal University of Brazil's programme for peace studies, has been a consultant on the advancement of women for the UK Secretariat for the Commonwealth of Nations, and has assisted with the government of Greenland's initiative to reduce gender-based violence. From 1998 to 2000 Professor Penn lived in Switzerland where he helped to design the 'Education for Peace Project' that assisted the children of Bosnia-Herzegovina overcome the effects of war and genocide. In 2004 he was appointed to the Board of Directors of the Pennsylvania Higher Education Assistance Administration by Governor Edward Rendell, and he currently serves as a member of the Permanent Board of the Tahirih Justice Center, which provides legal and clinical services to women and girls who are fleeing gender-based violence and persecution. Professor Penn was inducted into Phi Beta Kappa in 1986, is a former Ford Foundation/National Academy of Sciences Fellow, a former Aspen Institute Wye Faculty Forum Fellow, the recipient of several honours for teaching and community service, and was honoured with the John Russwurm Award for Scholarship from the University of Pennsylvania.

Lightning Source UK Ltd.
Milton Keynes UK
UKHW021929171221
5816UK00006B/233